DOORWAY TO THE WORLD:
The Memoirs of W. Cameron Townsend
1934–1947

Wycliffe
BIBLE TRANSLATORS

Hugh Steven

"God cares for those
who trust Him."
Nahum 1:7

Doorway *to* *the* World

The Mexico Years

The Memoirs of
W. Cameron Townsend
1934-1947

Hugh Steven

Harold Shaw Publishers
Wheaton, Illinois

ISBN 0-87788-891-4

Cover design by Nancy VandenBerg

Library of Congress Cataloging-in-Publication Data

Steven, Hugh.
    Doorway to the world: the memoirs of W. Cameron Townsend, 1934–1947 / Hugh Steven.
    p.   Cm.
    ISBN 0-87788-891-4
    1. Townsend, William Cameron, 1896–1982. 2. Wycliffe Bible Translators Biography. 3. Summer Institute of Linguistics. I. Title.
BV2372.T68S73   1999
266'.0092--dc21   99-26702

06 05 04 03 02 01 00 99

10 9 8 7 6 5 4 3 2 1

For Elaine Townsend
Uncle Cam's faithful wife, partner and encourager of thirty-six years.

Contents

Foreword

When I read Hugh Steven's book, I was amazed to discover a man of astonishing faith. That man was William Cameron Townsend. Steven's book gives the reader a superb historical account of the early beginnings of Wycliffe Bible Translators and the Summer Institute of Linguistics, but more than that, it reveals to us a man who learned to trust and obey his God.

"Cameron Townsend trusted God in situations where it was socially ridiculous and from every standpoint improbable. But nevertheless Cam knew that when something needed to be done, he, as a child before God, was going to do it, and he believed God would answer his prayers. When asked on one occasion how he could do the things he did with so little probability for it to work out, like starting out for Mexico with only ten dollars, he said, 'I like putting God on the spot.'" What a testimony of faith!

Another inspiring facet of Cameron Townsend we get to see is his deep Christian love for people and his desire that every lost sheep be saved. Cameron Townsend was reminded by our Lord that "some are called to shepherd the ninety and nine, while others, like himself, are called to go out into the wilderness in quest of the one lost sheep." And that is exactly what Cameron Townsend did. He never looked back, never regretted a moment the life chosen for him by God. He was motivated by his love for

God and for God's people and an abiding desire to obey the mandate of the Great Commission. This obedience led him to share the love of God with indigenous peoples world wide. It was his desire that all indigenous people groups should have the Scriptures translated into their heart language.

Cameron Townsend never wavered on the path God laid out for him. Rather, he walked by faith, and let God take care of the details. The Scripture he took as his standard to live by is taken from Paul's words in Romans 15:20, "So have I strived to preach the gospel, not where Christ was named." And this he did. What an example he has left for us to follow!

In reading this book, I was reminded how important it is that we all walk by faith. If I respond to only two truths in this story they would be: To trust God in areas where there is no earthly reason for things to work out, hence, "Putting God on the spot." And to put into practice the calling He has given to all His children, to share the gospel with all His lost sheep.

To those who feel they aren't able to share God's love to the lost, this book is a perfect reminder that God can use anyone to spread the gospel if they are willing and will make themselves available to God. God will take care of the rest. Just look at William Cameron Townsend.

Roy Peterson
Director, Wycliffe U.S.A.

Cameron Townsend and Kenneth Pike in 1973 at the University of Oklahoma, Norman. Cornell Capa photo.

Introduction

Linguistically, I was "born into" the 1934-47 decade covered by Hugh Steven's book. Camp Wycliffe was my "womb". Ten days of phonetics in 1935 set the tone of my academic writing until 1948. It was exhilarating, helpful to me, and profitable to others when I was brought back from studying the Mixtec Indian language of Oaxaca, Mexico, to teach phonetics in the 1936 summer of Camp Wycliffe. The surprise was heightened when at the end of that summer "Uncle Cam" suggested to me that I should write a book on phonetics. I did not want to write this book, but God arranged for me to break my leg, and in the hospital I started writing.

At the end of summer in 1935 several of us went to Mexico. And President Cárdenas (gracious surprise, indeed!) invited us to have dinner with him and others at the national palace in Chapultepec. (Cárdenas had already been impressed by visiting Townsend's work in the Aztec village of Tetelcingo where he with his wife Elvira were living and working.)

How could all this have happened? I found out, much later, when I read Steven's earlier book, *A Thousand Trails* (1984). It showed, through Townsend's diary, how as a young man, not having finished college, he was hiking around selling Bibles in Guatemala and was forced to see the need of learning Indian languages (which most missionaries then did not consider necessary.) He also learned that without knowing the Indian language, he could not discuss with the monolinguals there the purpose of his books. Townsend also determined to find a way to help the locals develop an ability to make products for sale. And he learned that sometimes he was forced to meet and talk with government officials in order to get permission to do his selling.

But another surprise awaited me. After a few decades it seemed to me (not necessarily to others), that we of the youthful Summer Institute of Linguistics had indeed "made the linguists sit up and take notice." In some senses, it seemed to me that we were years ahead in descriptive linguistics, by dealing with semantics, by analyzing texts (not just sentences), and by dealing with non-language behavior in ways (and with tools) analogous to the way we handled descriptive linguistics. The "emic" (my term, taking the last part of the word phonemic, and eliminating the phonological part so that I could use it as a more general term) structures of nonverbal behavior, needed the same kind of treatment that language did. Local structures, related to local purposes, were emic; but we also needed the more general universal approach to all behavior, as we did for a worldwide phonetic system. How could we have developed such an approach from our short-summer start? My answer: When Townsend pushed us to live in local Indian communities, we were forced, if we wished to survive physically and to get any analysis of the languages, to learn how they would eat, walk, do business, and talk. By this method, we were pushed into a HOLISTIC approach to human behavior, with language as a subsection of the analysis. This holistic approach pushed us, indirectly, to the advances I have mentioned. It forced us to treat as "science" the more local structures, not just the universal ones. And in this book by Hugh Steven, one can see the work in implicit process and progress.

The relationships of the Institute spread to various groups in contact with it. On the one hand, the American Bible Society became interested. Some of their interest related to the Institute's publications via its second organization, the Wycliffe Bible Translators (built to relate to church groups, whereas the Institute was built to cooperate with secular organizations).

In 1937, in order to add to us a deeper understanding of advanced linguistic principles, Townsend had me go to the linguistic summer sessions at the University of Michigan to study with Professor Edward Sapir, with whom Townsend had previously had some correspondence on linguistic matters. Sapir taught me (in a brief "coffee cup" session) how he had analyzed the tones of Navajo. This opened the way for me to understand the tone system of the Mixtec language, and helped me to assist my sister Eunice and her partner Florence Hansen with the tones of Mazatec of Huáutla Mexico (and help others later). The next summer in Michigan opened the door to contact with Professor Leonard Bloomfield, and eventually to a doctorate at that university, under the sponsorship of Professor Charles Fries. We now have a couple of hundred doctorates in our membership, and they have helped many of our beginners to publish 5,000 or more technical articles (or books) concerning several hundred languages of fifty or so countries, and to contribute to the publications of New Testaments in over five hundred languages. In addition, there have developed summer sessions of the Institute in various countries, as well as year-round training centers in Dallas, England, and Australia.

I once asked Townsend how he had been able to imagine so many things to do that had in fact worked out, under stress and danger. He replied: "I like to put God on the spot!" In Hugh Steven's book, one can see some of the paths Townsend took on the journey undertaken to serve God, underprivileged people, and governments, by language, linguistics, and Bible translation. One should also notice that instead of deliberately building for himself (or a board of directors) a power spot, Townsend insisted on building the organization so that the local SIL workers on the field should have ultimate control, under God.

Kenneth L. Pike, Ph.D.

Prologue

My object in each of the now three books on the life and times of William Cameron Townsend, *A Thousand Trails*, *Wycliffe in the Making* and *Doorway to the World*, is to provide a window into the heart, mind and soul of this most unlikely man who became one of the world's most distinguished mission statesmen.

I want, however, for readers to make this discovery for themselves. It is my desire that readers hear Townsend's own voice and discover his inner spirit through his personal correspondence, letters and diaries. I also want succeeding generations to meet a man who was fully alive with a clear vision and bold faith in what God could and would accomplish through a willing servant.

It is my prayer that readers will find inspiration in observing the life of a man who faced great trials and impossible adversities, including illness, the Great Depression, a sickly wife, two world wars, lack of money and social position, yet never allowed the times or circumstances to deter him from his vision. In fact, Cameron Townsend's vision for Bible translation became brighter with every passing year.

My second objective is, in a sense, apostolic. During the formation of the early canon of Scripture, the Church decided the standard of acceptance of any book in the canon was to be an unbroken chain of evidence and stories that were traced back to someone who could say, "I know this to be true because I saw it with my own eyes." This has been precisely my own criterion for the inclusion of any story, any anecdote or indeed any interpretation of Cameron Townsend's life and ministry.

While I was faithful in interviewing only "eye witnesses" to the life and ministry of Cameron Townsend, I do not regard the three books to be the final word on his life. There is a sense in which his story and the story of Wycliffe Bible Translators and the Summer Institute of Linguistics is opened-ended and ongoing. I do, however, submit that this trilogy, based on archival evidence from over 16,000 letters and other historical documents, will be a valuable resource for future books on William Cameron Townsend.

Hugh Steven
Santa Ana, California, 1999

Acknowledgments

I would like to pay special tribute to Cal Hibbard, longtime friend, colleague, former personal secretary to Cameron Townsend and Curator Emeritus of the Townsend Archives. Cal spent many hours reading the manuscript and made significant editorial comments. My appreciation to Beth Brennen and Gladys Zellmer, who, with the help of Dave and Vivian Robbins from the Townsend Archives, spent long hours photocopying and scanning hundreds of documents and thus providing me with valuable background materials for the book.

I wish to thank Dr. Benjamin and Adelle Elson and Dr. Kenneth and Evelyn Pike, longtime friends and colleagues who took time to read the manuscript and who made valuable editorial suggestions. My thanks also to Dr. Pike for writing the Introduction. Also to Elaine Townsend, Marianna Slocum, Dr. Dick Pittman, Bob Schneider, John and Isabel Twentyman and other colleagues and friends who contributed valuable insights and information.

My thanks also to Roy Peterson, Director of Wycliffe U.S.A., for his leadership, encouragement and for writing the Foreword. Teammates and partners all.

A deep word of appreciation to my dear wife Norma. She continues to be my best friend, editor, indispensable critic and encourager. I could not have done it without her love and support. Also, a particular word of appreciation to Prof. Ricardo Salvador for the use of his story about the "room of the mummies" in the epilogue.   Thanks, too, to Maggie Weatherstone for her encouragement and meticulous proofreading.

Norma and I are particularly grateful to the Missions Committee of Trinity Presbyterian Church, Santa Ana, California, and the many others, including our supporters, who faithfully prayed for the completion of this book.

Finally, my great thanks to Stephen Board of Harold Shaw Publishers for his friendship, his encouragement, and belief and willingness to publish, in his words, "significant books." In an age when many publishers, editors and management are more interested in the bottom line, it is heartening to find in Stephen Board and in Harold Shaw Publishers, colleagues who are friends of literature.

Camp Wycliffe 1934, Breezy Point, Arkansas. The "classroom" in the abandoned farmhouse rented for $5.00 a month. Standing: L. L. Legters, W. C. Townsend. Seated: Joe Chicol, Richmond McKinney, Oral Van Horn, Edward Sywulka.

Chapter One

Greetings from Camp Wycliffe

T he letterhead couldn't have been more explicit. Across the top were the words: "So Have I Strived to Preach the Gospel, Not Where Christ was Named, Romans 15:20." Centered in bold uppercase type were the words, CAMP WYCLIFFE. Written in italics was the camp's purpose: *A Summer Training Camp for Pioneer Missionaries*. To the right and below were the words "Founded in 1934," and on the left, the location: "Sulphur Springs, Arkansas." Below that were the words: "Sponsored by the Pioneer Mission Agency, 1201 Chestnut St., Philadelphia." The location for this summer training camp was listed as Breezy Point, Sulphur Springs, Arkansas from June 14 to September 7, 1934.

Cameron Townsend's decision to begin his long-dreamed-of school to train potential missionaries in the art of linguistics and Bible translation began near Sulphur Springs, a small rural farm community in the northwest corner of Arkansas. His decision to begin in Sulphur Springs, came about, as did many of Cam's projects, through a series of unplanned circumstances.

In 1922, Cam's brother Paul and his wife Laura, missionaries with the Central American Mission, had joined Cam and his wife Elvira at San Antonio, Guatemala. Paul, an experienced carpenter and handyman, was in charge of building. Laura had the responsibility for the Cakchiquel children's home. When Cam began to move toward independence from the Central American Mission, Paul, in his own memoirs wrote, "I saw the handwriting on the wall and decided I should also make a move." In 1927, Paul and Laura transferred to the Presbyterian Mission in Guatemala City where Paul became the director of a new industrial college for young men. Six years later, in 1933, during the height of the Depression, the Presbyterian mission board was forced to close the school. Paul and Laura returned to California for a furlough. That same year, Paul took a position with the John Brown Schools in Siloam Springs, Arkansas.

In February 1934, while Cam was conducting a linguistic survey of Mexico's ethnic peoples, word reached him from Chicago that Elvira was gravely ill and not expected to live. In his diary Cam wrote:

> I didn't have enough money to fly, so took a second-class railway coach part way, and then a first-class coach to Arkansas to where my brother Paul was living. Paul let me use his car, and with my nephew Russell White, we drove night and day to reach Chicago. We returned to the Ozarks almost immediately with Elvira reclining in a bed we had improvised in the car.

In the thirties, the warm sulphur spring water, laced with lithium and other minerals that bubbled out of the pine and oak-studded Ozark hills, drew people from all across the country. The popular notion then was that the spring waters contained curative minerals for a large variety of ailments, real or imagined. People came, they said, to "take the waters." There is no record that Elvira actually "took the waters." Cam simply believed the rustic beauty and the calm quietness of the Ozark hills would aid in restoring Elvira's health.

Cam was also in need of the calm recreative atmosphere of country living. When he arrived in Sulphur Springs, greatly burdened about Elvira's ongoing health problems, he was seriously underweight. There is not much recorded about Cam's feelings during those first weeks in the Ozarks. There is reference, however, to the immeasurable help of Dr. and Mrs. George Bast (an osteopathic physician) who, in order to give the Townsends their full measure of his medical skill, invited Cam and Elvira to live with them in their home.

But what is uppermost in Cam's mind in March 1934 is not his health, for which he seems to have little regard. Rather, it is his desire to make a fresh start. He was spending considerable time in meditation, writing articles on Mexico, and corresponding with his colleague L. L. Legters and others about opening a Linguistic Institute. While Cam still has cordial relations with the Central American Mission, his passion is to begin a school (later to be called Camp Wycliffe) where young men can be trained to do Bible translation in a cross-cultural setting. This plus Elvira's health occupies practically all his thinking. The Central American Mission, however, apparently did not share that passion. On April 13, 1934, on official mission letterhead, Karl Hummel, the secretary for C.A.M., wrote:

> My Dear Cam and Elvira,
>
> Yesterday our Executive Committee held its monthly meeting and we discussed your resignation from the C.A.M. Since you feel clearly led of the Lord to pursue your plans for the Translators Training School and the translation work and not return to Central America, the Committee voted to accept your resignation. However, it was accepted with keen regrets, with an expression of deep gratitude to God and to you for the years of faithful labor, and with the assurance that the doors of the Mission are open to you should you ever feel led to reapply for appointment.
>
> We will likely take the liberty of calling on you from time to time for counsel and possibly some special service. And, of course, we desire to keep in touch with you regarding the translation work and possibly to use some of the young men [on our own field].

As difficult as it was for Cam and Elvira to completely sever their official relationship with the Central American Mission, Cam knew he was obeying the will of God for him, even though he was not certain of the outcome of the school. It was truly a step into the unknown, an adventure of faith. On May 4, 1934, Cam wrote to tell the council of the Central American Mission that even though his resignation from the mission had finally been accepted, he deeply appreciated that the "latch-string" was being left out. He then wrote an amazing postscript:

> You all know the details behind why we have resigned. I need not say anything more, except to say that we do indeed love each one

of you. We will continue to support you every chance we get. I am going to take special pains not to sidetrack any Central American Mission contributors to our new undertaking, at least not until you have a few thousand surplus in your treasury.

In March and April of 1934, Cam was unsure how successful this new school idea might be. He had personally hand-delivered his new prospectus titled, "Summer Training Camp for Pioneer Missionaries," to Dallas Seminary and Columbia Bible College. Eight students indicated their interest that first year, but only two showed up for the course—Richmond McKinney from Dallas Theological Seminary, and Edward Sywulka from Columbia Bible College. Cam actually picked up Ed at the college and drove him to Sulphur Springs. Richmond had canceled a trip with his parents and brothers to the Holy Land in order to take the course. Joe Chicol, one of Cam's co-translators of the Cakchiquel New Testament, served as a language assistant.

On June 27, 1934, two weeks after the first Camp Wycliffe opened, Ed Sywulka, secretary for the camp, wrote a detailed account of the students' activities to interested friends and supporters:

> Greetings from Camp Wycliffe. We have chosen this name in honor of the great English Bible translator [John Wycliffe, 1328-1384] because each of us hopes to follow his example among the Indians of Latin America.
>
> Our present group of students include J.M. (Joe) Chicol, a Cakchiquel Indian from Guatemala. Joe came to the United States about six years ago to assist Mr. and Mrs. Townsend in the translation of the Cakchiquel New Testament. During the last four years, he has been a student at the John Brown University in Siloam Springs, Arkansas. He is teaching Spanish and other subjects, as well as taking some courses. Richmond McKinney of Memphis, Tennessee, a graduate of the University of Tennessee, has completed the first year of his seminary training in the Evangelical Theological College at Dallas, Texas. Edward Sywulka was born in Africa of missionary parents and is a graduate of Columbia Bible College. Oral Van Horn, of Gravette, Arkansas, is beginning his preparation for missionary work. [Oral Van Horn only attended classes for the first three weeks.]

Our camp schedule begins at six a.m. with private devotions. Breakfast is at eight-thirty after which we have a time of united prayer for the unreached fields of the world and our own problems at camp. The rest of the morning is spent in classes and study. At twelve we have dinner which is prepared by the other shift. In the afternoon, we usually have one or two classes and time for study.

Three times a week we take long hikes of about ten miles into the beautiful hills and valleys surrounding Sulphur Springs. Supper is at six, or as soon as we can prepare it after returning from the hike. Our evenings are free for study or gathering up the loose ends of the day. The exhilarating Ozark atmosphere draws us to our board bunks early.

After being with our teachers for these two weeks, we think that none better could be found, and we praise the Lord for giving us this opportunity for specialized training under such competent instructors. We also praise God for bringing us together according to his own purposes in Christ, and that He has thus far made the camp financially possible through the Pioneer Mission Agency of Philadelphia.

We ask prayers for: 1. The complete restoration of Mrs. W.C. Townsend's health, if it be the Lord's will. 2. For God's guidance in the plans and his provision of funds for two projects: /a/ A time of visiting several Indian tribes here in the U.S. this summer. /b/ For a time of the study of phonetics with Dr. E.L. McCreery [This required a trip to California].

Yours for the unreached Indians,
Edward Sywulka,[1] Secretary for the Camp.

Ed Sywulka should have also asked prayer for Cam's health. On August 20, 1934, Cam wrote his friend Karl Hummel to tell him he had been suffering from a bad case of poison oak that had turned into a terrible case of boils. Cam's ill health, in fact, occasioned the closing of Camp Wycliffe two weeks before the scheduled time. His correspondence revealed that a Dr. Bast had removed twenty cores from the back

---

1 Edward Sywulka went on to have a distinguished career in Guatemala. He joined the Central American Mission and translated both the New and Old Testaments for the Huehuetenango and Ostuncalco Mam people.

of his head and neck, with an added note that "this area looked like a scarred battlefield."

On September 21, Cam wrote to Bill and Etta Nyman in California expressing his appreciation for allowing Ed Sywulka and Richmond McKinney to stay in their home (they had driven from Sulphur Springs to Glendale, California) to take Dr. McCreery's phonetics course. It was, said Cam, a perfect ending to the summer school:

> As I look back it all seems like an evil nightmare. I guess Elvira wrote you about my studying Job, so I won't go into any more detail. Except to say that I sympathize with the old boy as never before. The back of my head is still draining, but the holes are healing and I am not in pain. I just have to tell you that I am glad to be in the land of the living, although a few weeks ago heaven looked awful good to me.

While Cam admitted that he was sometimes dizzy and found it difficult to write and think, there is no evidence from his copious correspondence during the summer and fall of 1934 that gives the slightest hint of his not being in full command of himself. Nor was there any indication that his faith had faded or that he doubted that God was with him in this project. In a general letter to supporters he wrote: "Though our path is not clear very far ahead, it is a joy to advance one step at a time with the assurance of His guidance."

That only two full-time students who attended the first Camp Wycliffe in 1934 seemed in no way to deter Cam's enthusiasm to move forward in the building of his two-pronged dream. The first prong was, of course, the training school for potential Bible translators he and co-founder L. L. Legters called Camp Wycliffe. The second was a dictum that former U.S. President T.R. Roosevelt had coined: "The test of our worth is the service we render."

From the beginning of his ministry in San Antonio, Guatemala, Cam wanted to alert the government that his presence and program would be beneficial to the country. Now, with the launching of Camp Wycliffe, Cam began to look for positive ways to serve the governments of Guatemala and Mexico and make them want the services of the trained linguists.

In the fall of 1934, Cam wrote the President of Guatemala, Gen. Jorge Ubico, and proposed that Edward Sywulka go to Guatemala to develop a fish hatchery as a way of building Guatemala's economy. Cam told President Ubico that Sywulka had gained fish hatchery experience in South Carolina and would be privileged to serve Guatemala in this way. Cam would provide the fish if he could find a way to get them there. After much correspondence, and no official word from the president, the fish hatchery idea collapsed. Still this did not blunt Cam's imagination in looking for new ways to serve.

In the meantime Cam had received an official letter of appreciation from Professor Rafael Ramírez, head of Mexico's department of rural and primary schools. The letter came in response to Cam's highly informative and positive article he had written and published on June 30, 1934 in the *Dallas News* on the splendid progress of Mexico's rural education programs. He had found a new way to be useful to the government of Mexico.

If Cameron Townsend was the dreamer and visionary for Camp Wycliffe, L. L. Legters, Cam's longtime friend and public spokesman for the cause of Bible translation, was the midwife who helped Cam bring the dream into reality.

For historical purposes, it must be made clear that in 1934 and 1935 Cam's vision for a school to train potential Bible translators was not always clearly understood even by those who supported him. He and Elvira had resigned from the Central American Mission in order to develop the school free from any denominational restraints. While Cam was now a free agent, he had cut himself off from financial support. However, L.L. Legters, Field Secretary for the fledgling Philadelphia-based Pioneer Mission Agency, had come to Cam's rescue with financial aid.

In a letter written on October 8, 1934 by Legters to the board of directors of the Pioneer Mission Agency, we get a fuller understanding of this agency's pivotal role in Cam's life. The letter is remarkable for the notion of funding national people to do Bible translation. Such a program would take almost three decades for Wycliffe Bible Translators to implement this as a major part of their own ministry:

> Just one year go we [Mr. Townsend and I] were preparing to go to Mexico. The purpose of the trip was to seek permission from the

government to bring men into the country to learn the Indian languages and then to translate the Bible into those languages.

We did not get all we wanted, but the Lord gave us a favorable trip. The roads which were impassable three weeks before our arrival, were put into fine condition for a motorcade from Canada. We were the first to follow them. They thought the government had prepared the roads for them, but we knew the Lord had prepared the roads for us. Some of the government officials were not at all interested in having us come into the country. The Lord, however, gave us favor in the eyes of other important government officials and we were able to enter the country.

My wife and I left Mexico City about the middle of December while Mr. Townsend remained and visited the larger Indian areas. His purpose was to gain information about the need for Bible translation, to make further linguistic studies, and to learn about the resources among the Mexican people themselves for doing translation work if we can furnish some of the funds to support them while they are engaged in this work.

The one thing that is clear, however, is that whoever does translation work must be specially trained. Seminary and Bible school training will not adequately prepare them for this specialized work. Mr. Townsend has long been convinced of the need for a special linguistic school that would give such training, but no funds were available, nor was there a place to hold a school.

However, the first week after my return from Mexico, the Lord gave me a sum of money to use as the Holy Spirit directed. I set it aside for the school. Soon after this, Mr. Townsend was urged to return home from Mexico because of his wife's illness. He was led to take her to Sulphur Springs, Arkansas in the Ozark mountains where to a great degree she has been recovering. It was there we began the training camp for pioneer missionaries in an abandoned farmhouse near a beautiful stream.

Legters continued at length with his report to the board with figures of how much the next session of Camp Wycliffe would cost--a modest $350 to $400 for food and miscellaneous expenses. He was quick to point out that no instructor was paid for his work, nor was he reimbursed for his travel expenses, or room and board. "And," wrote Legters:

"it is understood that this work is under the Pioneer Mission Agency and not under some independent offshoot." He also said that Edward Sywulka was being sent to work in Guatemala under the Central American Mission and would receive support funds from the Pioneer Mission Agency. At the close of his four-page typewritten report, Legters gave a classic understatement about his own speaking ministry when he said: "Because of my trip to Mexico, I have spoken fewer times this year than in previous years. I have spoken only 474 times, besides the personal conferences with individuals."

To read Townsend's correspondence in the fall of 1934, is to feel his rush of optimistic idealism. Clearly his desire was to make the idea of his linguistic school work for world mission and his host country. In his diary he wrote:

> The original plan is not only to train the young pioneers in linguistics but also to improve them physically for the hardships they encounter in pioneer work. We believe that hiking, swimming, wood-cutting and other outdoor exercise will be a kind of test to see if they can "endure hardness" *before going to the expense of sending them to a distant land.*

In the fall of 1934, Cam learned that the believers in Panajachel, Guatemala were particularly anxious for his return. When friends asked about Elvira's health, his response was that she was gaining strength and was looking forward to revisiting her brother Carl Malmstrom at the Robinson Bible Institute at Panajachel. And then there was the further possibility that Cam could spend a month or so allocating Ed Sywulka in a new mission station. Wisely, or unwisely, Cam thought that if they took the trip in easy stages to Mexico City and then flew to Guatemala City, "Elvira would be able to make it." Reading Cam's letters from the balcony of history one might conclude that Cam's natural optimism had talked him into believing that all was well with his wife when in fact she was still ill.

In October 1934, Cam and Elvira began their long drive to Mexico City via Dallas, and then on to Mexico. Just about a month later, on November 22, Cam wrote to tell Karl Hummel that he and Elvira had arrived in Monterrey, Mexico and were staying at the Regina Courts. Their plan was to remain there for two to three weeks before venturing on to Mexico City.

Although there was major road construction underway and the roads were not officially open, Cam thought he could get through. But then parenthetically he said: "Since no money has come for the trip to Mexico City and Guatemala, we may have to return to the States."

But it wasn't for lack of money that Cam and Elvira would have to return to the States. On January 23, 1935, three months after arriving in Monterrey, Cam wrote the following to Karl Hummel:

> Elvira's condition has taken a serious turn for the worse. Her feet and abdomen are swelling and the doctor doesn't think she will last many days. Elvira thinks she can stand the trip to Dallas and wants to go (a nurse will travel with us). In spite of the risk, we are starting out at noon today. (I sent you a telegram last night.) We plan to reach Laredo today, Temple or Austin tomorrow, and Dallas on Friday. Much love, Cam.

The second Camp Wycliffe

Back row: W. C. Townsend, Kenneth Pike, Brainerd Legters, Max Lathrop, Bill Sedat. Front row: L. L. Legters, Elvira Townsend, Mrs. Legters, Richmond McKinney.

Kenneth, Evelyn, and Judy Pike in Mexico, 1941.

Chapter Two

Couldn't You Send Us Someone Better Than This?

After Adolf Hitler became Chancellor of Germany in January 1933, he spent
[3]4 laying the groundwork for the conquest of Europe. His dream was to build
empire that would last a thousand years. His dream, however, was the dream
a lunatic, a deranged madman.

In 1934, Cameron Townsend was laying the groundwork for his dream. His
am, however, was the complete antithesis of Hitler's. One wanted to enslave and
jugate the human spirit to an Orwellian nightmare. Cameron Townsend wanted
give people the gifts of healing, joy, peace, education, and freedom and a new
se of self awareness and spiritual vitality. This, Cameron Townsend believed,
uld be the result of giving the translated Scriptures to people in their heart lan-
age.

But the question a logical and practical person might ask was, "How, without
ney or organizational support, at the height of The Great Depression, do you plan
accomplish this?" To which, Cameron Townsend with a smile would say, "By
h." In fact the theme song that L. L. Legters led the small group in singing that
t summer, and which was sung every summer thereafter, was called "Faith,
ghty Faith."

Faith, mighty faith, the promise sees and looks to God alone.

Laughs at impossibilities and shouts, "It shall be done."
And shouts, "It shall, it shall be done,
And shouts, "It shall, it shall be done."
Laughs at impossibilities and shouts, "It shall be done!"[1]

By faith indeed. At the end of the first Camp Wycliffe in 1934, after all expenses were paid, the Camp bank account had eight dollars and fifty cents with which to bring Cam's dream to reality. He owned almost nothing. He had traded in his Whippet car and was given an old Buick that drank oil almost faster than gasoline. Said Cam with tongue in cheek, "The Buick was always stopping beside secondhand auto parts places to get yet another part that had broken."

At the end of 1934, Cam's health wasn't much better than his old Buick's, and worst of all, neither was Elvira's. In January 1935, when Cam and Elvira arrived in Dallas from Monterrey, Mexico, where Elvira had come dangerously close to death, Cam wrote in his diary:

> Elvira became so ill that the doctor instructed me to prepare for a funeral. I went to the pastor of the Monterrey Baptist Church, who told me that the restrictions on religious services were so exacting, it would be impossible to have a funeral service in his church. I then asked him if we could have a service at the cemetery. The pastor said this would mean that all who were present would be liable for imprisonment.
>
> I then went to the owner of the tourist court where we were staying and asked if we might at least pray and have a Bible reading and sing some hymns. The owner said his property would be subject to confiscation if he permitted such things on his premises. [At that time thirteen of the twenty-eight Mexican states had closed all churches and many had expelled all priests and ministers. A law had been signed by the new President, Gen. Lázaro Cárdenas, prohibiting the use of mails for religious literature of any kind. As a result many boxes of Bibles were quarantined in warehouses in the port of Veracruz.]

---

1 Composer unknown. From *Word of Life Chorus Melodies,* compiled by Jack Wyrtzen.

Repelled at the thought of laying away my dear wife without even singing one of her favorite hymns, I asked if she would try to stand a trip back to the States. She agreed. Accompanied by a Mexican nurse who knew how to drive, we traveled day and night (stopping over only for a few hours rest in Laredo) until we reached Dallas, Texas.

Cam's letter of February 7 to a director of the Pioneer Mission Agency (PMA), Mrs. J. Harvey Borton, explained what happened next:

We got Elvira to the hospital [in Dallas] not a moment too soon. The dropsy that began in Monterrey developed so rapidly that by the time we arrived in Dallas, Elvira could hardly breathe. Three times the doctor tapped her lung and drew off about two gallons of fluid. This relieved her breathing. Thus she was able to survive the rest of her treatment for dehydration, although for several days her life hung in the balance.

I have rented a small apartment near the university. As soon as Elvira is able to leave the hospital, I will bring her there. The Mexican nurse who accompanied us from Monterrey has promised to stay with us for a while longer to care for Elvira. Our prayer is that Elvira will be strong enough to travel back to Sulphur Springs in a week or so. I feel the Lord would have us return to Sulphur Springs as soon as Elvira can stand the trip. I have a good bit of writing to do in preparation for next summer's Camp Wycliffe.

Cam's chief concern at this moment was, of course, Elvira's health. He wrote that under no circumstances could he leave her side. But never far from his mind was the upcoming Camp Wycliffe. His concern was that adequate publicity be delivered to a variety of seminaries in time for students to make a decision to attend the summer session. He asked PMA's Harvey Borton if he could help with Camp Wycliffe's publicity by sending out the brochures and application forms. "It is my desire," said Cam, "to get these posted in every Christian college and Bible School in America."

By early May 1935, five young men had applied to take the course at Camp Wycliffe. One letter dated May 2, 1935, came from a Kenneth L. Pike:

Dear Mr. Townsend,

I received your letter yesterday accepting me to Camp Wycliffe for the Summer. The Lord willing, I shall be there. Thank you for suggesting that I write Mr. D.B. [sic] Legters in Philadelphia.

I have not planned to go with the group to Mexico because I have not the financial means. Should this situation change, I shall, Lord willing, apply for the trip.

Should there be any change in the date of the opening of the Camp, please let me know since I have to make plans for leaving school early.

Yours in His glorious ministry, Kenneth L. Pike.

Just a few days after his twenty-third birthday on June 9, 1935, Kenneth L. Pike stuck out his thumb in his hometown of Woodstock, Connecticut and began to hitchhike his way toward Sulphur Springs, Arkansas. En route, Ken stopped at his brother's home in Rolla, Missouri. Knowing that Ken was almost penniless, and that room and board was to be six dollars per month, Ken's brother gave him thirty-five dollars and drove him the rest of the way to the second session of Camp Wycliffe at Sulphur Springs.

The correspondence from Legters and Cam had informed Ken that students should be prepared to live in primitive conditions. Ken's father had been a medical doctor to the Metlacatla Indians in Alaska, but after the strain and load of caring for people in the throes of a measles epidemic, Ken's father's own health broke. He then returned to Woodstock and became an old-fashioned country doctor on an old-fashioned country doctor's wages. In order to feed his large family, Ken's father grew a large vegetable garden that provided much of the family's food. He also grew his own hay for his buggy horses.

Like most boys growing up in a country town, Ken had daily chores, one of which was to keep the wood box filled. Thus, Ken was no stranger to rustic living. However, even after growing up in a rural village environment, he was not prepared for what he found at Camp Wycliffe's Happy Valley Farm. At one point in its history, the farm may well have lived up to its name. But not in 1935. The outbuildings were dilapidated and overgrown with vines and grasses. But it was almost rent free (only five dollars per month) and while the buildings were in need of much repair, Cameron Townsend thought it would be "just the ticket" to train and toughen would-be missionaries. Years later, Ken wrote:

> I remember when my brother and I drove up to the farmhouse and converted chicken coop that was to be used as a classroom, I was a little taken back. I had never seen such rickety, tumbled down buildings.
>
> There were five of us taking the course that summer. Nothing was ready for us. Four of the fellows had to make wooden beds out of old lumber (I found an old wooden bed left over from the previous year). I did, however, make my own mattress. We stuffed straw and dried oats that grew on the hill behind the farmhouse into muslin bags.
>
> But the memory that is most vivid are the nail kegs that we used for chairs. I sat for hour after hour of classes on nail kegs. I did try to upholster my nail keg with a little straw and a burlap sack. This, of course, was part of our training and would become part of SIL's basic principles. Mr. Townsend and L.L. Legters wanted to introduce us, and all subsequent students, to pioneer living as well as pioneer linguistics.

Without any noticeable trace of a sense of humor, the serious, no-nonsense L.L. Legters had little tolerance for mischievous or prank-loving students. So when, on one of the first days of the second year of this school for "serious and purposeful" missionary candidates, he saw one of these so-called serious students sitting twenty feet up a maple tree with a silly grin on his face, he shook his head and prayed, "Oh Lord, couldn't you have sent us someone better than this?" Unknown to Legters, Ken's reason for climbing the tree, was to make himself useful by collecting dead branches for firewood. He also wanted to demonstrate his mastery over a fear of heights.

Someone better, indeed! How could Legters possibly have known or predicted that Kenneth L. Pike, this skinny tree-climbing student, this most unlikely of persons in Legters' view, was destined, in the providence of God, to become one of the most significant and pivotal shapers of this "training camp" that was to become the Summer Institute of Linguistics

(SIL). Or, that Pike would become one of the world's preeminent linguists and pioneer in the areas of basic linguistic theory, phonetics, tone, intonation and grammar. In Eunice Pikes's biography of her brother, she wrote:

> [Ken] was a student of Sapir and Bloomfield, Sturtevant and Fries. Yet he has analyzed more languages than all those worthies. If we count the work of his students, he has probably done more than anyone else to broaden our knowledge of the tongues of man.[1]

And how could either Legters or Pike know at that moment that for thirty-seven years (1942 to 1979), Pike would be the president of the Summer Institute of Linguistics, called then simply "Camp Wycliffe"? And how could anyone have known that the school which began with just two full-time students would become a world-renowned institution that would train thousands of young men and women in the sciences of socio-linguistics, anthropology and Bible translation, and would be accredited as the best training ground in the world for field descriptive linguistics?

In 1933, during his senior year at Gordon College in preparation for what he thought would be the pastoral ministry, Ken renewed his interest in China as a potential field of mission service. This happened after Hudson Taylor's son and daughter-in-law spoke one day in chapel. Several years before, Ken had discovered in his father's library a biography of Hudson Taylor, the founder of the China Inland Mission (CIM). The book challenged Ken's spiritually-sensitive soul, and he became concerned that China's millions needed to have a gospel witness. Speaking about that moment Ken said:

> A year earlier, on December 25, 1932, believing with deep conviction that it was the will of God, I wrote a letter to the China Inland

---

1 Eunice Pike, *Ken Pike, Scholar and Christian* (Dallas: Summer Institute of Linguistics, 1981), p.1. Leonard Bloomfield (1887-1949) was one of the most respected linguists of the first half of the 20th century. His book *Language* (1933) was for years the standard summary of the dominant approach being taken toward linguistics in North America. Bloomfield believed that Linguistics should be an autonomous, empirical science and that language should be studied in isolation from nonlinguistic influences.

Mission board and offered myself for mission service. This was my Christmas present to God.

Through his senior year at Gordon College, Ken waited on tables and was in charge of the kitchen crew. Daily Ken prayed for China. To familiarize himself with that great land, he memorized the names of the provinces and the number of inhabitants in each. After graduating from Gordon College in 1933, Ken left for the China Inland Mission's candidate home in Philadelphia. There, with a number of other hopeful candidates, he was introduced to mission policy and given lessons in Mandarin Chinese. Wrote Eunice Pike:

> Ken loved hearing about China. He admired his teachers, and wanted to learn all he could. In his eagerness, he stayed up late night after night studying. That was a mistake. Without adequate rest, he was noticeably nervous. His brothers would have called him "jittery."[1] (Ken was the next to the youngest of eight children.)

Years later, as he reflected on that moment, Ken said:

> I had offered myself with deep conviction that it was the will of God for me to become a missionary. But after six months, the people at the mission said they thought my temperament was too fragile, that the pressures of the mission field would cause me to have a nervous breakdown. In their judgment, I was not a good risk for overseas service. I was rejected.

The profound hurt from that rejection became the greatest and most serious struggle of Ken's life. It wasn't just because he was rejected by the mission. Ken now had to deal with a greater question. What does God want of me? And how do I, as one who wanted above everything else in life to do the will of God, find guidance?

So sure was Ken that God was directing his life toward missions in general and China in particular, that for a year, while he was at Gordon, he told everyone with great enthusiasm about the spiritual needs of China. "China was," as Ken told his sister, "written on my teeth!" When Ken

1 Ibid: p. 10.

graduated from Gordon in 1933, he took Ezekiel 3:18 (KJV) as his personal mandate:

> When I say unto the wicked, Thou shalt surely die; and thou givest him not warning, nor speakest to warn the wicked from his wicked way, to save his life; the same wicked man shall die in his iniquity; but his blood will I require at thine hand.

With the words of Ezekiel running in his mind like a never-ending tape, and the pain of dealing with the most devastating disappointment of his life, Ken returned to his home in Woodstock. Said Eunice Pike:

> Dad was a nice person to go home to at a time like this. He knew Ken was nervous and that just maybe the CIM leaders were right, but now the question was, how to help Ken pick up the pieces? They were both convinced the Lord would use him somewhere, doing something, but where and what? What training did he lack if he were to fill the spot the Lord had for him?[1]

Just as a person forever remembers a serious fall as a child, Ken never forgot the shock and pain of this rejection. Much of Ken's later poetry explored the nature and subject of pain. In the meantime, Ken had to deal with the reality that he was shy and could be distant and standoff-ish in his personal relationships. He admitted his nervousness and lim-ited physical energies. In fact, the major reason given by CIM for rejecting Ken was poor physical health. Their recommendation was that he find outdoor work to build up his strength. In the face of this psychological, emotional and spiritual shock, Ken made two important decisions. The first was to place himself in what he described as a spiri-tual hospital:

> I was determined to resist all "internal leading" for a year except via the Scriptures and suggestions from advisers until I could reconcile all that had happened and get my feet back on solid ground. This was vitally important, because the alternative was to reject God, and I couldn't do that.

---

1 Ibid: p. 11.

Ken's second decision was to take the CIM's recommendation and find outdoor work. And while he wanted to find footing on solid ground, the work he chose left him completely unsteady on his feet. One of Ken's curious anomalies was his fear of heights. He once wrote a friend explaining that he would almost collapse in fear if he had to look over a banister from any height. In her book Eunice Pike explains the kind of work Ken found:

> Ken took a job with the CWA (Citizens Workers Administration) in their attempt to eradicate the gypsy moth from New England. At that time, the gypsy moth was causing whole forests to die. They attached their eggs in clusters to the underside of branches. The job of the crew working for the CWA was to kill the eggs by painting them with creosote.[1]

In 1933, the mood of America reflected Ken's depression and uncertainty. A quarter of all heads of households in the United States were unemployed. But then in March of that year, came the newly-elected president's inaugural address that heartened millions. Said Franklin D. Roosevelt, "There is nothing to fear, but fear itself."

Ken Pike undoubtedly heard that address, although there is no mention of it in his correspondence. But this idea of overcoming and controlling one's fear took root in Ken's thinking. Little by little he conquered his fear of heights by sheer grit, determination and prayer. Said Ken:

> I took a year out and tried to build up my strength by climbing trees and hunting for gypsy moths [in his home town of Woodstock.] I would climb a little bit, stop, pray, climb some more, stop, pray and climb. People on the ground could see that I was scared, but I climbed in spite of my fear and the shame my older brother said he felt when he saw me struggling to climb a tree.

Ken's brothers may have had their doubts about Ken's ability to get a job done, but not Ken's father. When he saw his son's determination to overcome his fear of heights, he said, "I am not at all concerned about Kenneth. He's got intelligence, courage and determination. He will succeed in anything he does."

---

1 Ibid: p. 11, 12.

These were not idle words from a doting father designed to charm Ken's imagination. Rather they were words from a competent critic who had a keen appreciation of his son's tenacity and budding interest and genius for languages and linguistics. When Ken's year of joyless tree climbing was over, he and his father sat down for a serious talk about Ken's future. His father reminded him that Greek had always been relatively easy for him, and suggested that further study of Greek might be something he should consider as a next step in his training.

That "next step" was for Ken to return to Gordon for a postgraduate course in Greek. While he was there, three minor but life-changing events took place. The first was hearing someone from India casually mention that a little knowledge of phonetics could help missionaries learn a new language faster and with less difficulty than those who had not studied this particular branch of linguistics that deals with the study of human speech sounds. Since Ken had difficulty with the sound system when he was trying to learn to speak Mandarin at the CIM candidate school, he thought surely phonetics would be the "magic bullet."

The second event that built on the first came from one of Ken's professors. "Ken, you have a logical mind and a retentive memory." This remark, along with an "A" in his Scriptural Exegesis class and an invitation from the secretary of the League of Evangelical Students to write some expository lessons from the Gospel of Luke, began to rebuild some of Ken's beleaguered self-esteem.

The third casual event was meeting Sam Fisk, a returned missionary from the Philippines. Fisk had been on staff at John Brown University and had received a copy of the brochure announcing the linguistic course at Camp Wycliffe in Arkansas. In 1935, Fisk taught at Gordon College and told Ken about a tiny school called "Camp Wycliffe" that had started the summer before. "It's a special school where they study linguistics to prepare prospective missionaries to do Bible translation."

The more Ken thought about Bible translation, the more interested he became. For the next several months he wrote to all eleven mission boards listed by the Interdenominational Foreign Missions Association (IFMA) asking where he could go to find training in Bible translation and technical linguistics.

When Ken's letter of inquiry arrived on the desk of L.L. Legters, he sent it on to Townsend in Sulphur Springs who answered immediately (Ken's only positive answer to his letters of inquiry).

The prospectus Cam sent to Ken explained that the school's distinctive was to teach young men how to translate the Bible for Latin American Indians. It also said the student would learn such things as the description of an Indian language, some anthropology, and phonetics. Ah, phonetics! This was exactly what he felt he needed to complement his training.

Of that summer in 1935 and his memory of using the hard nail kegs for chairs, Ken said there was another memory he never forgot. It was Cameron Townsend's dream:

> When I hitchhiked to Sulphur Springs, I was tired, hurt and still brokenhearted over my rejection from the China Inland Mission. I felt a half man. And then I met another half man, Cameron Townsend. He too was tired, had been sick, and had a wife at home who was almost an invalid.
>
> But that's not what stood out in my memory. What I remembered most about Cameron Townsend was his incredible dream. He told us students that all the tribes of the world should have the Scriptures in their own language and the French Academy had listed 2,700 different languages. However, seven hundred of these were dying out and not profitable to reach and that perhaps a thousand of these languages or more were overlapping dialects. Thus, he calculated, there were a thousand languages that needed the Scriptures.
>
> With the help of another student, Max Lathrop,[1] Mr. Townsend wrote a little pamphlet called, "A Thousand Tribes Without the Bible," and when he said, "Let us tackle half of those," I thought that there had never been a bigger dream dreamed under more difficult circumstances. Alexander conquering the world was small compared to that. (At one point, I have to confess that I thought it was something of a pipe dream.)
>
> At the same time he was talking about five hundred languages, he was talking about translation and science. This man, who had only had three years in college, was saying, "In fifteen years we will

---

1   There were five students who took the course in 1935. They were listed on Camp Wycliffe's letterhead as: Maxwell B. Lathrop, Jr., B.A.; D. Brainerd Legters, B.A.; Richmond McKinney, B.A.; Kenneth L. Pike, Th.B.; William Sedat. William (Bill) Sedat was a German citizen and was working on securing his American citizenship papers.

make the scientists sit up and take notice." In addition to his scholarship and Bible translation, he dreamed of being a practical servant to governments and wanted to institute a vigorous literacy
program that would teach people to read. He was dreaming of this
when I was there in 1935.

It was true SIL would one day make the scientific world sit up and take
notice. But Kenneth L. Pike, the man who would most dramatically
bring this about, still had to convince the cofounder of the school, L.L.
Legters, that his interest went beyond climbing trees.

*Elvira Townsend, Evelyn Griset, Cameron Townsend with the old Buick
and housetrailer given them by friends in Gravette, Arkansas. Photo
taken on Coyoacan, Mexico City, the fall of 1935, as they were preparing to travel to Tetalcingo to set up their language project among the
Nahuatl Aztecs of Tetelcingo.*

Chapter Three

Ten Dollars and God

He was a soldier, a general, a great hero and leader of the Mexican Revolution. His name was Lázaro Cárdenas del Rio, and in 1934 he became the president of Mexico. Given the nature and history of Mexican politics, a sitting president hand picks his successor. As the presidential elections of 1934 approached, the then president, Plutarco Calles, often referred to as the "iron man" and known for enforcing harsh anticlerical policies, gave his support to Cárdenas.

Calles, a shrewd political manipulator, had installed three previous puppet presidents. He now believed that in Cárdenas he had installed a fourth. Calles could not have been more wrong.

In his November 30, 1934 inaugural address, Cárdenas said, "You have elected me to be your president. Your president I will be."[1] Immediately Cárdenas set about to implement the social reforms promised by the Mexican constitution of 1917. A highly principled, idealistic man dedicated to social reform, Cárdenas broke with tradition by choosing to live in his own private house, rather than moving into the presidential mansion "Los Pinos" (The Pines) in beautiful Chapultepec Park. He cut his salary in half

---

1 Josephus Daniels, *Shirt-Sleeve Diplomat* (Chapel Hill: The University of North Carolina Press, 1947), p. 59.

while raising the salaries and benefits of those in the military. He then began to implement land reform and improve the educational system.

At first, some observers thought Cárdenas would be a rubber stamp for Calles, but the Mexican people and foreign observers were surprised one day in early summer of 1935 to learn that Cárdenas had taken a drastic political step by requesting the resignation of every member of his leftist cabinet. Further, Cárdenas announced the dismissal of two top ranking generals on charges of "seditious and rebellious" activities.[1]   The years under former President Calles, once described by Dr. Frank Tannenbaum, the noted sociologist and political science professor from Columbia University, as "debased and clouded," were over.

Such news, of course, was observed with great interest by the U.S. government. Josephus Daniels, U.S. Ambassador to Mexico, hoped the New Deal Cárdenas proposed for Mexico would run concurrently with Roosevelt's New Deal in the United States. And the shake-up of Cárdenas's cabinet did not go unnoticed by Cameron Townsend or the students at Camp Wycliffe. On June 19, Ken Pike, while enduring Sulphur Springs' oppressive ninety degree heat (in the shade) wrote a lengthy letter to his mother:

> We had a great day here yesterday. A week ago, no missionary or preacher was allowed into Mexico. Two of the men who are here who had spent some time in Mexico were almost bounced from the country when someone from the States addressed a letter to them as Reverend (they were not ordained). On Saturday morning and Sunday afternoon we had a special prayer meeting about this situation. We also prayed for guidance as to where each of us should work when we go to Mexico.
>
> On Sunday, Mr. Legters prayed that the Lord would put God's seal of approval on our work by giving us one man *that* night to support us fellows. On Tuesday we invited a number of neighbors who were interested in the work for another prayer meeting. Our prayer was especially for God to open the door to Mexico for Bible translation. That very day the newspaper reported that President Cárdenas had demanded the resignation of his entire cabinet. Many of these were the very men who favored the antireligious

---

1 Ibid. p. 61.

laws. One of those who resigned was governor of the state of Tabasco. He especially was hard against the church. We took this to be God's leading and praised the Lord for answered prayer.

The next day President Cárdenas announced his new cabinet, and none of the new men were in favor of the antireligious laws. One of the men he appointed to be the governor of San Luis Potosi has an evangelical wife and mother-in-law.

The other good news came from a letter addressed to Mr. Legters from a friend in California who offered financial support to one of us five fellows. The amazing thing is that the letter must have been mailed at least by Sunday night! All these things remind me of King Nebuchadnezzar from Daniel 4:25 [KJV] "...and they shall make thee to eat the grass as oxen, and they shall wet thee with the dew of heaven, and seven times shall pass over thee, till thou know that the most High ruleth in the kingdom of men, and giveth it to whomsoever he will."

Ken ended his letter by saying that Mr. Townsend wanted him to consider working among a particular group of Aztec people. Years later Ken told how Cam got him committed to joining the group that was going to Mexico.

One afternoon as I was walking up a little Ozark hill, I met Mr. Townsend. He asked me what I was going to be doing when the course was over. I told him I wasn't sure and that I had been turned down by another mission who worked in Asia because they determined my health wasn't strong enough to take an overseas assignment. Mr. Townsend just smiled and said, "Well, I don't know about that, but why don't you come with me to Mexico?" And that was it. No health examination, no formal examination or letters of recommendation, no board to go before or extensive interviews. Just a simple invitation, "Why don't you come with me to Mexico?" and I was in.

Ken did not then share these details with his mother. He said simply: "The ideas of what I will do and where I will work are somewhat nebulous at the moment. At this point I don't care where I work, except it must be the place I am supposed to be."

Twenty-five years later, on May 10, 1959, at a special meeting where Cameron Townsend was speaking about God's faithfulness over those years, Townsend recalled the events surrounding that pivotal prayer meeting in the hot summer of 1935.

> When I asked Mr. Legters how the students were going to get to Mexico, without a blink he said, "The fellows can hitchhike." Then I said, "How are we going to get into the country? The doors to Mexico are closed. The government says they have too much religion. They don't want any more." When two of our men, Maxwell Lathrop and Mr. Legters' son Brainerd were about to graduate from seminary in April, they both wrote and inquired about their chances of entering Mexico to work with a minority people. Both men had received positive invitations to work with other organizations.
>
> In my reply I told them in all honesty that we had no human assurance whatever of their being able to enter the land to which they felt called. In fact, I said the human restrictions that faced us were insurmountable except for God. But then I told them of how God had led us thus far and of my conviction that He would go before us and open the door. Amazingly they felt this assurance was sufficient and both took the summer linguistic course.
>
> One day that summer we set aside a day of prayer to ask God to open the doors to Mexico. It was a summer of great heat, drought and hot, dry dust storms. All that summer the weather was miserable. But we needed to pray. We went outside under those dry oaks, with hard nail kegs for chairs, and listened while Mr. Legters opened the Word to us. We then got down on our knees and asked God to open the doors to Mexico.
>
> Can you imagine a weaker human situation? We were calling on God to do the impossible, to open closed doors to the Gospel. And then, to our amazement, that very night we heard over the radio that President Cárdenas had dismissed his entire cabinet. When Mr. Legters asked me what I thought all this meant, I said I wasn't entirely sure. What I did know was that the intensely antireligious men were no longer in power. And for that we could be thankful. I was also certain this cabinet shake-up would result in improved government relations, and that God was opening the doors to Mexico.

In many ways, the summer of 1935 was a mixed blessing for Cameron Townsend. He had a great deal for which to thank God. Elvira's health improved to where she was able to speak at a conference in Atlanta and sing two solo numbers. The publishing company, Fleming Revell, was interested in publishing a book Cam was writing about the physical and spiritual needs of Guatemala's ethnic peoples. John Brown University allowed Cam to present a weekly missions message on their radio station. The five young students of Camp Wycliffe's class of 1935,[1] plus many in the surrounding Arkansas communities of Sulphur Springs, Gravette, Southwest City, and Maysville were captivated by Cam's charisma and vision. Many saw this as a practical program around which both career translators and lay persons could rally. Cam rejoiced when people from several churches visited the Camp and brought not only the contribution of their prayers, but also their "dietetic" relief in the form of homemade pies and ice cream. Several mission leaders visited the Camp as well and later wrote glowing reports. One said:

> I consider this school to be the fourth great missionary movement of the past half century. In order they are: the Moody Schools for training missionaries, the Student Volunteer Movement, the Layman's Missionary Movement, and now Camp Wycliffe and its plan to train men to translate the Bible into all languages of earth.

Another said he thought this training was "the most practical thing he had seen in preparing people to be missionaries." On the other hand not all mission agencies shared these positive endorsements. It seemed Cam's idealism and sense of responsibility for ethnic peoples to have the Scriptures in their own languages sometimes put him at cross-purposes with other established mission agencies. In a letter to Rev. R.R. Gregory of the American Bible Society on July 12, we see a candid Cameron Townsend outlining his vision with clarity, precision and a touch of frustration. Cam sent the letter in response to criticism from those who did not share or understand his vision:

> It has been my hope [from the beginning] that after the students [learned the techniques of Bible translation] they could carry on

---

1 Maxwell (Max) Lathrop, David Brainerd Legters, Richmond McKinney, Kenneth L. Pike, William (Bill) Sedat.

through established mission agencies. Mr. Legters and I do not want to form a new organization, and if at all possible, will stay clear of doing so. Both Mr. Legters and I want to see these men go out under established mission boards or, if it were possible, under the American Bible Society.

Thus far, however, it seems hopeless to hope for either. My fellow missionaries in Guatemala do nothing but either throw water on the scheme, or else show nothing but their indifference. The Presbyterian board wrote to say that they only have money to send out one or two educational or medical missionaries this year. The Nazarene Board showed more interest and I anticipate their cooperation. However, before we can have mutual cooperation from the mission boards, it will be necessary for someone like yourself to visit the Camp and see firsthand what God is doing.

In the meantime, we are going ahead with great blessing from on high. If it's impossible to make the contacts with the established mission organizations, we will ultimately have to go ahead and organize [our own] translation society.

On July 25, just weeks after his 39th birthday, Cam wrote his constituents to bring them up to date on the activity of the school and his future plans:

It is our prayer that as a result of this summer's linguistic training, six New Testaments will be translated into six languages. Elvira and I plan to join the students on their trip to Mexico. Our hope is to spend eight or nine months in Mexico with a new tribe of people. Our summers will be spent in the States at Camp Wycliffe where we will continue to train prospective missionaries for Bible translation.

This session of Camp Wycliffe has been singularly blessed with five God-picked men. Each is exceptionally well prepared. Dr. McCreery believes the birth of this school will become a movement that will go forward until every tribe on the face of the earth has received God's Word in their own language.

This month we celebrated the 18th anniversary of Elvira's arrival on the mission field by spending four hours studying phonetics under Dr. McCreery. Just a few months ago she almost died. Now she has the strength to study four hours a day in preparation for a new task. Truly a miracle!

Along with praying for our health, you also have prayed for an open door to Mexico, and God has answered. A month ago the hinges on the door began to creak. A new president has come to power and the antireligious laws have been relaxed. Many who favored the laws have been dismissed from prominent positions in the government. Another miracle!

Cam then added two paragraphs in which he asked for money, not for himself, but for another. He first mentioned that his niece Evelyn Griset had taken a year out of her studies at U.C.L.A. (her major was Spanish) to go with them to Mexico to help Elvira (who obviously wasn't as strong as Cam wanted to believe).

Years before, Cam, who enjoyed playing Cupid, had introduced his sister Lula to his bachelor Sunday School teacher, Eugene Griset. The result was a marriage, as Cam hoped. Eventually Cam had a niece, Evelyn (Evie). Evie was, in the words of her U.C.L.A roommate, Ethel Wallis, "Cute, always cheerful, upbeat, vivacious, energetic and with a passion for drama and football."

None of this was in Cam's letter, of course. He said simply that Evelyn was a talented missionary volunteer and needed support for the year she would be tending to Elvira's special diet and other duties. Cam also asked for "sufficient support [money] for the splendid young men who were going with me to Mexico." But as for money for himself, Cam said:

Elvira and I urgently request you do not help support any of these that I have asked for, if by so doing you should have to reduce your contributions toward the precious work of God with whom we were formerly connected, the Central American Mission. Prayer is what we must have! Nothing else can see us through in this tremendous undertaking.

Cam ended the letter by saying he and Elvira planned to leave for Mexico on August 15, and since he wasn't sure exactly what town or village they would settle in, all mail after that date should be sent in care of the Pioneer Missionary Agency. He then said, "Please do not address me as

'Reverend.' I am not ordained and the title might occasion me serious difficulties in Mexico."

Cam's insistence that money normally designated for the Central American Mission should not in any way be diverted to himself, the school or any of the students, came out of a blistering attack earlier that summer. Elvira's brother, C.A.M. missionary Carl Malmstrom, had objected to Cam's designation of a small amount of money to Joe Chicol and Ed Sywulka. Joe had been part of the Camp Wycliffe staff and had returned to Guatemala to work among the Cakchiquels. Ed Sywulka also returned to Guatemala and was to work among the Mam people.

During the years Cam and Elvira worked with C.A.M. in Guatemala, Mr. A.E. Forbes, an elderly tea and coffee merchant from St. Louis, had been an enthusiastic and generous supporter of Cam's work in San Antonio. After Cam and Elvira resigned from C.A.M., they were scrupulous in sending all monies to C.A.M. that had come directly to them for the C.A.M. work. The one exception occurred when Cam allocated fifteen dollars each to Joe Chicol and Ed Sywulka out of a five hundred dollar gift from Mr. Forbes. This was considered an arbitrary use of funds and Cam was soundly criticized for so doing. On June 29, Cam wrote Karl Hummel to partly answer that criticism:

> Joe Chicol wrote to tell me that because of the poor coffee harvest this year, the San Antonio School is practically without funds. I have sent him and the others at San Antonio the last bit of the Forbes money to help out. Mr. Forbes should send another five hundred next month, but I believe I had better send it on to Carl Malmstrom. He and others have criticized me so severely in the Chicol-Sywulka matter, I feel I need to protect myself against further misunderstanding. I prize the friendships of my C.A.M colleagues more than I can tell you. I don't want in any way to add to their burden, nor to my own misunderstandings. Therefore, I have concluded that I had better not try and control the expenditures of funds which I am instrumental in raising, nor guide the activities of those, who like Joe, go to the field through my instrumentality.

There was a postscript to his letter that gives a unique window into Cameron Townsend's inner soul. Part of his character was the abiding belief that "all things work together for the glory of God," even his own sickness.

> Did I tell you that my nephew Ronald White is developing into a successful Presbyterian preacher? I am glad I had T.B. That illness forced my return to California at just the right time which in turn allowed me to influence him for the ministry.

On August 5, Elvira gave Karl Hummel an answer to her brother's criticism concerning the Forbes money:

> Enclosed you will find the A.E. Forbes check for $500.00 which my brother Carl returned to us from Guatemala. As you know, we have carried A.E. Forbes funds on our books. I believe you realize that through these many years Mr. Forbes has been sending us money, we have never used a cent of this fund for our own personal needs. We are happy to forward this check to you for distribution for C.A.M. missionaries working among the Cakchiquels.

Elvira concluded her letter by saying they had a wonderful summer with the "boys" at Camp Wycliffe, and that the study of phonetics under Dr. McCreery was great. "We are counting the days until we all leave for Mexico."

It goes without saying that the most fundamental item any traveler must have before undertaking a lengthy journey, especially to a foreign country, is money. But Cameron Townsend was not just any ordinary traveler. He seldom took into account the "normal" circumstantial hazards associated with travel. Such hazards, whatever they might be, were to be given over to God and His intervention. In his diary he wrote:

> At the close of the 1935 summer linguistic session the entire student body decided to make the trip to Mexico. The only stipulation was that we required them to have at least fifty dollars apiece in hand before we would consent to their going. That small sum would allow a person to go and return after a short visit. For those who desired to remain, we felt God would demonstrate His approval by sending more funds after they had crossed the border if He had not done so before.

The only problem was that of the ten people in their party, only Elvira, Cam and his niece Evelyn Griset knew that between them they did not have fifty dollars. Since Cam believed it was God's will for him to go to Mexico with Elvira, his niece and the students, he began their journey to Mexico with not much more than ten dollars and God.

The car Cam drove was an old 1929 Buick with a motor so badly worn that it burned a quart of oil every twenty to twenty-five miles.[1] Hitched to the Buick for the trip to Mexico was a lumbering two-ton boxcar-shaped trailer that had been given to Cam and Elvira by Tom Haywood who ran the local Peoples Hardware store in neighboring Gravette, the same Tom Haywood who suppled the nail kegs for chairs at Camp Wycliffe.

When the little party reached Dallas, they stopped at the C.A.M headquarters over Sunday to visit Mildred Spain, C.A.M financial secretary, Karl Hummel and other former colleagues. About ten o'clock Monday morning, Mildred asked Cam if he was planning to leave that afternoon for Mexico. (The other members of the party had started early that morning.) Cam replied with a time-honored, "Well, Lord willing, we hope to."

"What do you mean, hope to? Don't you have any money?" asked Mildred.

Cam smiled and said, "We have a little over five dollars between the three of us." Cam remembered that Mildred expressed such astonishment that at first it seemed to border almost on disgust. "But then," he wrote, "with her customary enthusiasm, she entered into the fun of waiting to see how God would provide for our need."

About an hour later the postman arrived with the day's mail and Mildred went to Cam and Elvira's room and said, "Well, you can thank the Lord. Moody Memorial Church has just sent you a check. It's for ninety dollars!"

Years later, Ken Pike would wonder out loud about the incongruity of Cam starting out with a wife who had heart trouble, his young niece to help take care of her, a lumbering old car and trailer, and a dream to translate all the languages of the world with ninety five dollars in his pocket!

What Ken may have forgotten was that Hudson Taylor, Cameron Townsend's model for mission, had returned to England from a first term

---

1   Ethel E. Wallis & Mary A. Bennett, *Two Thousand Tongues to Go* (New York: Harper & Row, 1959), p. 53.

in China deeply discouraged. But then after a new experience with God on a lonely beach in Brighton, Taylor opened up a bank account in the name of the China Inland Mission. The amount deposited was five pounds (about ten dollars US). Taylor had no mission organization, no missionaries and no money. That was in 1855. By the end of the century, Taylor had over seven hundred missionaries in the interior of China!

But Ken Pike himself might have considered the incongruity of his own act of faith. Mexican law required a visitor to have in hand or in the bank thirty-five dollars for every month they would be in the country. When Ken's brother learned he was going to Mexico and was low on funds, he gave Ken thirty-five dollars.

Ken, with Bill Sedat and Max Lathrop, crossed the Laredo border for the first time on August 20, 1935. Cam, Elvira and Evelyn crossed several hours later[1] and overtook Ken and the others sleeping beside the road. John Dale, who had helped them in Laredo, drove ahead with Richmond McKinney as did Brainerd Legters with a traveler named Moody.

However, when the customs official discovered Ken only had sixty dollars in hand and a bank statement that showed a balance of one hundred dollars, he issued Ken a two-month visa with the provision that if he could demonstrate his financial security, he could renew his tourist visa in Mexico City. The other "near miss" occurred when the customs official read a shipping label on Ken's luggage. Ken later recalled:

My heart sank when I saw "In Care of Central American Mission" on the shipping label of a box I had sent express from Sulphur Springs to Dallas. The woman inspector stamped the label twice, then clucked her lips and said, "Mmm! Mmm!"

There were to be several more "near misses" before Ken and the other fellows reached Mexico City. One of the first for Ken was wandering range cattle crossing the narrow Mexican highway. Unfortunately, their 1929 car wasn't equipped with modern sealed-beam headlights (they weren't invented until 1942). The ink black darkness seemed to swallow up the weak light from their headlamps and only by the grace of God and some fancy last-moment maneuvering did the fellows miss some rancher's laconic steer.

---

1 Curiously the big old oil guzzling Buick proved to be something of an asset at the Mexican border. The border officials were so impressed with the big Buick and large two-ton trailer, they were embarrassed to ask if Cam had enough money to live on during their stay in Mexico.

Headlamps were not the only weakness of the car; so were the brakes, and then one of the headlights broke. But this was only the beginning of their troubles. Wrote Ken in his diary on August 21 and 22:

> After dinner with the Townsends and getting the car's brakes and lights fixed, we left [Cam was delayed by having new rings put in his Buick and the front end of their trailer repaired]. August 22 was a day of great trouble. Ran out gas at noon. Hailed a car and they gave us enough gas to reach the next village. About six that night I left the rut in the road and the front wheel dropped to the axle. At the same time the starter locked. For fifteen pesos, a bus pulled us thirty kilometers to the town of Valles (the rate of exchange was three to one). This somehow resulted in breaking a headlamp and the bumper on both sides. It seems the best insurance for travel in Mexico is a heavy rope, a complete set of mud hooks and a two-gallon can of gasoline. (Sometimes a brass stomach and a bottle of quinine doesn't hurt as well.)

Ken's diary records they tied the broken bumper to the sides of the car and started on their way, only to hazard a dangerous river crossing:

> We came to a ferry. I could not guess where the power was. Cable was strung across the river. There were two wheels big as barn doors. Tackle blocks to the front and back of the ferry. By tightening the rope on one end, the ferry was swung at an angle to the current which was very swift.

The ferry worked like a sail, and was pushed sideways. The cable kept it from drifting. At the opposite shore the other cable would be tightened and the ferry straightened to run aground by its coasting momentum. Then the nose would be lowered onto the gravel, and with a bump, a car would go off. The ferry was only big enough to hold two cars. The charge for this crossing was fifty centavos.

Ken learned that the cables and ropes on these ferry crossings sometimes broke. For this reason, Ken and the others were not too unhappy when they had to wait five hours at the village of Tamazunchale to let the river recede in order to make a safer crossing. In the meantime, Cam had experienced his own travel problems. On September 23, after arriving in Mexico City, he wrote:

> Elvira stood the trip surprisingly well. But we did have some difficulty along the way. In many places the roads are under construction. This not only makes it hard on the traveler, but dangerous as well. At one point on our trip, I was afraid the car and trailer would both drop into a canyon. The right rear wheel of the Buick actually went over the edge and was suspended in thin air. But God took care of us. There was a big steam shovel nearby and with true Mexican hospitality, they pulled us back on the road.

Cam's letter also revealed that in a remarkably short period of time, each of the five fellows, along with himself, was already involved with an indigenous group of people:

> We each seem to have received definite guidance regarding our respective fields of labor. McKinney goes to the Otomi people, Pike to the Mixtecos, Brainerd Legters to the Mayas in Yucatan [Max Lathrop went with his new wife Elizabeth to work among the Tarascan people on the shores of Lake Patzcuaro in the state of Michoacan]. Bill Sedat went to Guatemala. Elvira and I will go to Tetelcingo, an Aztec town about two hours south of Mexico City. I have been spending so much of my time getting the other fellows settled in their various areas, that I haven't had much time for language study. Elvira, on the other hand, has jumped right in and seems to be enjoying herself.

There is a short paragraph in that letter that in passing seems like an "Oh, isn't that nice," but in reality it represents one of the most defining moments in the history of the Summer Institute of Linguistics in Mexico, and beyond. It also uniquely defines Cameron Townsend's own career as a mission statesman and friend of presidents:

> The Lord had a special treat in store for us when we first arrived at the end of August. The Seventh Inter-American Scientific Congress was being held at the Palace of Fine Arts. Representatives were to come from every country in the Western Hemisphere. One

of the subjects under discussion was the situation of the Indian tribes. We presented ourselves as SIL. When the leading friends of the Indians of Mexico, like the Secretary of Labor, and the founder and director of the Mexican Institute of Linguistic Investigations and others learned we wanted to assist the government in improving the Indians' living conditions besides carrying out a thorough study of Mexico's ethnic languages and to give them some portions of the Bible and promote literacy among them, we were taken in as members. We were seated in the section devoted to Indian affairs and took part in the discussions. It was all most instructive.

What Cam failed to mention in that particular letter was the name of the man who for that opening session was seated at the presiding officer's desk. His name was Lázaro Cárdenas, President of the Republic of Mexico.

Chapter Four

"This is Townsend. He has come to translate the Bible"

It is unlikely the five new young translators who went to Mexico with Cameron and Elvira Townsend in August of 1935 realized how pivotal Pike's and Townsend's participation in the Seventh Inter-American Scientific Congress would be for their future. While both men attended the same congress, they each focused on different aspects of that historical moment. Said Pike:

> After my trip to the state of Oaxaca and it was established I would work among a group of Mixtec people of San Miguel el Grande, I returned to Mexico City just in time to join Mr. Townsend at the Congress. The caucus on Indian affairs met in a room about fifteen feet wide and twenty feet long. Seated at the head table were the dignitaries including the Minister of Indian Affairs, Dr. Vasquez, a Zapoteco Indian. He was the former Rector of the National University of Mexico and is now the director of the Indian Linguistic Institute.

As we came to this particular meeting, I sensed Mr. Townsend was under considerable tension as he wondered out loud to me just how he was going to make it plain to the officials that he wanted to translate the Scriptures for Mexico's many ethnic minority peoples. Mr. Legters had stated the board of the Pioneer Mission Agency wanted it clearly understood that there be no subterfuge with respect to our reasons for being in Mexico. The board had insisted the Mexican government understand what we wanted to do, and that we do it out in the open. Legters concurred that nothing be done underhanded.

Mr. Townsend, too, did not want to work clandestinely, yet he knew the attitude of the government toward expatriates working with ethnic peoples was negative. At the same time, he wanted the government's blessing, which seemed an impossibility.

As we walked into the room and faced a dozen or more high level ministers, Mr. Townsend immediately spotted the Minister of Rural Education. He was the man who had at one point told Mr. Townsend to stay out of the country, that Mexico did not need any more religion. To my surprise, Mr. Townsend walked straight up to the minister, smiled and gave him a big *abrazo* and said, "Don Rafael, I am delighted to see you."

To my astonishment, Professor Rafael Ramírez returned Mr. Townsend's *abrazo,* then turning to the others in the room said, "This is Townsend. He has come to translate the Bible."

That particular incident was forever etched in Ken Pike's mind, and he took delight in retelling (always with passion) how God had performed a miracle:

Do you now see why I say God has been at work in SIL from the very beginning? This simply could not have just happened. Each of us would have been willing to dig ditches to get the translation done. Instead, rather than having us dig ditches, the government asked us to do science and linguistics for them. Again and again Mr. Townsend said, "They paid Moses' mother to nurse Moses." We had to do linguistics in order to do the translation, and the government and the universities invited us to do linguistics.

While Ken focused on the outcome of being an official member of the Scientific Congress, Cameron Townsend focused on Mexico's chief executive:

> My first encounter with President Cárdenas was in August 1935 at the opening of the Seventh Inter-American Scientific Congress in the Palace of Fine Arts in Mexico City. There at the presiding officer's desk sat a man just past forty with dark curly hair crowning a high receding forehead, large kindly eyes, a short bushy mustache, a physique radiating energy, and a serious military bearing.[1]

Two months later, on October 8, 1935, Cam wrote a letter to the office secretary of the Pioneer Mission Agency on what appears to be the first letterhead that bears the full name and seal of the *Instituto Lingüístico De Verano* (Summer Institute of Linguistics).   Ethel Wallis, longtime Wycliffe member and writer of several important books on Wycliffe and SIL, including the *Dayuma Story* and *Two Thousand Tongues to Go,* wrote:

> Less than a year and a half after the first Camp Wycliffe, Cameron Townsend had a plan and a format for formalizing the field work of his linguist translators in Mexico under the name of the Summer Institute of Linguistics, INSTITUTO LINGUISTICO DE VERANO (SIL). It is clear Townsend, even then, had the vision of starting a scientific society which would be acceptable to Mexican scientists and educators and the Mexican government.

That Townsend was moving ahead with all speed was evident. The outcome of his attendance at the scientific Congress resulted in his being elected a member of a newly-formed Linguistic Society. This in turn led to a formal request by the Director of Rural Education that Cam prepare primers to be used by government teachers to teach ethnic people to read in their language. Cam noted that membership in this society was limited to twenty Mexicans and ten expatriates.

Additionally, Cam had sent a formal request to President Cárdenas through the Secretary of Labor asking permission for him to bring in ten

---

1 William Cameron Townsend, *Lázaro Cárdenas, Mexican Democrat* (Waxhaw: International Friendship, 1979), p. 4.

more young men to work on Mexico's ethnic languages. Cam, of course, did not have ten young men. It was for Cam an audacious leap of faith. In a letter to Legters that dealt with some housekeeping details about moving Camp Wycliffe from Breezy Point to a more suitable location thirty miles away in Siloam Springs, Arkansas, Cam asked Legters to covenant together with him in prayer that God would provide ten men[1] from those who would be coming to the third Camp Wycliffe to be held the next June.

Cam concluded the one-page letter with, "Mrs. Townsend and Evelyn are all well and we plan to settle next week in an Indian town called Tetelcingo." In another letter written on that same October 8 to Karl Hummel, Cam's description of Tetelcingo was less than complimentary. At the same time, he was characteristically optimistic:

> We feel led to settle in an Aztec-speaking town called Tetelcingo. This little village of a thousand people at just a little over 4,000 feet is only two hours drive from the capital.

Never passive, Cam wanted to give his full attention to the issues he felt the Mexican government wanted to address. Cam knew President Cárdenas had cast himself as the "friend of the peasant" and wanted economic and social reform for all citizens of his country. Thus Cam was eager to demonstrate his solidarity with the goals and desires of the government. In a letter to Legters, Cam wrote:

> You know how important it is to the overall Indian work to break down prejudice. The time spent helping the government will, in the long run, be a direct advantage to our overall work.

Cam believed that to talk about God and personal salvation apart from addressing the physical and social needs of downtrodden or exploited people was to bear a hollow witness. And in the case of the village of Tetelcingo in the state of Morelos (the very state that produced the revo-

---

1 Note the emphasis was on men. Within a year, the issue of single women serving as translators would become a point of contention between Legters and Townsend. Townsend, the young visionary aware of the social reforms sweeping both Mexico and the United States, realized women as well as men could serve as translators. The older more conservative Legters held an opposing view.

lutionary fighter Emiliano Zapata), the needs were massive. The town was the poorest of the poor: hot, dry, treeless; without paved roads, electricity, running water, hospital or clinic and a high infant mortality rate. The Aztec-speaking citizens lived in simple adobe dwellings that were, like the village school house, on the verge of collapse. Further, there was little local land for the men to farm. In his diary Cam wrote:

> Poverty is extreme. People only eat twice a day and seldom more than tortillas, chile peppers and herbs. In spite of the fierce heat, the women wear a heavy costume made from wool. The square where we parked our trailer (after asking permission from the mayor) is barren, except for the stone *pila* (water tank) in the center where people come to draw their water. At one side, of the square stands the schoolhouse; on another side the town hall and jail and one of the seven Catholic churches in the area. Over the entrance of the church is a painted cross. On the right of the cross is a painted sun, and on the left a painted moon. I learned the people called the sun "our holy father," and the moon they call our "holy mother."

While Tetelcingo was only two hours from fashionable Mexico City, this sleepy village was considered so miserably poor that even the tax collector passed it by. This fact may have been in Cam's thinking when he wrote Legters on November 14 to ask him to pray about a serious situation:

> A complication has arisen which demands prayer. The man in the government who is our chief sponsor advises us (almost orders us) to sleep in the city of Cuautla until a band of marauders in this region is captured or scattered by government forces.
>
> We don't have enough money to rent a room there unless we could get one very cheap. Furthermore, it would cripple our work here. If it's the Lord's will for us to be here, He will send in the funds, and if it isn't, He will take care of us. We do, however, urgently need your prayers. The town of Tepoztlán, not far from here, was looted the other night.

The work Cam referred to as in danger of being crippled was two-pronged. Prong one was a request by the Department of Education for Cam to prepare and print five thousand copies of a his Aztec primer that would be sent to school teachers in every Aztec-speaking town in the region. In addition to the primer in Aztec, the government wanted ten thousand copies of a Spanish primer Cam had prepared employing the same literacy principles he used among the Cakchiquels when he was in Guatemala.

When Cam, Elvira and Evelyn Griset first arrived in Tetelcingo, there was no house to rent. Cam was, however, given permission to park his house trailer in the central square between the school house and the Catholic church. To give them some privacy, and reminiscent of their first cornstalk house in San Antonio, Cam built a shed next to the trailer, then fenced in the trailer and shed with bamboo stalks. Also reminiscent of their work in Guatemala, Elvira opened up their yard to visitors and spent each afternoon reading a chapter of the New Testament to the wife of the town's mayor. Besides her reading classes, Elvira began a sewing class. While she was dealing with sewing and reading classes, Cam was struggling with what to officially call the group of people he had taken to Mexico. Some, including American Ambassador Josephus Daniels, referred to the little group as the "Townsend Group," a name Cam disliked intensely.

On November 11, 1935, in view of Mexico's anticlerical posture, Legters, speaking for the Pioneer Mission Agency, suggested that Townsend use a nonreligious name for his letterhead. He suggested "The American Linguistic Society." Legters then asked Townsend if he might have a more appropriate name. What is curious about this correspondence is that Townsend was using the name *Instituto Lingüístico de Verano* informally a full month before Legters wrote to suggest he use a nonreligious name for the group in Mexico. The group was to be known as the Mexico Branch of the Summer Institute of Linguistics.[1]

A week later Cam wrote Legters to tell him he thought it premature to think about a formal organization, and that the situation in Mexico was developing far more satisfactorily than he had expected. What wasn't developing satisfactorily, however, were their finances. Wrote Cam:

1 The term "Summer" was coined by Townsend to identify the linguistic courses that were then held only during the summer months. While SIL still offers summer linguistic courses, there are also year round courses.

I have noted the extra funds we have needed for living, traveling, building, etc., above the $78.67 we receive each month from the churches, come mostly from your own pocket. I fear you have stinted yourself too much to do it. Yet you can readily understand that three people cannot get along on $78.67 a month when demands are made on them for travel, contacting officials, etc., etc. I also fear we have imposed too much on the missionaries in the Capital and others because of our lack of funds. An organization might solve this problem.

While the legal incorporation of SIL and WBT would not happen until 1942, the need for Cam and Elvira to be formally connected to a recognized mission organization was uppermost in Legters' mind. On December 5, 1935, the Chairman of the Pioneer Mission Agency, J. Harvey Borton, formally invited Cam and Elvira to become members of both the Pioneer Mission Agency and the Keswick Colony of Mercy. On January 6, 1936, Cam and Elvira returned their signed doctrinal statements with a note saying they would try in every way possible to cooperate with the aims of the P.M.A.

The year 1935 concluded with a letter from Elvira and an important report from Cam. Elvira's letter was to supporters and friends, and gives a closer look into their new village home and activities. She notes that her health has improved and that she is most appreciative of Evelyn Griset's help. She also mentions that Tetelcingo has no post office, and there is extreme poverty, yet the people are "friendly, jovial and have welcomed us into their midst." Elvira then describes their living situation:

The house trailer serves as our "room deluxe." Mr. Townsend has erected a lean-to at the back and left side of the trailer, which serves as kitchen, dining room, living room, study and guest room. The floors are rough boards covered with native woven straw mats. The walls are bamboo stalks lined on the inside with cheesecloth for protection against the mosquitoes. The roof and ceiling are of canvas. Our dishes are small earthenware jugs, pitchers and bowls. The shelves for dishes, a stand for a gasoline stove and the dressing table are made of boxes covered with either plain cloth or oilcloth.

The letter concludes with Elvira giving thanks for their "cozy home."

Cam's eight-page report was for Ambassador Josephus Daniels. One Sunday morning in mid-December Cam had met the Ambassador at Union Church in Mexico City. In the course of their conversation, Ambassador Daniels asked Cam how he was getting along in Tetelcingo. Always optimistic and positive, Cam told Daniels that he was receiving wonderful cooperation from the National University, and from the General Director of Rural Education. "Look," said Ambassador Daniels, "I am going to Washington next week to give a report to the State Department. I have received so many bad reports from Americans about the Cárdenas administration, that I would like to have a brighter side to my report. Could you give me a written report of your activities since your arrival in August?"

Cam's report was filled with lofty ideals mixed with concrete actions he had begun or hoped to begin as a way to help make the aims of the Mexican Revolution become part of his own vision for Mexico and his little linguistic group.

Parallel to Cam's vigorous and ambitious proposals in this report is the emergence of one of SIL's foundational principles in working with governments. Namely, do not be timid in demonstrating one's scholarship, expertise and academic credentials. (This principle would become the special focus for Ken Pike, who, more than Cam, pushed his SIL colleagues to "publish or perish." This was much more than a mere slogan, it was indeed a matter of survival. Pike understood that if SIL were to be taken seriously by the academic world, his colleagues would soon have to publish their linguistic and anthropological findings in recognized scientific and academic journals.)

The first part of Cam's report carefully mentioned the resistance he first encountered at the border and his subsequent travels throughout the republic at the request of Rafael Ramírez, head of Mexico's Department of Rural Education. He told how his findings from that trip had been published in Dallas in the June 1934 issue of *School and Society*. He outlined his analysis on the deterioration of Mexico's rural school system that had occurred under the previous radical anticlerical cabinet. He then presented his vision and reasons for coming to Mexico:

> As a teacher of philology, I led an expedition of graduate students from the Linguistic Institute where I teach on the subject of Indian affairs in Mexico. After my students returned to the U.S., it was my

desire to spend the fall and winter in a particular Indian town or village studying one of the many Indian languages still spoken in Mexico.

I hoped also that some of my students would decide to settle in Mexico for a few years, and in cooperation with Mexican linguistic agencies, carry out a thorough investigation of different languages. Indo-America presents a vast field for linguistic research which is almost untouched. My institute hopes to locate five hundred trained linguists during the next two decades to work among the ethnic groups, not only in the Americas, but also in the Philippines, the East Indies, Africa and sections of East Asia.

My second objective is a desire, prompted by Christian convictions, to serve my fellow man. I despise scientists who use humanity as laboratory instruments in their research, but think nothing of the welfare of those they are studying. In the same way, I detest ecclesiastical emissaries who seek only to inject their dogma while leaving the people in economic, intellectual and moral stagnation. I am determined not to engage in the propagation of sects but rather simply to give the Bible to people with whom I come in contact. Especially do I desire to see at least portions of this Book of good will and brotherly love translated and published in all of the Indian languages.

My third desire is to have a part, though small, in the great movement being carried out by the Mexican government on behalf of the two million or more Indian people who as yet are foreign to the life of the nation as regards language, customs, social standing and economic progress. I feel my students should learn the methods Mexico has developed and thus be able to introduce them into other countries where their linguistic research might take them.

Throughout his life Cam looked for ways to esteem others better than himself, and this included his host government. Thus, whenever he found a particular governmental program or philosophy or idea that benefitted a local community, he would seize the opportunity to commend or acknowledge in some way the person or department responsible. He did exactly that in his report to Ambassador Daniels:

When we came to Tetelcingo, we found the benefits of the revolution had somehow bypassed the local citizens. In a town of a thousand, perhaps thirty people know how to read. The standard of living is exceedingly low. There is no doctor or drugstore, infant mortality is high and the local crops are poor. When I made known these conditions to the Department of Labor, Professor Uranga, an unselfish and talented leader in revolutionary thought and action, visited Tetelcingo as the personal representative of the Secretary of Labor. As a result of this visit, the following steps and recommendations are being taken.

A new pipe is being laid to bring in drinking water to the section of town without water. An old truck is being secured for me to teach the Indians how to run it in order for them to have low cost transportation. Many of the women go on foot each day into the city to sell tortillas. This leaves them almost no time to care for their own homes and families. Trees, flowers and vegetables have been planted in the town square which serves now as a park and an experimental station for new crops.

In her book, *Ken Pike, Scholar and Christian*, Eunice Pike adds:

Cam had hired a team of oxen and a wooden plow and plowed up enough of the town square to make a small garden. He planted cabbage and lettuce and a few other vegetables. The plants had come up in pretty rows and made a beautiful sight. [When the men and women gathered to look at the garden] Townsend would hand them a head of lettuce or some other vegetable and tell them how to eat them. In that way he was demonstrating [these vegetables] could be grown in their own area.[1]

In all, Cam presented twenty specific proposals that were to be, or had been, implemented. They included a plan to eradicate the dangerous fire ants, homes were to be whitewashed inside and out, plus road improvement. The Department of Reforestation had promised to donate five hundred trees for adornment, fruit and firewood. The school was

---

1 Eunice V. Pike, *Ken Pike, Scholar and Christian* (Dallas: Summer Institute of Linguistics, 1981), p. 27.

to be repaired and given new equipment. Cam concluded his report with:

> As you can see, my contacts with the Mexican officials have given me renewed confidence. I doubt if there is a country in the world that would show as much interest in helping such a backward town. The men from my Linguistic Institute and myself are being commissioned as Honorary Inspectors of the Department of Labor and as Linguistic Investigators of the *Instituto Lingüístico de Verano*. One of our young men has gone to work among the Mixteco people. Another is going to the Mayas of Yucatán, and a third to the Otomis [of the Mezquital].
>
> It is my hope that next summer more of our students will decide to come here on the same basis of cooperation with the Mexican government. I consider it an unusual privilege to participate even in a small way in one of the greatest surges forward recorded by any people.
>
> In closing, let me say that any success in this undertaking will, under God, be due in no small measure to Mrs. Townsend's willingness to live in a bamboo house far removed from relatives and comfortable amenities.   All this in spite of serious heart trouble which on several occasions during these past three years brought her close to death.   She adds her invitation to mine that you and Mrs. Daniels honor us with a visit at your convenience. [Cam and Elvira had been the ambassador's guests for tea some weeks before.]

It is common knowledge to anyone who has worked with words, as Cam did, that an overworked word or phrase can soon lose its significance and become merely a cliché. Yet from August 1935 through March of 1936, almost every letter Cam wrote included some variation of "Our work is moving very fast and as for cordial relations with the government, there is no fly in the ointment. We simply marvel at what God is doing."

"What God was doing" was opening doors of service and welcome that Cam and the young soon-to-be translators hadn't even dreamed of. Besides being made a member of the Inter-American Scientific Congress,

Cam was invited to serve on the board of directors of an international society organized in Mexico that included many high-level government officials called *Amigos del Indio* (Friends of the Indian).

So interested was the University of Mexico in the service of linguistic research Cam had outlined that they promised to pay fifty pesos per month to each of the five translators to do research on Indian languages. And much to the surprise and bewilderment of L.L. Legters, who was of the opinion that only men should be involved in pioneer linguistic work and translation, the head of Mexico's rural education offered salaries to Evelyn Griset and Evelyn's friend at UCLA., Florence Hansen, if they would also go to an Indian town or village to do linguistic research.

But the most startling and far-reaching of all surprises came one Saturday afternoon, January 25, 1936, when two shiny black motor cars made their way into the village of Tetelcingo and stopped in the center of the square. The townspeople stood in awe, amazement and bewilderment as the President of the Republic of Mexico, Gen. Lázaro Cárdenas, accompanied by his personal aide, two generals and two captains of the army, stepped out to greet them. Cam said when he heard the cars enter the village, he had been working in his vegetable and flower garden he had planted around their trailer and was plucking a chicken in preparation for their Sunday meal. Later Cam wrote :

> There was no time to change my clothes. I was anxious to see this circuit-riding ruler hold court in the village schoolhouse. Crossing the square, I presented myself, work clothes and all, to where the president stood talking with the teachers who were still gasping from surprise. "Mr. President," I said, as I extended my hand, "I am glad you are a friend of the peasant, for you have found one today."[1]

---

1 William Cameron Townsend, *Lázaro Cárdenas, Mexican Democrat* (Waxhaw: International Friendship, 1979), p. 5.

Chapter Five
Wide Open Doors

W hen Cameron Townsend walked across that hot, dusty plaza in the Aztec village of Tetelcingo on January 25, 1936 and extended his hand to greet Mexico's president, Gen. Lázaro Cárdenas, much more happened in that moment than a mere perfunctory clasping of hands. In that moment, the future of the Summer Institute of Linguistics (SIL) in Mexico was formed. Indeed, the history of thousands of Mexico's indigenous peoples would be forever altered in new and dramatic ways when the New Testaments, translated into their vernacular languages, would become available to more than one hundred and eighty different indigenous groups throughout that great country.

What happened at that moment was the beginning of a lifelong personal friendship between President Cárdenas and Cameron Townsend. On that Saturday afternoon when President Cárdenas drove into Tetelcingo, Cam wondered exactly why he had come. At first Cam thought that since the president was known as a tireless traveler and bent on visiting communities throughout the Republic, he was simply visiting this village as part of his planned itinerary. Later Cam was to learn the deeper reason for the president's visit. Ambassador Daniels had translated the report Cam had given him and sent it to President Cárdenas. Cárdenas was so impressed with Cam's practical ideals and ideas that he decided to meet this man and see for himself what he was all about. In his diary, Cam wrote:

> I did have a chance to wash my hands and when I introduced my-self, he said he was glad to see me and told me he would call on me as soon as he was finished talking to the school teachers. This he did for nearly an hour. And then we had the undreamed of privi-lege of entertaining the chief ruler of the land in our tiny quarters.
>
> When I showed him my linguistic notes, the president looked them over with more interest than anyone else had ever shown ex-cept a linguist. He expressed appreciation for the primer and the reading classes we had organized among the adults and older chil-dren who did not go to school. As an aside, he assured us that his government was going to put an end to religious persecution. When he looked at my garden, he asked pointedly if the young people we wanted to bring into Mexico to translate the Bible would help the In-dians in practical ways, just as we were doing. I assured him the young people we would bring in would be non-sectarian. I said the desire of our young people was to follow the example of their Mas-ter, "who had come not to be ministered unto, but to give his His life for others." The President replied, "That is just what Mexico needs. Bring all that you can get to come."

From that day on General Cárdenas became Cam's staunch friend. Within a week after his visit to Tetelcingo the President sent a truckload of budded fruit trees. In addition, in an effort to improve the livestock of the village he sent some thoroughbred pigs, and according to Cam a "fancy bull and cow."

Two months later on March 28, 1936, he sent Cam a letter that clearly indicated his warmth of friendship toward Cam. It began, "Very Es-teemed Sir and Friend." In the letter, Cárdenas expressed his appreciation on behalf of Mexico for what Cam was doing in Tetelcingo. He further ex-pressed his personal appreciation for the arrival of Max and Elizabeth Lathrop who were assigned by SIL to work among the Tarascan people in his home state of Michoacán. Then in a single sentence, Cárdenas gave Cam an official *carte blanche* to bring as many young people as he could into the country:

I wish to congratulate you upon the noble service which you are accomplishing among the Indian towns in connection with your research studies. I earnestly desire that you may be able to carry out your project of bringing a brigade of university trained young people to engage themselves in the same service as that which you are accomplishing. To that end, my administration will give you every aid that might be necessary. I remain your attentive friend and faithful servant.

(Signed) Lázaro Cárdenas.

It was true the president had extended an invitation for Cam to bring in a "brigade" of young people, but in March 1936, Cam had only five young people committed to his threefold vision of linguistic research, Bible translation and service to governments by cooperating with them in their humanitarian efforts to disenfranchised ethnic peoples. That there were only five men to carry on this bold program did not seem to cause Cam concern. In fact, about six weeks after Cam had received the Cárdenas letter, Cam wrote an ecstatic letter from Atlanta, Georgia, to his friend William Nyman in Glendale, California to tell him about the "remarkable" ways God was guiding and blessing, ways that far exceeded his wildest dreams:

Elvira has sent you an extract from the president's letter, so you know how wide open the door is. We have been on a rush trip these past two weeks from Mexico City, speaking at colleges, churches, Bible institutes and state universities. Several talented young people have expressed a desire to come to Camp Wycliffe and prepare for work in Mexico or to whatever pioneer field the Lord may lead them. Our hearts are running over with gratitude to the Lord for the miracles He has performed. We realize all of this is entirely of Him.

What was most certainly "entirely of the Lord" was the summer enrollment at Camp Wycliffe. Cam estimated it would be from twelve to twenty students, some of whom would be single women.

In most everything that had to do with mission strategy, Cam and L.L. Legters were agreed. However, there were a couple of important exceptions. They centered around *who* should do Bible translation. Legters argued that only men, by that he meant seminary-trained men, should be involved in Bible translation. Legters held strongly to the notion that women should do "women's work." In his opinion, that certainly did not involve a couple of single women living in an isolated Indian village far removed from the normal amenities of civilization and protection and care of a man. His reasoning had come from the extreme living condition he had endured during his exploratory and survey trip to Brazil's Xingu National Park in June 1926.[1]

Cameron Townsend, however, did not hold to the notion that women must occupy prescribed domestic roles. He was enough of a mission historian to realize that single women like Amy Carmichael, Mary Slessor, Gladys Aylward, Florence Nightingale and many others had made outstanding contributions to world mission. Furthermore, Cam agreed with his mentor Hudson Taylor that single women were fully able to "manage distant mission outposts without the help of male missionaries." Cam might easily have cited the astonishing growth of the China Inland Mission (CIM) and pointed out that in 1931 the CIM language school had graduated sixty women. "And as far as restricting Bible translation to only seminary-trained men, he himself had set the example that if a person had a good Bible background and strong enough passion, he (or she) could, with scholarly assistance, do a good translation."

Cam's consuming vision for Bible translation convinced him that women, as well as men, could be challenged to use their talents in this grand venture of faith. Furthermore, this was 1936, and the United States had First Lady Eleanor Roosevelt as a proactive model of a modern woman making a dramatic contribution in such areas as urban renewal, child and family support and equal rights. And then there was President Cárdenas himself who actively supported the United Front for (Mexican)

---

1 See chapter seventeen of *Wycliffe in the Making* (Wheaton: Harold Shaw Publishers, 1995), pp. 181-189.

Women that was formed in 1935 and would grow to a membership of over fifty thousand by 1940.[1]

But more compelling to Cam than the social foment about woman's rights were letters of inquiry from two single women who had expressed an interest in attending the summer session of Camp Wycliffe. [2]

The first letter was from Florence (Florrie) Hansen, a pert Phi Beta Kappa graduate from the University of California at Los Angeles (UCLA) with a major in French and a minor in Spanish who was looking for a satisfying place to use her talents for God. Florrie belonged to the same Bible club at UCLA as had Evelyn Griset. During the months Evelyn was in Mexico helping her Aunt Elvira, she wrote to the members of the UCLA Bible Club about a new sense of purpose and adventure she was experiencing. The prospect of being in Christian ministry and being able to help people know God better by using her love of language captured Florrie's imagination. Two weeks after she graduated, Florrie, at the invitation of Cameron Townsend, was on her way to the third session of Camp Wycliffe that was to begin June 1. She was twenty-one.

The second woman to receive an invitation from Cam to attend Camp Wycliffe was Ken Pike's sister Eunice. Actually Ken Pike, like Evelyn Griset, had also been writing letters. Ken's were to his younger sister Eunice. Intrigued with what Ken told her about Camp Wycliffe, Eunice volunteered to be the camp nurse. Ken, the ever practical New Englander, suggested that Eunice combine this with taking the linguistic course. Ken had been invited by Cam to return to Camp Wycliffe to teach phonetics. This was over the protest of Legters and several others who considered Ken to be too jocular and "kiddish" to be on the camp staff. But Cam's genius for spotting a person's potential said, "You haven't seen the exceptional possibilities of this young man."

Ken reasoned that a background in linguistics would help his sister learn whatever language she might study on whatever field the Lord would direct her to. Little did Ken realize that Eunice would take to lin-

---

1 Michael C. Meyer and William L. Sherman, *The Course of Mexican History* (New York: Oxford University Press, 1983), p. 613.

2 In 1936 classes were held in an old country schoolhouse two and a half miles outside of Siloam Springs, Arkansas. The women students lived in a house in town and drove back and forth each day to classes. The men made use of an old farmhouse and barn. One of the chicken houses was cleaned out and converted into a bedroom and nicknamed, "Lingua Lodge."

guistics like the proverbial duck to water, and would one day be given an honorary doctorate in linguistics.

Another UCLA graduate to become interested in that third session of Camp Wycliffe was twenty-two-year-old Eugene Nida. (He also belonged to the same Bible club at UCLA as Florrie.) Nida, who held an MA in Greek, had talked to both William Nyman and Evelyn's Griset's father, Eugene, about Camp Wycliffe and the work Townsend had done in Guatemala. Nida was intrigued with Cam's vision to carry the gospel to Mexico's minorities through the vehicle of Bible translation.

Like Florrie Hansen, who had given him a brochure on Camp Wycliffe, Nida was looking for a place where he could specifically use his talent and interest in Greek. Bible translation seemed to be a perfect fit. In a letter written to Cam on May 25, 1936, Nida wrote: "Recently I spoke to Mr. Nyman of the Church of the Open Door about [your] work, and if it's God's will that I should go, I shall count it a great privilege to be able to witness for my Lord."

And like the previous camp session, several of the students drove to Mexico at the conclusion of the summer course. This was to include both Florrie and Eunice. When Cam and the new group of students arrived in Mexico City, word had preceded them that Cam had brought two young inexperienced women who were going to live and work in an area where no outsider had gone before. One missionary with years of experience in Mexico who learned of this was so upset and alarmed that he asked if Cam really understood what he was doing. "Look at how young and good looking they are. It's too dangerous to send them out alone."

Legters, of course, had objected to accepting single women on the same grounds. Now with this added pressure, Cam thought he should consider the warnings of the more experienced missionaries. When he approached Florrie and Eunice with what he had been hearing about the dangers of sending out two single women alone to a hard and difficult place, they looked at him in surprise. Their simple statement of faith and confidence in God's faithfulness has become a part of SIL's corporate history. The two women looked Cam in the eye and said: "If God can take care of a man in difficult circumstances, surely He can also take care of a woman." In his journal Cam wrote, "When they asked the question,' Will God not take care of us?' I had no reply but to say, "Well, if you put it that way, go ahead."

To help the reader see how Cam and Legters understood the ministry of Camp Wycliffe, it's helpful to examine the document that gives us the clearest statement of their mission purpose—their recruitment brochure. Printed lengthwise on legal-sized heavy bond paper were the words:

CAMP WYCLIFFE

(THIRD SESSION)

SUMMER TRAINING SCHOOL FOR PIONEER MISSIONARIES

SILOAM SPRINGS IN THE OZARK MOUNTAINS OF ARKANSAS

JUNE 1ST TO SEPTEMBER 1ST, 1936

CONDUCTED BY THE PIONEER MISSION AGENCY

Under this were nine subheadings. The first of these was *need* in which Cam listed the large number of ethnic groups in Latin America, Africa and Asia who were without God's Word in their own language. Then, in not so subtle language, Cam laid the blame for this neglect on the doorstep of the Church:

> The Pioneer Mission Agency, in its program of helping other societies meet this need, found it necessary to open Camp Wycliffe because the specialized training it offers is essential to a pioneer missionary, especially to one who looks forward to translating the Bible, and yet cannot be found in any seminary or Bible school.

Both Cam and Legters continued to see themselves and Camp Wycliffe as an arm of the Pioneer Mission Agency that offered a much needed service to the Church. This was clearly emphasized in the second subheading, *Requirements*. This detailed the kind of person Camp Wycliffe was looking for. The ideal student was a single male between twenty and thirty years of age who had some Bible and language training, college and seminary preferable. (By the end of the summer, the assumption that only men should do Bible translation would be challenged and made forever obsolete): "Students who are to be motivated by a desire to translate the Scriptures into some unwritten language (no matter what board they plan to work with when they go out) are invited to apply. A very limited number will be accepted; no modernist need apply."

"No modernist need apply." At first glance this harsh exclusionary phrase appears to contradict the very nature of the man who had championed the causes of tolerance and goodwill during his ministry in Guatemala. Modernism, in Cam's mind was, however, something altogether different. Cam viewed modernism as a serious virus that had infected the Church as well as many universities and seminaries. Cam's early letters in the twenties to his brother Paul warned him of the rising danger of liberalism, higher criticism and philosophical idealism, synonymous with the rise of modernism. Thus, Cam wanted it clearly understood that anyone who compromised the authenticity of the Scriptures in any way had no place in an organization dedicated to Bible translation.

The brochure continued with what the students were to expect at Camp Wycliffe. Under *Courses* was listed "Initiation to Pioneer living, Ethnology, Linguistics and Pioneer Missionary methods." As to the camp's underlying philosophy, the reader learned under *Organization* that this was a faith mission, that they were themselves responsible to do everything from preparation of their own food to the publication of a monthly newsletter (called *Camp Wycliffe Chronicle*). There was also an order of the day that included a four-mile hike, swimming and baseball.

Being prepared in body, mind and spirit was for Cam a fundamental assumption for all who took the course at Camp Wycliffe. If the students were faulty in any one of these areas, the implication was that the students' ministry on the field would or could falter.

Thus, there was a scheduled time for the students to play games and go on hikes in order that their bodies might be "prepared" for the hard steep mountain trails they might be required to traverse on the field. The rustic setting of the Camp itself was part of a plan to train field workers in how to work together in less than ideal living and working conditions. The student's spiritual life was nurtured through corporate and private prayer and study of the Word, plus the opportunity to minister on weekends in a variety of ways at local churches. They also visited a nearby Cherokee Indian reservation where students could practice their language skills.

Under *Expenses*, the cost for this summer training camp was listed as six dollars per month for room and board. This, however, was "not compulsory." There was the *Optional Trip To Mexico*. This, the brochure said, was designed for those who planned to study Indian tribes [sic]. The expenses for this three-week trip were between forty and fifty dollars.

Contrary to what was advertised in the brochure, Camp Wycliffe ended not on September first, but a month earlier on August second. There is no recorded reason for this change. One reason may have been the heat. All summer long the students had fairly sizzled in the stifling one hundred and ten degree Ozark heat. While the students may have lacked the enthusiasm to continue studying for another month in the heat, enthusiasm for the trip to Mexico, which they considered the next phase of their adventure of faith was high.

All eighteen students who attended that third summer course wrote a brief testimony in the August *Camp Wycliffe Chronicle* of what the summer training had meant to them and their expectations for the future. Some used the words of a new camp chorus composed by Cameron Townsend and sung to the tune of "The Bells of St. Mary's" to express their reasons for attending Camp Wycliffe and their hope for the future:

> March onward, Camp Wycliffe,
> With Christ as your leader,
> Till tribes long neglected,
> The message they have heard.
> And in *every language*
> Is told His salvation,
> Haste forward, O Camp Wycliffe.
> With God's saving Word.

Of the eighteen students who attended that summer, eight signed up to go to Mexico with Cam. They included three single women: Florrie Hansen, Eunice Pike and Ethel Mae Squire (Cam's niece, and Evelyn Griset's first cousin). Eunice, a graduate nurse from the Massachusetts General Hospital, and Florrie had formed a partnership and had early decided how they were going to divide their workload. With her background in languages, Florrie said she would do the translation; Eunice, with her background, would help the people medically.

There was one newly married couple. New Zealand-born John Twentyman and Isabel, his American wife of six months, had heard Legters speak at the Church of the Open Door in Los Angeles. They approached Legters after the service about mission service. In a casual way, John and Isabel said they were interested in the linguistic school he talked about. "Splendid," said Legters, "you are accepted. Go, and tell them I have accepted you." And they went. The single men were Walter Miller, Eugene Nida and Landis Christiansen.

While Cam was delighted with these eight new recruits who were going to Mexico, he was equally delighted that the other students who had taken the course were intending to work in countries other than Latin America.

In later years, there would be criticism that the leadership of Camp Wycliffe, which was to become The Summer Institute of Linguistics (SIL) was only interested in Latin America. The August 1936 *Camp Wycliffe Chronicle* clearly dispels that criticism and shows, with the following paragraph, an established policy of service that continues to this day:

> Camp Wycliffe stands ready to accept volunteers for any pioneer field in the world to dispel the idea that we are concerned only with the Indian tribes of Latin America. The field is the world. It seems that Camp Wycliffe's field should be the pioneer world, the small ethnological groups hidden away among the mountains or jungles "for whom nothing is prepared."[1]

One of Cameron Townsend's special gifts was his ability to discern a person's potential long before that person was aware of his or her own gifts. When he spotted such a person, he made it his business to provide an avenue for that gift or talent to develop. Cam had early recognized Ken Pike's intellectual prowess and had invited him back from his Mexico assignment among the Mixtec of San Miguel to teach phonetics during the summer of 1936. Ken enjoyed the challenge of that summer. He and his new friend and star pupil, Gene Nida, had become kindred linguistic spirits. In her book, Eunice Pike writes that before the end of the summer Nida had turned teacher and was lecturing on morphology and Greek.

Nida actually went through some of Ken's Mixtec grammatical materials and gave him some helpful suggestions. One of the important contributions attributed to Nida was to introduce Ken Pike to the important

---

1 Nehemiah 8:10a: "Go and enjoy choice food and sweet drinks, and send some to those who have nothing prepared."

work of Leonard Bloomfield [1] and his eminent work, *Language*. Nida is also credited with introducing Pike to the word "phoneme."[2] Ken would later write that the notion of the phoneme was completely new to him. And that it was "exciting to be contributing to the knowledge of the whole human race by doing pioneer work and stretching the knowledge of language, and hence the knowledge of man."

If Ken had any doubts about the importance of Nida's suggestion to study Bloomfield's book, they were swept away by a letter Ken received from Dr. Miles L. Hanley of Harvard University's Department of English. Dated August 24, 1936, Dr. Hanley wrote Ken a lengthy letter in response to Ken's letter of inquiry about the best schools available for the students at Camp Wycliffe to do postgraduate work. Dr. Hanley offered a variety of suggestions about where and who was doing the best work in Indo-European linguistics, anthropology, comparative philology, folk music and phonetics. At the conclusion of his letter, he said that, in his opinion, the best book on linguistics was Bloomfield's book, *Language*.

While Ken Pike had enjoyed his summer teaching experience, he realized he was a long way indeed from being an expert in phonetics. He had, in fact, only ten days of formal phonetics study in the summer of 1935. While Ken enjoyed teaching, he was also keenly aware of the danger of

---

1 Leonard Bloomfield and Edward Sapir were the most respected linguists of the first half of the 20th Century. Bloomfield's book, *Language* (1933), was for years the standard of the dominant approach being taken toward linguistics in North America. Bloomfield taught at three universities: Illinois, Ohio State, and Chicago. He served as professor of linguistics at Yale from 1940 until his death in April 1949.

His masterpiece, *Language*, deals with, among other subjects, descriptive phonology, grammar, and language change.

2 In his book *Bible Translation* published in 1947 by the ABS Nida says descriptive linguistics covers all branches of language study: (1) phonology (sounds), (2) morphology (the words), (3) syntax (the arrangement of words), and (4) lexicon (the meaning of parts of words, words, and combinations of words). The translator cannot neglect any part of descriptive linguistic studies if he or she is to make an adequate translation."

Thus, to fully understand a language the translator must be able to identify and organize all the phonological different types of sounds in a language into phonemes, which, Nida said, are the "psychologically significant units of sound." Or to say it another way, a phoneme is the smallest phonetic unit in a language that is capable of conveying a distinction in meaning, as in the *m* of mat and the *b* of bat or the *s* in cats.

masquerading as an experienced linguist. It seemed, therefore, somewhat ludicrous to Ken, when at the end of the summer, Cam asked him to write a book on phonetics. Cam wanted it to be a book that would be a helpful tool for any field worker interested in learning to speak an unwritten language.

While Ken laughed at the idea, he nonetheless wrote five pages. He gave them to Cam with a kind of "I told you I couldn't write anything" attitude and put the assignment out of his mind. While Ken may have thought the assignment was no longer an option, God had a plan that in a few weeks would galvanize Ken's attention to reconsider the assignment. In the meantime, Ken prepared to act as guide and leader of the eight people driving in two cars to Mexico.

Unlike Cam and Legters' first border crossing, the eager young people in the two cars were treated like visiting diplomats. The reason was simple. President Cárdenas had seen to it that Townsend and the young people he had asked to come into the country were sponsored by the University of Mexico and the Mexican Ministry of Labor. While the border crossing went smoothly and without complications, the trip to Mexico City was filled with a variety of misadventures. Almost immediately after crossing the border, the sky broke loose with a torrential downpour. As the two cars sped along the narrow two-lane highway toward Monterrey, the sky turned ominously dark. At times the windshield wipers were overwhelmed with the pelting rain. The men drove more by faith than by sight! After spending the night in Monterrey, the little party began again, in the rain. Eunice Pike recalled that experience:

> It had been raining for several days not only in Monterrey but farther on as well. Actually, it had been raining so much that two bridges were washed out and we were caught on a stretch of road between them. For two nights we slept in our cars while the Mexican army built a temporary means for crossing the river.
>
> Even after we were beyond the flooded rivers, we traveled slowly. We were pulling heavily loaded baggage trailers and they kept having flat tires. Ken and Gene did most of the heavy work changing the tires. The six days it took us to go from Laredo to

Mexico City were especially hard on them. (Years later, even a bus made the trip in less than twenty-four hours.)[1]

President Lazaro Cardenas (center), Cameron Townsend (right), at a "Good Neighbors International Picnic" Townsend organized at Auga Caliente (near Tijuana), Mexico, July 7, 1939. One hundred fifty Americans met a delegation of Mexicans headed by the President.

---

1 Eunice V. Pike, *Ken Pike, Scholar and Christian* (Dallas: Summer Institute of Linguistics, 1961), p. 42.

After the group arrived in Mexico City, they spent much of their time going with Cam to call on government officials. Cam wanted to personally introduce the new people to the officials in the Ministries of Labor, Education and other government agencies. And then one day Cam told the little group to get themselves ready for an extraordinary event. All had been invited to a presidential banquet. They were to be the honored guests of President Lázaro Cárdenas!

Chapter Six

Dinner on Grasshopper Hill

B y October, the seasonal rains in Mexico City have stopped. The rarified air of the mile-high capital was, in 1936, clean and pure. And if on that October day in 1936 you had walked along the fashionable Paris-like *Paseo de la Reforma* on your way to Chapultepec Park, you would have passed beautiful buildings, statuary and bubbling fountains. There would have been well-trimmed lawns and flower gardens ablaze with roses, gladiolas, marigolds, carnations, lilies and more. And as you walked, dipped in dappled sunlight under gracefully arched Cypress-like trees, you would have shared the same enjoyment of these ancient trees as Montezuma II, the last Aztec emperor of Mexico did over four hundred years before.

It's almost impossible to walk a block in Mexico City without coming face to face with Mexico's rich and fascinating history. Names like Grijalva, Cortés, Alvarado, Juárez, and Hidalgo are mixed with Aztec names like Quetzalcoatl, Cuauhtémoc, Oaxaca, Texcoco, Tenochtitlán, and Chapultepec (which in Aztec means "grasshopper hill"). These are more than mere names etched in stone monuments or street signs or over the doors of government buildings. Rather, they represent a living, persistent and deeply intrusive dialogue between the events and heroes of Mexico's past and the citizens of the present. And if anyone was tempted to forget or disavow the roots of his rich Mexican Indian heritage, there are the magnificent twin snow-capped mountain peaks of Popocatepetl (Fire Mountain) and Ixtaccihuatl (White Princess) that stand guard over the valley of Mexico City in their silent splendor.

When the invitation came for Cam and his group of young people to dine with President Cárdenas in the banquet hall of the elegant Chapultepec Palace, Cam knew history of another kind was about to take place. Curiously, the invitation had come suddenly and without notice on the very morning the group was expected for a three o'clock dinner.

Among the women of the group there was a kind of mild panic mixed with the high excitement. The invitation had come so soon after their long trip from the states that none had unpacked or ironed their nicer dresses. Fortunately, the young women were able to borrow dresses from Elvira.

Ever aware of preserving these moments for posterity, Cam asked Ken Pike to be the official photographer and rent a camera from American Foto in downtown Mexico City. Arrangements for transport were frenzied. Seven people crammed into Townsend's car. Others took taxis and the remainder went in a special car sent by the president and driven by Colonel Romón Beteta (he would later become a special friend to Townsend and SIL). Ken wrote:

> We all headed for Chapultepec Castle, the prettiest place in Mexico City and the home of about all the presidents and the one emperor up until the time Cárdenas came into office. Cárdenas now lives in a small private home in Chapultepec Park.
>
> After we arrived, Colonel Beteta (the president's chief of staff) took us upstairs in the palace and showed us around, even though most of us had seen it before since it is now a museum. We waited for some time downstairs. Then at three o'clock we all stood with our heels lined up on the carpet and greeted the president as he came through the door. He was attended by two older men and a younger man. Cárdenas shook hands all around and then we were led into the waiting room. The room was lined with French tapestries and matching chairs with beautiful inlaid woods.
>
> From there we were led into the dining hall. Mr. Townsend sat on the president's right with Mrs. Townsend on his left. I sat across from Mrs. Townsend. We then began a nine-course meal. There was honeydew melon, doodads of cheese, ham and shrimp, a fish

course, a meat course, plus beans, an enchilada course, fruit, ice cream with peaches, coffee *demitasse*, and, oh yes, a soup course somewhere in there. I spoke with the young fellow on my left. He had noticed Nida's Phi Beta Kappa key and said to Nida that he too had one. It turned out that he was the under secretary of foreign affairs and had been the personal advisor to the president.

The most interesting conversation was going on between Townsend and the president. I learned most of what he said after we returned home. Townsend took the occasion to comment that the president did not drink liquor, and added that none of us did as well. He told the president that this was one of the reasons why we wanted to translate part of the Bible, because from his experience, he discovered that people who read the Bible often get over their drunken habits.

Townsend continued by saying that all of us believe the Bible, but we were not at all interested in any particular sect or denomination. When he learned Cárdenas liked to walk for exercise, Townsend mentioned that as a young fellow he had walked a lot in Guatemala selling Bibles. Townsend then mentioned we had come to Mexico to serve, and said we do this because the Lord Jesus Christ came to serve, not to be served, and to give His life for all people.

The president then invited Mr. and Mrs. Townsend to accompany him on a trip some time in the future to the State of Michoacán. He said he would like them to visit the home where he was born. Townsend suggested that he might write a biography of the president. The president accepted the suggestion and offered to place all relevant materials at his disposal.[1] After dinner was over and we were about to leave, the president told a number of us how glad he was to have us in the country. We all went home to walk on air for a while.

From Elvira's account of the dinner, we catch a woman's fuller and more artistic view of that celebrated event:

---

1 The biography on President Lázaro Cárdenas, written by William Cameron Townsend, was published in 1952 and was titled *Lázaro Cárdenas, Mexican Democrat*.

We could scarcely believe our ears when the president told Mr.
Townsend and me to sit at his left and right respectively. On the
long magnificent table were bowls and vases of baby breath, carnations and maiden hair arranged most artistically, as well as large
bowls of exquisite fruit. Above, on a mantel piece, stood the largest
and most gorgeous bouquet of gladiolas I have ever seen.

Besides our group of twelve, including the eight new recruits, the
governors of the states of Michoacán and Quintana Roo, and the
sub-secretary of foreign relations were present. We were at dinner
from three to five in the afternoon, and each moment was filled with
joy and happy fellowship. When it was over, the president said that
our coming to Mexico was of *transcendent importance to his land.*

Gene Nida's account of that occasion was similar to both Ken and
Elvira's. He spoke about the finely carved high back chairs with the
most beautiful hand-tooled leather he had ever seen. Like Ken, Nida
mentioned the young man who was the personal advisor to the president, who had earned a Phi Beta Kappa key. Nida said simply what a
good thing it was that he had the key, and that he was glad he had studied for it.

While Ken had almost missed commenting on the soup of their
nine-course meal, Nida identified the soup as asparagus and said it was
the most delicious he had ever tasted. Cam did not mention the soup in
his report, but never again did he forget its savoriness nor the fact that it
was served at the president's table. Forever after, whenever Cam had occasion to entertain high-ranking government officials in Mexico City and
was in charge of arrangements, he made certain asparagus soup was on
the menu. Nida was the only one to report that when Cam got home he
wanted a steak. He had been engaged in such animated conversation with
the president that he had hardly eaten anything.

Later in his journal Cam wrote that he knew the food was superb, but
he had so much to tell the president he spent more time talking than eating. "The result," said Cam, "was that I actually got up from the table
hungry." Cam also noted that he was astonished at how much the young
men were able to eat, especially Walt Miller. But with a note of good humor and understanding he wrote, "What else could you expect? Most of
our young men were so short of money they were living on fruit, milk
shakes and bread, and not too much of these."

The nourishment that came from the dinner on Grasshopper Hill was, of course, infinitely more than food for the body. The positive goodwill and ringing endorsement of Townsend's vision for practical service and Bible translation from Mexico's chief executive set a new tone of psychological energy for the fledgling linguists. The dinner also produced some much needed practical help. When the president asked Cam if the new recruits had enough money to live on, Cam said that only two of the ten had promised financial support. The president immediately assigned small rural school teacher salaries (about twenty U.S. dollars) to the remaining eight. (These salaries continued for about three years.)

While there were no marching bands or cheering crowds to send these linguistic explorers off into uncharted linguistic territory, the dinner was, if viewed symbolically, a kind of inspirational pep rally. However, within days after those magical moments of inspiration, the cloud many were on evaporated. The harsh reality was that once out in the real world they encountered unexpected dangers, pain, insecurities and confusion while traveling and exploring the intricate mysteries of Mexico's unwritten languages.

For one of the men, the experience of unexpected pain and confusion would cause him to dig deeper into the nature of God and the place of pain in one's life. Another would temporarily abandon his assignment. Elvira, unaware of the problems that lay ahead, wrote a friend ten days after the presidential dinner to say that with the exception of Landis Christiansen, who had brought a Totonac man to Mexico City to study the Totonac language, all the group had "scattered to their respective fields:"

> Besides the two young men in Guatemala, our Camp Wycliffe group is reaching ten different Indian tribes in Mexico, for which we indeed praise the Lord. It is most touching to see them all bravely and gladly going into these hidden away places.

One of those "hidden away places" was among the Tarahumara people who live in the sierras and canyons of the northern state of Chihuahua. It was to these people that Gene Nida had been assigned. In a letter dated October 15, 1936, to his parents, Gene told how it felt to leave Mexico City by train and travel alone to Chihuahua City for the first time:

I am told the people I am going to are rather exclusive [he meant the semi-nomadic Tarahumara do not live in villages, but in scattered isolated caves or plain pine board huts] and therefore I will live for two or three months in an *Internado* (a government-run boarding school for Indian peoples). After that I hope to live among them in one of their settlements and learn their language. While I am learning the language, I am to teach agriculture, carpentry and diet. I am told these people are difficult to reach, and it will be hard for me. Yet I am confident that when the Lord sends out his sheep, He goes before them.

I felt very much alone when I boarded the train on Wednesday. It was hard to say goodbye to the group and move out to a strange land. I found strength in Psalm 21:5: "My times are in His hands" and rested on that verse. Every fellow should have to start out this way. It makes one's faith grow.

Nida continued his lengthy letter by telling how after reaching Chihuahua City he was able to contact various missionaries and friends who helped him on his way:

The people I have met think I am undertaking a big job translating the New Testament into Tarahumara. Most are happy that I am going to try. As soon as my trunk arrives, I will leave for the government *Internado* at Tonachic. It will be a day by train and five days walking to reach Tonachic. I will have a mule to take my gear. So far the Lord has marvelously timed everything just right.

The Lord seems so much nearer to me during these past months. Never before have I gotten such wonderful nourishment out of His Word as I am getting now, particularly as I read the Psalms. I am constantly driven to the Lord in prayer, and he always provides just what I need.

I am realizing in a measured way just why God has sent me to do this work. My faith has been increased a hundredfold since I have been on this trip. I tell you, one just has to meet the Lord when there is no one else around. The one thing I need to learn is absolute trust. I do not believe I could have learned this in seminary. God seems to have his own modes of preparation for service.

Gene Nida was absolutely correct. God did have a plan and special preparation to train him for future service, but it wouldn't be entirely to Gene's liking. Meanwhile, some thirteen hundred miles to the south at a railroad siding in the state of Oaxaca, God was about to remind Ken Pike of a quote he had committed to memory: "Prayer and pain can accomplish much." Ken had begun his career in prayer; now came the pain. It would be the kind of pain Ken would reflect upon and one day explain why he felt it was an important ingredient in the life of faith:

> I believe God is imprinting us for eternity. Perhaps it is only through suffering that we can be imprinted for our eternal home, and for the tasks each will do once we get there.

Ten days after the dinner with president Cárdenas, Ken, acting as guide and village allocator for his sister Eunice and Florrie Hansen, to the village of Huáutla de Jiménez in the state of Oaxaca. With railway passes, letters of introduction and clearance from the Director General of the Department of Federal Education in the State of Oaxaca, the three boarded the night train in Mexico City on Wednesday October 14, 1936, that would become for the two women a remarkable journey into the heart and soul of the Mazatec people.[1] On the twentieth of October, after Ken had left Eunice and Florrie in their village allocation, Eunice wrote Cam to tell him of their safe arrival:

> We are here in Huáutla safe and sound. The house we have is wonderful. We have two rooms, one up and one downstairs. The upstairs room has three windows with shutters that can be opened and closed and can cut us off from everyone. The downstairs, our kitchen, opens onto the main street. The plaza where we get our water is only a three-minute walk down the street. The Lord certainly exceeded all my dreams when he found this house for us.
>
> Ken turned out to be quite a handyman. He made us a dresser for our clothes [from packing boxes], shelves for the kitchen, etc., besides a million little things to help us get settled. The way every-

---

1 For a fuller in-depth look into the story of this journey, I recommend two books by Eunice V. Pike: *Words Wanted*, published by Moody Press, 1958, and *Not Alone*, also published by Moody Press, 1964.

> one talked about the steep mountains and hard horseback ride
> made me expect something terrible. But I enjoyed it. The mountains
> were beautiful. First we would climb and be above the clouds [nine
> to ten thousand feet]. Then we would go through them straight to
> the river [to three thousand feet]. During that whole day and a half
> trip I never got tired of looking. Then we saw the village of Huáutla
> on top of the mountain before we climbed up to reach it [at six thou-
> sand feet]. When I finally arrived, I slid off the horse, staggered and
> hung on. He was a good old horse, but I hadn't expected to hug
> him goodbye! The Lord has been mighty good to us, and now I'm
> going to learn this Mazatec language just as fast as He will let me.

Florrie also wrote Cam, and she, like Eunice, said how comfortable they
were. Cam must have smiled when Florrie wrote, "Our place is fixed up
like a palace, much more luxuriant than Siloam Springs." This, of
course, was exactly what Cam and Legters wanted to achieve with their
philosophy of "hard knocks" at Camp Wycliffe. In contrast to the
spartan, rustic dorms at Camp Wycliffe, life in a rural Mexican village
did indeed seem "luxuriant."

Ken, too, wrote a report on October 29. There was much in the way of
his linguistic findings in the letter, and then he ended with:

> I came all the way from Huáutla to Teotitlán on (well, not always on,
> since my dumb beast kept lying down on me) in ten hours. The
> road is bad, and the burros tired. I sat with some Mixtecos in the
> second class coach to Parian. Two men, to whom I had tele-
> graphed and asked to meet me in Parian, have not shown up with
> the provisions I will need in the village.

The next communique was a telegram from Ken's friends advising of
Ken's accident. As Ken would tell it in years to come:

> I decided it was not in the will of God for me to be socially inept. To
> improve my skills, I went to the railway station where the men were
> off-loading sacks of corn on their shoulders. In addition to my inept
> social abilities, I was, at one hundred and thirty-five pounds, inept
> athletically. But I was discovering something new about myself.
> From the railway station, it was a four-day hike to the Mixtec village

of San Miguel el Grande. To reach the village, I had to climb a mountain pass of over ten thousand feet.

When I was in the village, I would, for the sheer joy of it and to build up my stamina, run down the side of the mountain to about eight thousand feet and run back up again. It was pure pleasure. For the first time in my life I was doing something athletically.[1]

When I saw the men off-loading sacks of corn, I made a deliberate attempt to be friendly and offered to carry a sack of corn. The men were delighted, and, amid a lot of good-natured joking and banter, they placed a hundred-kilo sack on my shoulder. Immediately I knew this was too heavy, and asked to carry a fifty-kilo sack. But even with this smaller sack, I wasn't aware of the mathematics. Namely, that the load on your shoulders (when you are not used to it) increases by the square of the distance. Thus, the men who were used to carrying the heavy sacks took off on a dogtrot across the railways tracks, over a bridge and around a corner out of sight. I was barely able to keep up. If I stopped and dropped my sack, I thought it would be unsociable, so I tried to hurry. In my haste, I stepped on a slanted rock, slipped and down I went. My foot went one direction, my leg in another and the fifty-kilo sack of corn on top. My left leg was broken, about three inches above the ankle.

When the men who were off-loading the sacks of corn saw Ken's predicament, they carried him back to the home of his Presbyterian friends where he was staying. There was no doctor in the little town, but they called a man who was supposed to know how to fix broken bones. The man removed Ken's boot and sock and covered his leg with honey (this home remedy was supposed to provide heat). The lady of the house gently bandaged Ken's leg between two pieces of cardboard and offered to keep him there until his leg healed. Ken said he preferred to go back to the Baptist-run Latin American Hospital in the city of Puebla, eleven hours away by train. Ken's accident happened at about noon. The next train wasn't due until nine-thirty the next morning.

---

1 Ken liked games of all kinds. Whether it was hopscotch, handball, volleyball, or basketball, he played with great intensity. When he was a professor at the University of Michigan, Ken joined the water polo club and became famous (or infamous) as a fierce competitor.

Ken was in considerable pain and was beginning to run a fever, but what concerned him more than the discomfort from the broken leg was the emotional pain from his overwhelming sense of failure. Ken believed he was doing the will of God by wanting to translate the New Testament for the Mixtec people. The question Ken now asked was, why had God stopped him? The accident did not happen, Ken believed, without the Lord's permission. After a long and difficult night, he believed he had the answer. He concluded he was frustrated in his attempt to return to San Miguel to translate the New Testament for the Mixtecs because Cam, his chief, had asked him to write a textbook on phonetics that students could use at Camp Wycliffe, and he hadn't done it. God must have wanted this book written before the New Testament.

Twenty-two hours after the accident, Ken was carried in a chair to the train and placed on the only remaining double seat left the in first class coach section. To his amazement, a helpful American tourist immediately offered to help him. The tourist turned out to be a man Ken had met days before when he had taken the night train to Parian after allocating Eunice and Florrie. And to his further surprise, the tourist was a surgeon from the Mayo clinic who specialized in fractures!

The surgeon succeeded in making Ken comfortable except for those times when the narrow-gauge rail car snapped around some especially sharp curves. About eight o'clock that evening, thirty-three hours after Ken had broken his leg, the train pulled into the city of Puebla. Dr. Dawson from the Latin-American Hospital was waiting for him. Ken's Presbyterian friends in Parian had telegraphed ahead. It was too late that night for Ken's leg to be set in a cast, but in a short time, Ken was in bed with his leg resting as comfortably as possible.

Two days later, with his leg in a cast and in a kind of half-sitting position, Ken, with his fountain pen in hand, was busy writing down the way sounds are made. He didn't stop even when an attack of malaria sent his fever up to a hundred and one. He worked on this book eight hours a day for three weeks. When it was completed, Cam sent the manuscript to Edward Sapir, the outstanding linguist and authority on American Indian languages (then at Yale University) with whom Ken would later study (at the University of Michigan). Curiously, Ken's material was never published as a phonetic volume. However, the work was an important link in the development of Ken's career. Later, a revised edition of this manuscript was incorporated into Ken's important textbook *Phonemics*.

Ken also had a major part in writing another important document during the spring of 1936. It was a kind of democratic Magna Carta under which the new group would govern itself. While it was never a public document, the executive committee of the Mexico Branch governed themselves by its principles.[1] Later when a lawyer was hired to draft the constitution of WBT and SIL when each was incorporated as separate and legal entities in September of 1942 he used the Mexico Branch's constitution as a basic structure.

On September 29, 1936, the Pioneer Mission Agency wrote a letter to Cam, advising him that at their last board meeting, a motion was passed requesting that a suitable council be formed to direct the translation work in Mexico to whom the workers in Mexico would be responsible. The letter also recommended that Mr. Legters and Mr. Marroquín of the American Bible Society in Mexico City be part of that governing council.

There is no record of what or how Cam responded to that letter. It is known that Cam strongly opposed the model of a board of directors governing and directing workers on a field when they themselves knew nothing about firsthand field conditions. After Cam received that letter, Ken Pike said:

> When Mr. Townsend learned the Pioneer Mission Agency was not legally incorporated to sponsor field workers and could act only as a channel through which funds could be sent to those on the field, he called us together for a meeting. He instructed me to write a constitution which I did with major help from Max Lathrop. Richmond Mckinney, Brainerd Legters and others also helped draft the document. Cameron Townsend then made what in my mind was the greatest moral decision of all mission history. Knowing full well that even at that early stage there were opposing opinions from the seminary men versus non-seminary men, and those who favored Legters' more conservative views about women in ministry, Cameron Townsend asked us to form an executive committee, and he would put this committee above him in power. [The form of the

1 The May 15, 1939, minutes of the Mexican [Mexico] Branch of the Summer Institute of Linguistics reveals that after considerable discussion and debate over wording, the *original* constitution was modified and ratified by the group. A June 15, 1939, document attached to the minutes contains the official seals and signatures of all voting senior members indicating their collective willingness to adopt this constitution as their official *modus operandi*.

administrative structure would be a director and an executive committee. Each was to be elected by the senior members of the group.
The chain of command intended by Townsend would be for the executive committee to be over the director.]

Over the years, Ken and others thought about that decision and wondered if there had ever been another leader who had so early in an organization's history given up power to a completely inexperienced group
of men. Townsend knew full well that society, as a whole, and organizations, in particular, function through a relationship of power. He also
knew that a personal lust for power on anyone's part would suffocate
this new organization which he believed deeply that God intended to
grow and become a force for good. Years later Ken wrote:

> Townsend deliberately put himself under the jurisdiction of the
> group as a whole. He did this knowing there were some who ac-
> tively struggled for ascendancy and were opposed to his ideas. The
> question then becomes, how can the organization move forward?
> The answer, as we were all to discover, was in Townsend's ability to
> persuade. As founder and general director, his vision for where we
> would work in the future and the guidelines on how to work with
> governments and serve them were seldom questioned.

While it was true Cam's persuasive powers centered in his unique charisma to convince, most who worked with him believed they could take
on the world and win. The word *most* is the operative word here. At the
end of 1936, the Twentymans and Gene Nida were no longer floating on
that high cloud of optimism generated by the presidential dinner. In
fact, John and Isabel Twentyman, after only living a month in the
Zapotec town of Comitancillo, tendered their resignation. They had
come to do linguistic and translation work but were assigned, as were
others in the group, the responsibility of rural school teacher.

Ken Pike had once said he would gladly dig ditches for the right to
translate. (This willingness to be a ditch digger came from a story about
some early Dutch missionaries in the West Indies who had been willing to
sell themselves into slavery in order to be able to teach the Word of God to
other slaves.) The Mexican government hadn't asked them to dig ditches,

only to act, in some cases, as rural school teachers while they studied an ethnic language.

When Walt Miller was officially commissioned to study the Mixe language in the state of Oaxaca, he was given official papers by the Director of Federal Education to study at the Indian boarding school (*Internado*) in the town of Ayutla. The final sentence of that commission stated "Mr. Miller has knowledge of various small crafts to which he can give his time when he is free from his linguistic investigations." This was to be the way he could serve the community.

John and Isabel, however, felt unprepared as educators, and were uncomfortable in that role. In addition, they had been in correspondence with a British Mission, (Evangelical Union of South America), and shortly after left Mexico, went to Peru under the auspices of the EUSA. Years later, they helped SIL establish their own presence in that country.

While Ken had come to terms with his accident, he nonetheless had severely stretched the limits of his emotional endurance. But he wasn't the only one. Gene Nida's emotional endurance was also being tested. In early November, Cam began receiving letters from Nida in which he said he was "encountering innumerable snags" in his ability to work among the Tarahumara. Chief among the snags was the absence of anyone who could or would spend the time needed to teach him the language. He did say that in spite of not having a regular teacher, he had been able to record five hundred words. Not having a regular person to teach him the language was compounded by having to give up his room in the *Internado* at the end of November. "Further," said Nida, "the food was almost unbearable. I would have gladly cooked my own food but there is no place to cook it." He also said he was suffering from the cold, frosty mornings and evenings, since there was no heat in his room. And while he said he felt the Lord had definitely led him to this particular spot, he also said he felt the Lord leading him to leave at the end of November and go to another *Internado* called "Sisoguichic." Nida also mentioned in one of his letters that his money was running out since nothing had come in for him. On December 2, 1936, in a letter to William Nyman, Cam closed a full-page letter with:

Say, Bill, Eugene Nida is a member of C.O.D [Church of the Open Door, then in downtown Los Angeles]. Since May he has covered himself with laurels. He is a genius linguistically with lots of linguistic training from UCLA (Phi Beta Kappa honors) and is able to take "roughing" as few can. He chose the terrifically hard Tarahumara field and is making tremendous strides. The first month he memorized five hundred Tarahumara words besides a lot of Spanish words. (He said Tarahumara was a cinch after Greek.) Please get the young people behind him in prayer. He is only twenty-two. Please get the church secretary to write him at "Internado Sisoguichic, Chihuahua, Mexico." He's way back in the mountains and mail takes a long time to reach him, so don't be surprised if they have to wait a while for an answer.

However, it wasn't the C.O.D. church secretary who was to be surprised. Much to Cam's surprise and silent displeasure, the next communique that came from Nida was dated December 19, 1936 from Garden Grove, California!

Camp Wycliffe 1938

Chapter Seven

Walking God's Crooked, Yet Straight Path

$\mathbf{M}$an needs difficulties. They are necessary for health," wrote Carl Gustav Jung. During November and December of 1936, Gene Nida was not at all disposed to agree with the famous Swiss psychiatrist. In December he broke a tooth and tried to get it fixed in Chihuahua City. In response to a letter from Cam urging him to come to Mexico City, Nida listed a number of health difficulties. In addition to his broken tooth, he claimed the dentist said that because of his poor diet, his teeth lacked sufficient calcium and he could lose his teeth. He also said he had secondary anemia, a serious skin rash, an irregular heart beat and blood pressure problems. Besides all that, he had lost twenty pounds. Since Chihuahua was closer to the U.S. border than Mexico City, Nida, with a train ticket provided by his father, returned to his home in Garden Grove, California.

Cam and Ken were concerned about Nida's health. Cam recognized Nida's linguistic potential and did not want him lost to Bible translation. At the same time, Cam wondered if Nida wasn't unduly anxious over his health. Both Cam and Ken were counting heavily on Nida's teaching expertise in morphology to be part of the fourth Camp Wycliffe to be held at the Arkansas Baptist Assembly Grounds south of Siloam Springs from July 19 to October 8, 1937. (The grounds were unavailable to Cam until after the Baptist annual assembly ended on July 12.) Interestingly, this fourth session was advertised not as Camp Wycliffe, but as the Summer Institute of Linguistics.

In a letter to his father, Ken Pike noted that while tuition for this fourth linguistic course would be free, there would be an increase in room and board from six dollars per month to ten. This was, for Ken, a substantial increase from expenses in the village of San Miguel where he was getting by on literally pennies a day. The extra expenses were caused by a drought in Arkansas that had raised the price of vegetables. Requirements for the students were listed as follows:

> The Summer Institute of Linguistics is not interested in the development of the swivel-chair type of linguist, but rather in the type which at the cost of hardship and privation is willing to settle among primitive people and thoroughly learn their languages. For such a virgin field (hundreds of extremely interesting languages about which very little is known, and long-sought secrets about the relationships of people and streams of migration) offers an opportunity for service and discovery seldom surpassed in the realm of scientific research.
>
> The Institute will be able to receive only twenty-five students this summer so that it reserves the right of selection. Character, brains, brawn, and fortitude of a pioneer, as well as a college diploma are desired in candidates.

A college diploma is desired." There was a great deal going on in this last statement. Cam himself did not have a college diploma. In the twenties, he had opted not to return for his senior year at Occidental College in favor of remaining in Guatemala. Further, Cam had great respect for the ordinary person who may not have had a college degree, but who had a passion and dedication for the work. At the same time, he knew the importance of academic scholarship and the role this would play in realizing his vision for SIL.

During the second Camp Wycliffe in 1935 in the old farmhouse in Arkansas, Ken Pike literally laughed up his sleeve when Cam said to the group of five students, "Gentleman, in fifteen years the scientific world will sit up and take notice of Camp Wycliffe." Two years later in 1937, Ken was no longer laughing, nor was he quite so willing to discount Cam's audacious dream of making Camp Wycliffe (SIL) into an organization that would make its enduring mark on the scientific linguistic community. By January of 1937, it was evident to Ken that Cameron Townsend was grooming him to become a man of linguistic letters, as well as Gene Nida. Cam knew if SIL was to be recognized in its field, it would need the proper credentials, and this meant graduate degrees. Cam had promised the Mexican government that his students would do linguistic analysis of Mexico's indigenous languages. Cam also said he wanted to do Bible translation. In a January 14, 1937 letter to his mother, Ken Pike explained how Cam wanted to accomplish this:

> Townsend has a plan of action here in Mexico. It involves doing scientific research for and with the government. In the bargain we will, of course, do [Bible] translation. But we do not want to masquerade as linguists and be anything else but that. Therefore, the only answer is to become linguists in fact, not just in theory, and deliver the real goods.

With Cam's encouragement, Ken had been in correspondence with Harvard, Columbia, Yale and Chicago. Ken had also been reading the defining linguistic work, *Language*, written by University of Chicago's Leonard Bloomfield. Since Harvard did not then have a department of non-Indo-European languages (its professor had died), the suggestion from Harvard was for Ken to write Dr. Edward Sapir of Yale who also taught summer linguistic courses at Harvard and had helped Cam on his Cakchiquel grammar.

Sapir answered Ken's letter on January 18 and suggested he write Professor Charles Fries at the University of Michigan in Ann Arbor, who was then the director of the summer linguistic institute there.

To give further credence to SIL's claim as a scientific organization, Cam, with the new workers plus a number of Mexican scientists, sponsored an eight-day SIL conference in Mexico City at the end of January. Cam wrote to his old friend Karl Hummel, general secretary for the Central American Mission:

The linguistic part of the conference (*La Semana Lingüística*) was held in connection with the University [of Mexico] and the government office of Indian Education. It was in every way a great success. Our intention is to make the work of the entire group thoroughly scientific. This linguistic conference helped greatly to push us in that direction. In addition, the conference helped the authorities understand we were in the country to serve them in a non-sectarian capacity. [Cam's own particular service was teaching a course in linguistics at the National University of Mexico.]

This year we didn't apply for a renewal for the eight commissions with salary since McKinney and the Twentymans had objected so strenuously. However, we asked the Lord to work a miracle and have the educational authorities themselves renew the commissions if it was His will, and He did. This now puts us much at ease about this policy. So far this has resulted in opening up splendid opportunities to witness one on one with cabinet officials and other government officers.

We plan to hold our fourth Camp Wycliffe again in the Ozarks. Pike plans to attend a special linguistic institute at the University of Michigan. Dr. Sapir and other outstanding linguists will be teaching. After their course is over, he will come back and help teach at Camp Wycliffe.

While Cam no longer had any official relationship with his former Central American Mission, he used his friend Karl Hummel of that mission as a sounding board and someone with whom he could joke and let off steam. In a letter to Karl written on February 12, 1937, Cam began his first paragraph talking about how many shaves he could get out of a single Ajax safety razor blade versus an old fashioned straight razor. His secret was to sharpen the razor blade in a drinking glass that once held Kraft's pimento cheese.

Cameron Townsend wasn't the only one who was interested in saving money by scrimping wherever possible. In his March 9, 1937, letter to Dr. Edward Sapir, Ken Pike explained that the men in the village of San Miguel el Grande work for the equivalent of three American cents per day. This, he said, was just enough for them to buy four eggs. "Thus the people eat very little, mostly fried dry corn cakes (tortillas) baked on a clay griddle and eaten with salt and chile. The rest of their diet is beans, then beans and beans with occasionally a piece of fruit or meat."

One of Ken Pike's interesting idiosyncrasies was his enormous capacity to lose himself in his work. This sometimes occasioned bizarre dietary customs. In a detailed letter to Cam about the complexity of the Mixtec language and the difficulty he was having trying to understand the importance of tone in the language, Ken said all in one breath, "Other exciting news of the day: Read seventy pages of *Language* and ate four boiled onions."

Cam's own capacity for work was also legendary and more than once he had been characterized as being a workaholic. Yet when it came to advising Ken and Gene Nida about their work load, he was remarkably solicitous. Perhaps, after twenty years on the mission field, Cam had come to understand the wisdom of his old friend, Lewis Sperry Chafer. Years before in Guatemala, Chafer had reminded Cam he could do more work in eleven months than he could in twelve. Thus Cam wrote the following to Ken about Gene Nida's heath problems:

> Gene has returned to California. He wrote me a brief note en route but didn't give us many details. His father wrote me a long, perplexing letter saying he didn't understand what had happened to Gene. I take this to mean a serious call to prayer. We can't afford to let this young man get sidetracked. Both of you must learn to take things easy–yes, be lazy!

When Cam suggested to Ken that he become "lazy," he didn't mean lazy as in slothful. Cam was giving him a principle that he himself would practice over the years, namely, not to consider one's work to be so important and all-absorbing that one would miss the joys of life and be in danger of burn-out. Or, more important, miss hearing God's still small voice to interact with people in need. In ways unlike most of his contemporaries and some of his SIL colleagues, Cameron Townsend knew how to, in the words of Gottfried Arnold, *"Walk God's crooked, yet straight path."* On March 18, 1937, Ken answered Cam on the notion of being lazy, plus Nida's and his own health problems:

> The health question is an interesting one. I was sorry to have Gene leave [the country]. If Gene refuses to work in the altitude or go to malaria country, there is not much of Mexico left. And without practi-

cal training and experience from the field, he cannot do the job at Camp. This is serious business. We will pray that the Lord will heal Gene's body alone, or else make him so he does not give a hang.

My personal health is different from what it was last year. My sleep in much improved now that I have an air mattress, a bed and blankets and flea powder. There are almost no fleas in contrast to the tremendous numbers in the house I occupied last year. At night in that house, when you pointed your flashlight onto the floor, it wiggled!

I have studied harder this year than for any similar consecutive period in my life. Up at the early hours and studying late, and liking it. (In the past I loathed study.) I think having good grub has helped. So far I have eaten lots of onions (every night this past week), some tomatoes, lots of fruit, two and half pounds of cocomalt, a can of milk every day and even a bit of meat. I usually average two to three tortillas per meal, and beans once a day. Every morning I have oatmeal (a frying pan so full it wants to run over) with an occasional change to Cream of Wheat. If you had not told me to be lazy, I might have stayed up late tonight to finish my manuscript for Sapir.

Lest Cam think he really intended to slack off from his linguistic studies, Ken's next letter began by telling Cam he had been burning the midnight oil. So much for Cam's admonition to take it easy and be lazy! Except that Ken did add a note in a subsequent letter that he was relaxing by reading Mark Twain's book, *Life on the Mississippi*.

After being accepted by Dr. Sapir to attend the Linguistic Institute at the University of Michigan and after learning that Cam had turned down the offer from Yale[1] to work for an advanced degree, Ken wrote Cam a most exuberant letter. It is interesting to note the many ways Ken addressed his letters to Cam. Some began with "Dear Mr. Townsend," some were "Dear Boss," some were "Dear Prof," and in this letter it was "Dear Cam":

---

1 In an April 7, 1937 letter to Ken Pike, Cam told him that the head of the Yale expedition offered him [Cam] a full scholarship at the Yale graduate school to study under Dr. Edward Sapir for a Ph.D if he could get his B.A. The man said it would take two years for Cam to complete his degree. Cam thanked him but declined in favor of Ken and Gene. Cam said he thought the courtesy might be extended to one or the other, or both.

You constantly amaze me. And this is the latest! I'll offer you my degree if you will use it to go ahead with Yale! I had always figured if the Lord wanted me to get a higher degree that He could arrange it so I would not lose a lot of time from my real work here. In that respect, I would still want to look for an arrangement which would not mean a whole resident year at Yale.

I am happy at least that Sapir will have the opportunity to see a bit of my work. I suppose I ought to get over it, but it continually surprises me how the Lord leads you to men like Sapir and others.

One of the "others" that God led into Cameron Townsend's life was Morris Swadesh, also from Yale University. In May of 1937, the twenty-nine-year-old Swadesh wrote (at the request of Dr. Sapir) to invite Cam and SIL to become part of the Indian section of the Linguistic Society of America and the American Anthropological Association which, said Swadesh, was in the process of being formed. Thirty-six years later, in 1973, SIL member Herb Whealy reflected on this invitation for SIL to join this prestigious society and noted that in the years since SIL had joined, SIL members had written more articles on linguistics than all the other linguists in the Society put together. Said Herb, "Cameron Townsend's prediction that SIL would one day make the scientific world sit up and take notice has come true."

As pointed out earlier, at Cam's suggestion Ken had drafted a set of guidelines under which the new group would agree to govern themselves. On May 28, 1937, Cam dutifully complied with the guidelines and submitted his first SIL report to Max Lathrop, Chairman of the SIL Executive Committee.

Cam began his report by saying, "I have been looking over the constitution of our organization. I find that I am supposed to report to the Executive Committee every three months on all important business." The single-page report noted the most important matter at hand was that Gene Nida had returned to his home in California and was still under doctor's care and was not expected to return to Mexico for another year. Cam mentioned that Legter's wife Elva was ill and had returned to the States. Otherwise, reported Cam, all the other workers were able to continue in their respective allocations and had been protected in the midst of dangers. The report concluded by saying that the head of Mexico's Office of Indian Education had asked that primers be prepared as soon as possible in all languages where SIL was working because the government was anxious to push the matter of teaching Indians to read in their own language.

By the summer of 1937, the fourth session of Camp Wycliffe was something of a major event for the little Ozark community of Siloam Springs, Arkansas. The community looked forward to the arrival of the students and faculty and began to feel a sense of ownership for the school. So much so that a group of businessmen under the direction of Legters had organized themselves into a Camp Wycliffe Committee to look after the interests of the school. One of the first things this committee did was to rent the Baptist Assembly Grounds in Siloam Springs. Unlike Cam and Legters, these men felt the school should have more livable quarters for the students and staff. Cam's only comment was that it surprised him that Legters decided to turn the Camp over to a local committee. Nevertheless, Cam described these new grounds in glowing terms: "We have the prettiest sight one could imagine. There is a long beautiful valley, countless trees, a sparkling spring, cabins and dormitories atop a skirting hill, cozy nooks below, a large swimming pool, tennis courts, and lots of green grass and wild flowers."

This, of course, was for publication. The new accommodations were indeed infinitely superior to the "rustic" accommodations of the previous three summer sessions. What Cam did not mention was the heat of that summer. Cam had experienced many discomforts, in some cases acute discomforts, but this summer's heat seemed to be almost unbearable to him. In every letter to Elvira, who had once again recuperated and was on a speaking tour, Cam began with a description of the one hundred degree sweltering heat and sultry humidity he and the eight students were enduring.

In some ways, this summer was different from the three previous Camp Wycliffe sessions. Some of the differences were subtle and reflected the maturing of the staff and students. Walt Miller returned with a new bride, the former Vera Stilwell of Frostburg, Maryland. Landis Christiansen, who was Cam's tennis partner, also returned with his new bride, Jerdice, and unlike the previous summers, married students, like Otis and Mary Leal, and single women outnumbered single men. Vern Bruce (a new student), Ken Pike and Gene Nida were the single men.

One difficulty of this fourth session of Camp Wycliffe had to do with Cam's personal finances. Cam had driven from Mexico in a borrowed car.

For a good part of the summer, he had his heart set on buying a new 1938 Plymouth four-door sedan for seven hundred dollars. Legters had promised two hundred dollars toward it. But by the end of August, Cam was discouraged. He confessed to Elvira that the muggy heat, the pressure of heavy correspondence, plus the weight of writing the biography of Lázaro Cárdenas, was taking its toll on his time and creative energies. Additionally, he was often called on to speak to many of the local congregations. On September 1, he wrote:

> Dearest Elvira,
>
> I am still hoping that the way may open up for me to go to Chicago to meet you, but as yet no light has come. Mr. Legters is praying for money for the car, but still no answer. I don't how we can go to Mexico with the group now that Evelyn doesn't feel led to stay. I wonder if we should publish the book first? Well, it's only one step at a time that's requested of us. I must not plan too far ahead until He gives light. That is one lesson we have learned the past few years. The faculty meetings have turned out fine and it was just lack of faith that caused me to lose four hours sleep over them.

Cam wasn't the only one that summer to be concerned about money, so too were Otis and Mary Leal. Otis, as a student at Westminister Seminary in Philadelphia, had heard Max Lathrop speak enthusiastically about the challenge and need for people to be involved in Bible translation. When Otis, a smallish young man with a ready smile and wit to match, heard Max's presentation, Otis said, "A light went on in my mind, and I said, `This is it. This is what I want to do.'"

Otis and Mary had met during their years at UCLA. Otis had proposed to Mary on the basis that one day they would go to the mission field. And now in the summer of 1937, they were married students at Camp Wycliffe preparing for service in Mexico. Since Mary's major at UCLA was Mathematics, she was elected to be the Camp treasurer and hold the "purse" (the students each paid daily for their own meals). What no one knew was how little money Otis and Mary had. They had no local church or friends who were at that moment willing to be partners in their financial support.

Many years later, Otis, who became Wycliffe's Candidate Secretary, remembered what happened when they had used up all their money:

> Since Mary was Camp treasurer, no one knew that we had run out of money. And in a way, this was a blessing because it made us earnestly pray and evaluate ourselves and ask the Lord if He really wanted us to be involved with the ministry of Bible translation. After we had eaten our last meal, a meal for which we had money to pay, Mary and I walked back to our cabin and by chance met Ken Pike on the walkway. Since he had been away all summer studying at Michigan, we hadn't gotten to know him. We were just turning into our cabin when Ken said in a cheery voice, "Say, could you kids use some of the Lord's money?" And then he pressed some bills into my hand. When we counted it later, it turned out to be just enough to see us through to the end of Camp.

Like Ken, Cam also noticed Otis and Mary. Cam wrote Max Lathrop that both Otis and Mary's faith and "steadfastness of purpose" was an inspiration to everyone. Cam said he wanted them to come to Mexico and asked Max if he had an idea of where they might work. The one problem was that Otis and Mary didn't have enough money for travel or for living expenses in Mexico.

This was the kind of problem Cam enjoyed trying to solve, and by the end of the linguistic session it was solved. But then a completely new problem arose, toward the end of Camp, that Cam had never before faced. He was challenged by a group of discouraged, almost mutinous students.

Chapter Eight
Fiddling While Rome Burns

The trouble began at the end of August 1937 shortly after Ken Pike arrived at Camp Wycliffe from Ann Arbor, Michigan, where he had been studying phonetics under Dr. Edward Sapir. Throughout the summer Ken had been writing letters to Cam from the University of Michigan proposing rather significant changes in the way the school would test its first and second year students. "We need this," said Ken, "to safeguard our position as a linguistic school." This push for stricter evaluation undoubtedly came about from the intellectual rush of linguistic study and interaction with other scholars, including Dr. Sapir and Dr. Leonard Bloomfield.

Then, after his arrival at camp, Ken, ever aware of what he called his "overpowering sense of social inferiority," found in Gene Nida an intellectual soul mate. Further, Ken saw in Nida a certain poise and sophistication which contrasted with his own perceived lack of social skills. In a word, he was in "awe" of Nida and some of the others who had seminary training.

Cam had asked Ken and Nida to share the teaching load and codirect the Camp. (Cam was spending most of his time drafting the Cárdenas biography.) It was a heady responsibility for Nida and Pike. Both were aware of their budding scholarship. This gave Nida what one student said was a "cocksure attitude about his own intellectual prowess." There was also pressure from Brainerd Legters (L.L. Legter's son) and Richmond McKinney, both seminary men who, like Nida and Ken, felt that while Cam was the founder, he did not have the correct credentials to "operate" the school. The first time Cam mentions this is in a letter to Elvira on September 6, 1937, in which he says:

> Tomorrow morning I am constrained to bring a rather difficult message at devotions on youth not trying to get into the saddle. With the addition to our staff of Ken and Gene, I realize that someone has to be the responsible head. Mr. Legters wants me to be it. I realize that if Ken and Gene were given an equal vote with me, the outcome would be risky.

Cam and Legters had each exercised their individual leadership style in an easy informal manner. Cam had the statesmanship; Legters the down-to-earth realism. Their common denominator was their faith and rock-hard belief that this enterprise was within the will of God. They each exercised their respective gifts without regard to who was in charge or the need of an organizational chart. Cam was always suspicious of any kind of top-heavy management that might stifle individual initiative. Now a new element had suddenly appeared.

In 1937, Cam was forty-one years old. Nida was twenty-three: Ken was twenty-five. This was just about the same age as Cam when he nipped at the heels of the "older" more conservative missionaries in Guatemala at the innovative conference in January 1921 which came to be known as the Chichicastenango Twelve.[1] Then Cam had been the young innovative upstart. Now here were two young men challenging what they thought was a two-party system: conservatism and innovation. "Innovation is the salient energy; conservatism the pause on the last movement," wrote Emerson. No one could ever accuse Cameron Townsend with "pausing on the last movement." To the amazement and sometimes to the chagrin of his colleagues, Cam was forever fielding original ideas and thinking up new programs. Said Ken Pike many years later:

---

1 Hugh Steven, *Wycliffe in the Making, the Memoirs of W. Cameron Townsend,* 1920-1933 (Wheaton, IL: Harold Shaw Publishers, 1995), p. 34 ff.

Cameron Townsend trusted God in situations where it was socially ridiculous and from every standpoint improbable. But nevertheless Cam knew that when something needed to be done, he, as a child before God, was going to do it, and he believed God would answer his prayers. When I asked him on one occasion how he could do the things that he did with so little probability for it to work out, like starting out for Mexico with only ten dollars, he said, "I like to put God on the spot."

This observation by Ken Pike, however, came much later after years of reflection. In the meantime, Nida and Pike had come face-to-face with Cam's unique leadership style. When Cam placed himself under the direction of an executive committee, he intended decisions would be made by consensus rather than by an autocratic individual or two. While Cam believed he, as founder and General Director, was equal with individual members, he was more equal in terms of his history, institutional power and influence. He was, in a word, first among equals.

There was yet another aspect to Cam's leadership style, and it had to do with titles. In later years, he would be awarded many honors including an honorary doctorate from the University of San Marcos in Lima, Peru, but he never wanted anyone to address him as "Professor" or "Doctor." The honorific of professor, he thought in the early days, implied a status he did not have (on this point he agreed with Nida). More important, he felt such titles would separate him from ordinary people. And above all, he wanted people to be at ease with him and to know he was approachable. Cam believed it was his personal responsibility and the responsibility of the camp staff to "encourage all those whom God sends our way."

Because Cam was approachable and because the students knew he was on their side, they came to him to lobby against Nida's tough, and what the non-university students considered to be unreasonable, exams. On September 14, Cam wrote Elvira about the problem:

Nida gave a rather hard exam to the students just before he left to be a speaker at a Rotary Club. The result was that we heard plenty of indignation about this over the lunchtime. (The students didn't appear to be as upset with Kenneth as they were with Gene.)

To say there was a mutiny against Nida would be a bit too harsh, but there was a serious backlash against this young "cocksure" teacher who wanted to push the students toward academic excellence. Four days later on September 18, Cam wrote Elvira about a "crisis" that had occurred the day before and yet again on the day of his letter:

> I won't bother you with the details about the big crisis we had here at camp until you get back. Just to say that the classes were moving along so fast that over half of the students were terribly discouraged. I gave several devotional talks and emphasized, "We can do all things through Christ." After each message, we discussed the problems with Kenneth present the first day, and Gene the second. It turned out that two students decided to quit and several others had decided not to recommend the Camp to their friends. When Ken and Nida heard this, they both promised to be a little more moderate about pouring on the work. They also promised to have a more understanding attitude toward those who don't have a strong academic background.

Cam's letter to Legters about this problem is significant, not only for its expanded details of the problem, but it appears to be the only letter in which Cam gives Legters a mild rebuke:

> Half of the students were so discouraged they didn't know what to do. It was a combination of too much work (classes progressing too rapidly) and the grading system which Eugene Nida felt should be up to University standards rather than Bible Institute standards. The result was that grades were very low for some of the students. Perhaps more serious was the attitude of Kenneth and Eugene toward students who did not have an adequate academic background. This made them feel as though it was a hopeless proposition for them to ever do translation work. We had two special sessions at which our grievances were aired and discussed and taken before the Lord. I am happy to say that our faithful Leader has given complete victory. There is now no more complaining and the spirit of encouragement once again prevails. Eugene took the criticisms very well.
>
> One further note. In the future I feel it is important for all of us to take a stand, and in every way help and encourage the men and

women God sends to us. This should be our attitude whether we feel the students are properly gifted or not. The attitude which has been taken by a number of our group, and encouraged to a certain extent by yourself, of making the person with few gifts or insufficient preparation feel that it is absolutely hopeless for him or her to attempt translation work, is greatly hindering our work.

God had most assuredly rebuked us for the attitude that was taken toward the women at Huáutla and others. In fact, this stand has proven such a hindrance to our work here at Camp this summer and in dividing our ranks in Mexico last winter, that I feel we should hereafter be very slow about discouraging people whom God has permitted to come and help us.

What is most curious about this situation is that on September 15, following the students' first complaint against Nida, Cam wrote a lengthy three-page letter to Dr. Eric M. North, General Secretary of the American Bible Society. The purpose of the letter was to explore the possibility of a reciprocal agreement between the Bible Society and SIL whereby both organizations might use Nida's linguistic talents. From conversations with Nida that summer, Cam knew he was unwilling to return to living in an isolated village situation. The letter once again shows Cam's vision and determination to make the scientific community sit up and take notice. It also shows his personal concern that a young man's talent not be lost to Bible translation. (Nida would eventually move on to work full time with the Bible Society):

Why shouldn't missionaries do a more scientific piece of work than secular linguists? We are, after all, dealing with God's Word. Of course, this is generally impossible unless very special training is given to Bible translators. We intend to build up a hands-on linguistic institute which is second to none in the field of practical linguistic research. It is my conviction that if the many indigenous groups in the world are ever to receive God's Word in this generation, all agencies with this burden on their hearts should cooperate. Strange to say we have found much more readiness on the part of governments and scientific organizations to cooperate with us than most missionary organizations.

Cam went on to write at length about how practical it would be for all concerned if a translation secretary could be appointed by the Bible Society to supervise the work of missionary translators and help them with their technical problems. Cam assured Dr. North that the expense for such a person would be minimal. In fact, said Cam:

> At the outset I don't think it would involve a great deal of expense for the Bible Society. If you were to appoint Mr. Nida for this position and would permit him to continue his teaching ministry here at our training camp, as well as to pursue his doctoral studies, I don't think it would cost you more than fifteen hundred dollars per year apart from traveling expenses.

By the end of September, the problems at the school were resolved and Dr. North had written to say he was in favor of Nida working with the Bible Society. What wasn't resolved was Cam's personal finances. Even after several letters of inquiry as to what may have happened, Cam and Elvira received almost no support money that summer.

In a letter to his friend Amos Baker, requesting financial support for the Leals, Cam, however, made no mention of his own financial need. (Amos Baker was secretary to the Executive Vice President of the Shell Company in Oklahoma. Cam had befriended Amos and won him to the Lord. After his personal commitment to the Lord, Amos made it a practice to help support first-time workers. He agreed to help the Leals.)

To Legters however, Cam was more forthcoming about his financial needs. In a letter to Legters, in which he reported that Elvira's speaking tour was well received in such places as Moody Church, Moody Bible Institute, as well as with students at Wheaton College and many other such groups, he confessed that the trip was a financial disaster:

> God has used Elvira's testimony in a wonderful way. Financially, however, the trip has eaten up most of our auto fund. However, the Lathrops [Max and Elizabeth] wrote and told us that we can continue to use their car. So God, as usual, is taking care of all the details.

There was always a steady rhythm to Cameron Townsend's life. He seemed never to panic or become unduly flustered. Not having sufficient money for one's daily needs, let alone money to expand his dream, was most assuredly a legitimate reason to be frustrated. Yet, in a remarkable way, Cam's and Elvira's lack of money did not hinder them from being magnanimous with what resources they did have.

In December 1937, after the Townsends returned to Mexico, President Cárdenas offered them twenty-five hundred pesos for the construction of a new house in Tetelcingo. In response to that monetary gift, Cam and Elvira together wrote the following letter:

> Our hearts have been profoundly touched by this latest thoughtfulness on your part toward us. It is quite impossible for me to adequately express our deep gratitude. Needless to say, we would be most happy to have a proper house in which to live in more comfort than our temporary shelter can provide. But we know that there are at least ten Indian families in this village without homes. Using a cooperative system of building, and making roof tiles in the workshop Professor Uranga has built, we believe that it would be possible to build ten two-room houses for $225.00 pesos each. Wouldn't it be better, Mr. President, to let us use the $2500 pesos which you so kindly designated for a house for us, to build small houses for the ten families who have no homes? These could be built on public lands where the five thousand orange trees will be planted along the federal highway. That way they could take care of the trees for the whole village while under the technical supervision of the government, forming an attractive subdivision very different from the old village.
>
> With the remaining twenty-five pesos for each family, they could build chicken houses, thus avoiding the present necessity of keeping chickens in the same house the people sleep in. We believe that those living on this public land would be able to repay the government within five years since they would be earning money, now that you, Mr. President, have given them fruit trees and an irrigation system. We would be very happy to help the women fix up their houses so they can live with a bit more comfort, convenience and cleanliness. We can assure you we would be much happier with

this arrangement than we would be with a single large house designated for our use.

We have written in this candid way because we believe the wonderful friendship with you with which you have honored us encour-
ages us to do so. It is a pleasure to assure you again that we will do
all in our power to improve the life of the Indians in this village, col-
laborating in the great humanitarian campaign of your government.

With fondness and admiration, we remain your affectionate and
humble servants,   (signed) Cameron and Elvira Townsend.

Cam and Elvira's letter to President Cárdenas requesting that money
allocated to them for a house be given to others reflects their view of the
great love God has for humanity. It was with this farsighted vision that
Cameron Townsend, in December of 1937, wrote an open letter to all
the evangelical mission workers in Mexico calling on them to give back
to Mexico a gift in the form of religious values and true spirituality by
supporting President Cárdenas's "crusade of reforms."

In his letter, Cam revealed that the president had said that the difficulty
with Mexico, and indeed the world, was the condition of the human heart.
Thus with the president's permission, he was writing to invite them to a
special meeting at the American Bible Society on January 3, 1938, at 10:00
a.m. to see how each might cooperate with the president's vision, aspira-
tions and reforms:

It seems to me the president's reform crusade needs now, more
than anything else, a spiritual force which can bring about a rapid
regeneration of man. This is true the world over. There are
well-known economists and sociologists who have maintained for
some time that what the world needs more than anything else is a
spiritual revival. Here in Mexico, apart from the personal example of
the president himself who has great regard for the poor, there is little in the revolutionary movement which serves to develop in the
people a spirit of self-sacrifice, absolute honesty, and the ability for
cooperating with one another in a democratic fashion.

I should make it plain from the beginning that my linguistic work
and writing prevent me from being able to serve you in this matter
other than to help the project get started and then present it to the

president. I conclude by saying that in these moments of great importance in the history of Mexico, we evangelical believers should remember the Bible says "pure religion and undefiled before God and the Father is this, to visit the fatherless and widows in their affliction, and to keep himself unspotted from the world." I believe we get great inspiration from the president himself for living this very kind of life.

It's not entirely clear from the archival record how this letter was received by the evangelical community. It does appear that one or two meetings were convened, but there is no indication how many people came. There are, however, some important clues written by Cam on the back of his original letter that said in cryptic fashion:

> Nothing came of it. Most missionaries are suspicious of Cárdenas. I went to one meeting after I had seen the president. I told them the president continues to be concerned for the poor. They were not impressed. I was not invited to return. Why is it that we Christians are more interested in "correct" theology and show no interest in the great social problems of this country? It seems to me they are fiddling while Rome burns.

Some may have accused Cameron Townsend of wishful thinking. If it were wishful thinking, it was the kind of thinking that rested on the eternal character and purposes of God. While Cam was often caught up in the idealism of his vision, he was also one who took seriously the practical admonition from the book of James, that says, in effect: If you see people cold or hungry or without clothes or anything to eat and say, "Well, God bless you. I hope you will be all right," what on earth is that kind of faith good for?[1]

Thus in 1938, in a gesture of remarkable practical friendship toward President Cárdenas, Cameron Townsend became a kind of roving ambassador for Mexico in an effort to explain why President Cárdenas expropriated Mexico's oil industry from seventeen foreign oil companies.

---

1 James 2:15-16

Elvira Townsend mixes with the ladies who quickly learned to use the sewing machine donated by the Mexican government. They proudly display some of the garments they have made (1938).

Chapter Nine

No Such Thing As a Small Friend

There is remarkably little reference in Cam's 1938 correspondence about the ruthless acts of violence by Hitler's Germany. Few in the West realized or wanted to believe that Hitler's absorption of Austria, and Italy's alliance with Germany, plus Japan's barbarous occupation of most of eastern China were a prelude to World War II.

When Cam's father wrote to tell him of the severe floods in California in March of 1938, and when Cam heard about rumors of war and the rising nationalism of Germany and Japan, he may have taken these geopolitical events to be consistent with Scripture that said there would be a time in history when there would be wars and rumors of war and nations would rise against each other.

There was, however, one important geopolitical event that very much occupied Cam's energies in 1938. It was the nationalization of much of Mexico's oil industry under President Cárdenas. It might be more correct to say that what occupied Cam's mind was the support of his friend, the president. By March 1938, Cam and the president had become close friends. In a letter to his father on March 6, 1938, we see just how deep this friendship had become:

We had a wonderful visit with the president and his wife in our home in Tetelcingo a week ago. The president has been having some serious problems with the foreign oil companies here in Mexico. He talked to me at length about the pressures the companies have brought on him to force the unions to comply with their wishes.

As we talked, it was apparent that he wanted to relax. He dismissed his two aides and sent them off to the nearby town of Cuáutla. We were then alone with just his wife and cousin. When I asked the blessing at the dinner table, I prayed also for Mexico and the rulers of the country. When I said " Amen," he gave me a most appreciative look and thanked me. After dinner the president and I excused ourselves from the others, took our folding camp chairs and went to the shade at the rear of our house trailer and talked. I could see the president was greatly burdened about the oil companies. He said he wanted to do the right thing and hoped the problems could be solved through arbitration.

Earlier, in February, Cam had written the president a three-page letter in the form of a personal testimony about how important his "Friend" was in his life and described all that He had done for him and mankind. Cam ended his letter by saying:

Mr. President, is it any wonder that I have dedicated my life and pledge my loyalty in a spiritual way to such a Friend? At least I can assure you most categorically that in Him I have found everlasting joy and peace and eternal life, because He has the facility of imparting His own abundant life and eternal life to His followers. As one of His biographers once explained, "But as many as received him, to them he gave the power to become the sons of God, even to them that believe on his name."[1]

During the conversation with the president in Tetelcingo, Cam had a further opportunity to reinforce the truth about his Friend and to tell the president how important prayer was in his own life. Cam said he de-

---

1 John 1:12 (KJV)

pended upon the guidance of God in all the decisions of his life. In a March 6, 1938 letter to his father Cam wrote:

> The president listened to me most attentively and told me how very much our friendship meant to him. He said he hoped it would continue after he left office in 1940. He then took out his fountain pen and gave it to me. This was the very pen the president had used to sign the most sweeping land reform bill in the history of Mexico. In fact, he said that for the past three and a half years, this was the pen he had used most often to sign all the important documents, bills and decrees affecting this great land.
>
> My first use of the pen was to write him a letter of appreciation. (I also included a page and a half about the Lord.) With the same pen I wrote a letter to President Roosevelt and one to President Ubico [of Guatemala]. Since this is an historic pen, I am not going to use it very often.
>
> I am deeply impressed with the way the president has dealt with the poor of this country. I believe President Cárdenas has been called of God to be a mighty instrument in His hands. He is, in fact, a great inspiration to me. More land has been given to the poor with this pen than any other pen in history.

Early in his presidency, President Cárdenas began to make good on his agrarian reform promises. He signed a bill (with the historic pen Cam now cherished) and distributed twenty-six million acres of land to the peasants. Later in his administration, he distributed another forty-nine million acres, seventy-five million in all. By 1940, approximately one-third of the Mexican population had received land under the agrarian reform program. It's important to note that the vast majority of the land distributed did not go to individuals or even to heads of households but rather to communal *ejidos*.

The *ejido* land was held in common by the communities, sometimes to be reapportioned to individuals for their use and sometimes to be worked by the community as a whole.[1]

Some economists would challenge the *ejido* system and argue that it was not the most efficient use of the land. Cárdenas does not seem to have

1 Michael C. Meyer, William L. Sherman, *The Course of Mexican History*, (New York: Oxford University Press, 1983), p. 599.

been concerned about these charges. His purpose was to make good a campaign promise and to meet what he considered a great social need. In his mind this took precedence. So also, when his hand was forced, was the nationalization of the oil companies.

The petroleum problem began innocently enough as a conflict between labor and management. At issue was the demand by the workers for higher wages and better working conditions. When a deadlock occurred, President Cárdenas ordered the dispute to be settled by an independent arbitration board. The board examined the records of the companies and living conditions of the workers and issued a decision ordering a one-third increase in wages plus improved pensions and a welfare system.

The companies said this would increase their operating costs by over seven million dollars and appealed the decision to the Mexican Supreme Court which ultimately upheld the decision of the arbitration board. When the foreign oil companies [Dutch and British, as well as a few American] refused to obey the Supreme Court's decision, President Cárdenas held they had flagrantly defied the sovereignty of the Mexican state, and on March 18, 1938, signed a decree expropriating and national-izing the holdings of seventeen oil companies.[1]

This unprecedented action resulted in congratulatory telegrams from other heads of state in Latin America. The greatest outpouring, however, came a few days later from the Mexican people themselves with a huge celebration in Mexico City to honor their economic independence. Cam wrote that as the president and his cabinet stood on the balcony of the Na-tional Palace, thousands upon thousands of Mexican citizens marched be-low in the grand *Plaza de la Constitución* in a steady stream that continued for hours and then flowed out into history as Mexico's second Declaration of Independence.

The U.S. press and American politicians did not share the sentiment of this public outpouring of support as something to celebrate. There were articles and pamphlets vilifying Cárdenas as a common thief. Calls came from some for gunboat intervention, but there would be no U.S. interven-tion. Franklin D. Roosevelt had come to the U.S. presidency enunciating a new "good neighbor" policy of nonintervention in Latin America.

American ambassador to Mexico Josephus Daniels did his utmost to urge the oil companies to negotiate in good faith. For months there was

---

1 Ibid. p. 603-604.

great difficulty over the issue of compensation since U.S. newspapers continued to press claims of compensation on behalf of the oil companies.

In an attempt to build a better understanding between the United States and Mexico, Cam proposed to President Cárdenas that he go to Washington and personally present Mexico's position to government representatives, congressmen and the oil executives. According to Jim Hefley in his book, *Uncle Cam*, Cam not only proposed that he be the president's spokesman in Washington, he further proposed that he try to recruit a corps of American young people (a forerunner of John F. Kennedy's Peace Corps) to help with Mexico's social projects. Cárdenas agreed with both of Cam's proposals and insisted the government not only pay his traveling expenses, but also provide a new automobile for Cam and Elvira. After President Cárdenas gave Cam a thousand U.S. dollars to buy a new car, Cam went to see Ambassador Daniels to discuss the trip. Daniels was in agreement with Cam's mission and wrote him a letter of introduction to President Roosevelt's appointment secretary.[1]

Cam and Elvira left by train the first week of April for Arkansas to purchase a new 1938 four-door Chevrolet sedan before Cam went to Washington and later to New York. Here was an amazing answer to Cam and Elvira's prayers. Most of the money Cam had saved for a new car was used to pay for Elvira's speaking trip during the summer of 1937. When it became evident that Cam would be unable to purchase a new car, he wrote to assure Legters "that God would take care of the details." At that time, of course, Cam had no idea how he and Elvira would ever be able to afford a car. But as God frequently did in Cam's life, He honored his faith and chose an unlikely channel through whom the blessing of faith would come.

As an aside, for years Cam and others drove that 1938 Chevrolet all over Mexico and the U.S. Finally in 1968, with an odometer reading of over 300,000 miles, the car was restored and retired. It now rests proudly on display as a symbol of international friendship at SIL's Mexico-Cárdenas Museum in Waxhaw, North Carolina.

In a curious way, Elvira was just as passionate to defend Mexico's right to expropriate foreign oil as was Cam himself. On May 3, 1938, Elvira, whose health continued to be a source of concern to Cam, wrote to Mrs.

---

1 James and Marti Hefley, *Uncle Cam* (Waco, Texas: Word Books, 1974), pp. 106-107.

Cárdenas from Chicago to tell her that she and a woman companion (who would drive the new car) were taking their own goodwill trip across the States:

> Everywhere I speak (I spoke five times last week) I notice a deep interest among the people to understand the situation as it actually exists in Mexico. On May 16, I begin speaking in North and South Dakota, Minnesota, Illinois, Michigan, Missouri and back to Arkansas. I will be speaking in women's clubs, over the radio, and at universities, colleges and churches. I hope after the people hear me they will have a better understanding of our southern neighbors.

Throughout the spring, summer and early fall of 1938, Cam seemed to be tireless in writing letters and pamphlets as a way to promote better relations between the U.S. and Mexico. One project he worked on to present to members of the U.S. Congress was an eighty-five page booklet entitled *The Truth About Mexico's Oil, As Observed by W. Cameron Townsend*. He also wrote an open letter to the U.S. press. The opening paragraph began:

> President Cárdenas is not anti-foreign. Far from being anti-foreign, President Cárdenas has invited a brigade of young Americans to work for his government among the peasants in his welfare projects. He desires to maintain friendly relationships especially with the United States. President Cárdenas is deeply appreciative of President Roosevelt's "good neighbor" diplomacy. He says there is no such thing as a small friend. And though Mexico is small, it will know how to be a big friend of the United States should the time ever arrive when, due to complications with European nations or Japan, the United States might need the cooperation of a friendly nation on her southern border. All Mexico asks in return for her friendship is due respect for her sovereignty.

By the end of the summer of 1938, Cam and Elvira had become ambassadors of good will for Mexico's international problems. On August 9, Cárdenas wrote Cam to express how deeply he appreciated everything Cam was doing to foster good will between the United States and Mexico:

The trips you have taken in behalf of a better understanding and a drawing closer of both countries are very important. You have done a great deal. Our deep appreciation goes out to Elvira and yourself as well as to the group of friends who so unselfishly have helped in this great task.

Signed, Lázaro Cárdenas.

While Mexico's president was deeply appreciative of Cam's efforts, they were not without some cost to Cam. To Mr. Marroquín of the American Bible Society in Mexico City Cam wrote that he had spoken thirty-eight times and had interviews with a number of oil executives in Washington. The letter also reveals that Cam's boundless energy had its limits. Further, it is the only letter to give an account of Legters' narrow escape from death in an auto accident:

I have been pleading Mexico's case so hard and long that I am just now so mentally tired that I can't write at length. In fact, I have had to postpone the completion of the book I am writing on President Cárdenas.

I also wanted you to know that Mr. Legters was involved in a serious auto accident. A drunken driver smashed into his car in Alabama. The car was a complete wreck, and he was hurt a good bit. His son Brainerd got to him a day or two after the accident. He didn't let his wife know he was hurt and in the hospital. Brainerd will take him home by train.

Cam may well have been tired, but it did not stop him from "seeking to be of service in diplomatic affairs." In July, U.S. Secretary of State Cordell Hull had sent a stiff letter to Mexico's ambassador to Washington, Dr. don Francisco Castillo Najera, over the question of "adequate and effective and prompt compensations." The letter (which was made public) also called for the payment of an old indebtedness. While the amount was never stated in the letter to the Mexican ambassador, a subsequent letter identified the amount to be ten million dollars.

On September 10, in response to this letter, Cam wrote his own insightful four-page letter to Cordell Hull calling on the United States, in the name of humanity, to be compassionate and show itself to be truly a good neighbor in the matter of pressing for payment of this outstanding loan. To alert Secretary Hull of his letter, Cam sent the following telegram:

> Why plague Mexico about a small debt when Europe owes so much? The friendship of Latin America is worth more than ten million dollars. Japan, Germany or Italy would give more for it. Furthermore, the American people are not Shylocks to exact the life blood of Mexico's undernourished masses. Let them pay when their bread and butter problems are solved. I propose that a committee of citizens be organized to discuss directly with a committee of Mexican citizens all our pending problems. (Letter to follow)

One of the chief methods Cam seems to have used for implementing new ideas and moving programs along was to form a new organization. For example, he had promised President Cárdenas that under the banner of a new organization he called the *Inter-American Service Brigade*, he would recruit young people, give them some beginning Spanish and cultural training, and then send them to Mexico as a kind of peace corps to help with Mexico's social problems. Ken Pike's letter of August 17 explained how this was working:

> Cárdenas has asked Townsend to bring in twenty-five young people at the expense of the Mexican government. They will work a full eight-hour day instructing in better farming methods, sanitation, etc. In their spare time they will be free to hold informal Bible teaching, or anything else they want. A check arrived the other day for one thousand dollars to help some of the students get to Mexico.
>
> We now have six young people being taught Spanish by Elvira and Vern Bruce and they will soon be ready to go. Any more will probably have to wait until next year. This project is not directly related to the translation program. But Cárdenas backed it because he saw the work some of the translators (especially W.C. Townsend) were doing on the side, in an effort to improve the basic living standards of people living in Indian villages.

When it comes to having an impact, a chance remark can sometimes have an impact out of all proportion to what the person meant or intended. The nickname, "Uncle Cam," as many thousands would affectionately come to call Cameron Townsend, came about via his niece Evelyn Griset. Evelyn had first accompanied her uncle and her Aunt Elvira to Mexico in 1935. The following year Cam's niece Ethel Mae came to Mexico and, of course, she called him Uncle Cam. Now, three years later, Evelyn, along with twenty-nine others, was herself a student at the fifth session of Camp Wycliffe. Given the informal atmosphere of the camp, the students picked up on Evelyn's reference to her "Uncle Cam," and Cameron Townsend became, for all time, Uncle Cam.

After Evelyn (Evie) returned from her year in Mexico, she completed her studies at UCLA. She then enrolled in the Bible Institute of Los Angeles (now known as Biola University). Her roommate in that tall grey building in downtown Los Angeles was Ethel Wallis. Ethel became a Wycliffe member in 1941. In her book, *It Takes Two to Untangle Tongues*, Ethel said that in spite of their dismal surroundings, Evie was a cheerful presence in their small, dark room. Ethel also gives us the first hint that Evie's reason for attending Camp Wycliffe may have had something to do with the phonetics teacher:

> One morning, before the cacophonous bell that jarred us awake each morning, I saw Evie's light on over the upper bunk. I looked up to see her staring into a hand-held mirror, her mouth wide open. When I asked her what in the world she was doing, she said, "I'm practicing phonetics. You see you have to watch your throat as you make the sounds."
>
> One day Evie interrupted her phonetic practice to share a message on a scrap of paper with me. "Look at this," she exclaimed, holding out a half a sheet of notebook paper, diagonally torn. "Here's a note from a fellow I met in Mexico. He's studying an Indian language, and he tells me I should keep practicing my sounds!" In a jerky scrawl, the brief note was signed, "Ken."[1]

Ken Pike's note to Evie may have been brief, but later that summer, Evie's letters to her family about Ken were anything but brief. And unlike Ken's prose that tended to mild sarcasm, wit and light mockery, Evie's prose was light, cheerful and full of inviting non-pretentious de-

---

1 Ethel Emily Wallis, *It Takes Two to Untangle Tongues*, (Huntington Beach, California: Wycliffe Bible Translators, 1985), pp. 38-39.

tails of the kind that two sisters might share over a cup of coffee. On a warm Sunday afternoon in August, Evelyn wrote her family in California about one of the interesting challenges she faced at Camp Wycliffe in 1938:

> I have tried all week to get a letter off to you, but if it isn't three things that have to be done, it's four dozen. Herman [Aschmann] and I are the stewards this week, and is it ever a JOB. We have to see that everyone has enough to eat, that very little is left over and that we don't go over budget. Thursday we planned a menu and first Uncle Cam objected to the cabbage. So we changed that. Then we found that we had something that Mrs. Fuller couldn't eat. She eats almost no protein, and Aunt Elvira eats no starch and Uncle Cam can't eat pickles, etc., so you see it's a great life. The menu was changed so much that day that it was a joke.

In the interest of more fully understanding the man Cameron Townsend, it's helpful to pause for a moment and explain that Cam had normal dietary preferences. However, if he thought his *not* eating something, no matter how bizarre, would offend a person who had given him something to eat as a gift, he would eat it with a smile. On one occasion a new believer in Tetelcingo brought him, as a gift, a bowl of cooked tadpoles, and with a smile and a warm word of appreciation, Cam consumed the tadpoles without a grimace. Evelyn continued writing her parents and mentioned an important luncheon:

> Kenneth let me and Uncle Cam read a letter he received from Bloomfield of the University of Chicago. It was a bombshell! Bloomfield and Sapir are the two biggest men in linguistics in the United States. Kenneth gave an hour and a half talk at the Linguistic Society of America luncheon on something or other. Anyway, the big fellows from all over attended the lecture.
>
> After Kenneth finished, Bloomfield congratulated him and asked that he publish it right away because it was the first real analysis that had ever been made and would prove to be very valuable. In another letter, Bloomfield said he was forming a committee of five men to consider giving Kenneth a Ph.D. Kenneth was certainly surprised. He hadn't even dreamed of getting a Ph.D without taking

several years to do it. It takes three years of research and two years of residence or four summer sessions to get a Ph.D at Ann Arbor. Kenneth has two of the latter and all of his thesis completed. Bloomfield said that his talk at the luncheon was more than sufficient for his thesis. So it looks like it will go through all right.

The mystery of what Ken spoke about at that special luncheon and his enrollment in a Ph.D program are solved in two letters dated July 10 and July 14 to his parents:

A good bit of my time this summer has gone into studying Mixteco [and how to analyze tone in this language.] I have to give a talk at a special linguistic luncheon conference. My topic: the problem of tones in Mexican Indian languages. Most of my material comes from the Mixtec [of San Miguel where Ken worked], but I will also use some from Mazateco [the language where Ken's sister Eunice and Florrie Hansen worked]. I need to add that it was Professor Fries, director of the Linguistic Institute, who, after seeing my material [on tone], asked me to speak at the luncheon conference.

By the end of July, Professor Fries from the University of Michigan had formed a special committee to oversee Ken's preparations for the Ph.D degree with himself as chairman. The remaining four were Professor Bloomfield from Chicago, Professor Morris Swadesh, who was now at the University of Wisconsin, plus two professors from Michigan representing the English and Anthropology departments. Ken had asked if he might substitute a foreign language exam in Spanish for German and the dean at Michigan agreed. In a July 22, 1938 letter from Fries outlining the particulars of Ken's program, he said:

It is our intention that the particular fields of study to be covered in the examinations will be determined by this committee. As you will see, your degree will not be in one of our departments as presently organized but will be in linguistics much as it is organized in the Linguistic Institute for the summer. The dean is favorable to your substituting an examination in Spanish for the examination in German. This substitution must be ratified by the executive board of the Graduate School to be final. I do hope you will have a good summer.

Ken was indeed having a good summer. One of the best he had ever had. He may have considered himself ill-equipped to handle some kinds of public social encounters, but in private he proved himself skillful enough to overcome this handicap and fall in love and propose marriage to Cam's effervescent niece, Evelyn Griset.

To celebrate the occasion and inform her friend and past roommate, Ethel Wallis, Evie sent her brother Lorin with a box of chocolates to Ethel's home and asked that she share them with her old friends from the Bible Club at UCLA. Cam's only recorded reaction to his niece's engagement to Ken Pike was a kind of, "Oh, by the way," comment at the conclusion of a letter to his friend Karl Hummel:

> Did we write you about Evelyn and Kenneth Pike being engaged? They plan to be married soon [on November 17] after their arrival in Mexico City. We are very happy with them in their love for one another.

And so Ken, who had poked fun at his single male colleagues for "taking unto themselves wives, tut, tut," now had them returning the good-natured razzing. And if Cam seemed less than attentive to this happy event, he had every reason to be preoccupied with other matters. The summer and early fall of 1938 were filled with mammoth responsibilities and demands on his time. Legters, who usually assumed teaching responsibilities, was suffering with a leg that troubled him with swelling if he walked too long. In addition to the thirty students at the fifth SIL who demanded Cam's time, there was the ever-present controversy over the Mexico oil crisis that he vowed to champion on behalf of President Cárdenas.

Yet despite his best efforts, Cam was realistic enough to know that with the avalanche of newspaper articles and the oil industry's financial and political power, his efforts to change American public opinion were pathetically small. Cam may have felt his efforts had accomplished very little and he indicated as much in a letter to Mr. Marroquín. But by actively championing the interests of his friend the president, and the country he led, Cam showed once again a basic premise of what was required of a true friend, namely: Ask yourself what you want people to do for you, then seize the initiative and do it for them.

Chapter Ten

Listening to the God Who Speaks

The invasion of Poland on September 1 by Hitler's Nazi forces and the declaration of war by France and Great Britain that would begin World War II was certainly the major world event of 1939. The United States, while dismayed by the events in Europe and the threat of another world war, nevertheless continued an uneasy policy of neutrality for two more years.

Cameron Townsend was also trying to teach his new recruits the meaning of neutrality. It was the neutrality toward criticism of Mexico's government policies (which by extension would include all host countries where SIL had a presence). But in 1939, not all the recruits agreed with Cam's position, and there arose some serious policy disagreements. But I am a little ahead of the story.

On January 9, 1939, all appeared calm and well within the group. Cam's circular letter from Mexico addressed to the "Camp Wycliffe Family" began with a quote from Cam's father who was known as "Father Townsend." During several of the previous summers, Father Townsend had served Camp Wycliffe as camp cook and had written appreciatively of the kindness and acceptance he felt by the students during the summer sessions. Whenever he wrote to Cam, without fail, he would express his deep love and appreciation to God for the "gift of His Son Jesus Christ." As a tribute, Cam quoted his father's New Year's prayer:

> May the Holy Spirit be my personal guide always so that I will live only for Him. May I overflow in love so as to draw others to Christ and may His strength be perfected in my weakness.

Cam's letter also paid tribute to Ambassador and Mrs. Daniels for providing a large turkey and "all the fixings" for their Christmas dinner, a dinner Cam and Elvira shared with a number of Tetelcingo's townspeople. And never forgetting why he had come to Mexico in the first place, Cam announced that his friend and new believer, don Martín Méndez, the mayor of Tetelcingo, had told the Christmas story in Aztec and in Spanish for the first time to the villagers.

In the letter Cam also shared highlights from reports and letters he had received from other SIL members. One such report came from Bill Bentley, a gifted and dedicated young man who had attended the fifth session of SIL and was assigned to work among the hostile lowland Bachajón Tzeltal people:

> Bill Bentley picked up some dysentery on his way out to the "sticks" of Chiapas, but he is now recuperating and enjoying German food, electric lights and a radio on a German coffee plantation.

Cam went on to tell how Florence Hansen and Eunice Pike were making amazing progress in the Mazatec tonal language, plus tidbits of information about each of the other teams living in isolated villages. Most of the reports received from the new recruits were amazingly detailed and full of local color. Bill Bentley's was no exception. He included an incident in his report that came to be part of a book written fifty years later in 1988 by Marianna Slocum and Grace Watkins:

> Bill ducked his head as he entered the smoky little Tzeltal house. The wind rattled the reed walls in a dismal dirge. [Inside, Bill saw a man] Pancho, hunched in a corner, his clothes bloodied, his head wrapped in dirty rags through which seeped a bright red [stain]. At [the man's] feet burned a candle. Bill gave an awkward greeting to

his young wife who knelt anxiously by her husband's side. She did not reply or look up.

Even before Bill unwrapped the head covering, a wave of nausea swept over him. Before his unaccustomed eyes gaped an ugly six-inch wound made by the slash of a machete. Part of Pancho's brain was exposed through the cranium and the separated bones pulsed with every throb of the victim's artery.[1]

It's difficult to know exactly why Cam included the graphic details of this incident in his letter except that he held an unyielding commitment to the notion of partnership and togetherness of the SIL team. Without the benefit of management training, group dynamics, or the ethos of social groupings, Cam instinctively understood an important basic fact about human nature: namely, that in order for individual members to experience a sense of well-being during their isolated field assignments, each needed to know they were needed. And equally important, Cam wanted each member to know he or she was inexorably linked to a larger whole. That in fact, they were a team, part of a group, part of a family.

For many years the SIL members referred to themselves as the "group." What was inherent in this term was not just a handy way to define themselves professionally. The term also served to define themselves socially. For all his push toward getting the job of translation done in "this generation," Cam understood that a happy, enthusiastic, upbeat group of people could, in fact, energize, strengthen and support each other emotionally and psychologically, particularly during lonely difficult, and sometimes harrowing experiences. This was why Cam continually called on the group to put as much "pie in pioneering," as they could.

The notion of togetherness and partnership in Cam's mind did not stop just with "the group." In recent years the watchword for mission has centered upon partnership—partnership with other missions, as well as nationals and with the national church as part of the translation equation. In some countries, some SIL members believed this was a departure from original SIL policy. But in a letter dated January 12, 1939, in response to a

---

1 Marianna Slocum with Grace Watkins, *The Good Seed* (Orange, Califonia: Promise Publishing Company, 1988), pp. 1,2.

fund-raising letter Legters had written asking for prayer and money to be used to print initial Scripture translations, Cam wrote the following:

> I think this request by you for funds to print initial Scriptures must have been an oversight. Last summer I told you my feeling that it is a mistake for us to undertake the publication of our translations when the American Bible Society is so willing and better able to do this for us.
>
> I feel most strongly that if the thousands of tribes of the world who are still without some portion of God's Word are to be reached, it will be necessary for all organizations interested in this task to co-operate. That being the case, we should stick to our job of Bible translation and let the Bible Societies do the publishing. The missions, where there are missions established, can take care of the church planting and teaching. May I urge that all funds that come in answer to this request be turned over to the American Bible Society for them to use in the publication of translations designated by donors.

Almost immediately after establishing this working procedure with the Bible Society, Cam had to correct yet another procedural problem. In his letter to Legters, Cam was able, in a single page, to effect a change. His next letter, sent to Max Lathrop, chair of the Mexico Executive Committee, was five pages of single-spaced type.

The essence of the conflict had to do with some fundamental changes in the original SIL constitution that Max Lathrop had inserted to more precisely indicate who were qualified to become SIL members. Max Lathrop, Richmond McKinny and Brainerd Legters were seminary trained and believed strongly that men (not women) so trained in the "arts, sciences, linguistics, Bible, and Greek should be considered for SIL membership."

Actually, the debate centered around a small change in a section of the original constitution which read, "Only those persons who are members of the parent organization in the U.S.A., the Summer Institute of Linguistics, shall be eligible for membership." The change that greatly upset Cam read, "Only those persons who are qualified graduates of the parent organization, etc." Max Lathrop had substituted the words "qualified graduates" for the word "members."

In clear, precise language, Cam pointed out that if this amendment were passed, it would eliminate over half of the present SIL membership, including himself. Then with a slight barb,[1] he added: "Under your proposal, those who would be denied membership would be our most successful workers." (Cam also pointed out in another letter that the two women, Florence Hansen and Eunice Pike, had remained in their allocation the longest that year, and as far as he was concerned, had accomplished more than any of those who had opposed him in allowing women to join SIL.)

Here was a critical moment in the beginning of SIL's early history which could easily have taken an elitist route. All the pressures were there. Max and the other seminary men, as well as Nida, and to some extent Pike, favored the constitutional changes that would reflect the academic seriousness of their mission and calling.

Certainly Cam understood the necessity for good scholarship and training for all who would join SIL. But Cam believed these men had forgotten the social conditions of the times. A world war was looming on the horizon and the pool of young men would soon be siphoned off to war. Cam knew that without new recruits, he was powerless to implement his Bible translation dream of reaching every ethnic minority with the Scriptures in their own language. There was also something else, something more essential in the Townsend character that Max and the others may not have taken into consideration, or didn't understand. Namely, Cam knew how to listen to God who speaks. This gave him the grace, purpose and courage not to be afraid of moral aloneness. If he believed an action was within the divine purpose of God, Cam, in humility was willing to stand alone, to think and act differently from the crowd. In a letter to Max Lathrop Cam wrote:

> Let me review a bit our history. From the beginning we sought to attract people who possessed diplomas from both college and seminary. In the second SIL session, God sent us five students, four of whom were qualified more or less to the standards of our current bylaws. Of the five, only one man did not come up to the set standards. The interesting thing is that he, of the five at this point, has been the most successful of all in language learning and doing actual translation.

---

1 According to Cam's February 1939 memo, there were thirty-two people from Camp Wycliffe working in Mexico. Twenty-six of these were allocated and working in ethnic minority language groups.

The following summer we expected God to send us more seminary students since we had such a high percentage the previous
year. It was true that we made an effort to secure seminary students because we were not always satisfied with the work done by
the non-seminary men. But much to our disappointment, God did
not send us a single student who had graduated from either a university or seminary. Mr. Legters felt that few of them would be able
to do translation work. The question now was, "What should we
do?" God had opened the doors to Mexico in answer to prayer and
we needed workers. Should we take what He had sent us, or bring
in none at all?

There is one thing I have followed very carefully these past three
years and that is to *follow* and not dictate to the Lord about where
and how He leads. He has given many surprises and upset many
old ideas but I have endeavored always to be deaf to my own and
others' counsel and listen only to His. Several of the old time workers from other missions in Mexico scoffed at some of the early
workers we brought down. Richmond McKinney insisted and insisted that none of the group was qualified. Interestingly, these
several years later the two people against whom there was great
objection have already produced a primer and the gospel of John,
and many other portions.

The question is, were we correct in bringing to Mexico those who
graduated from a Bible institute rather than a seminary? If we had
not brought them down, three tribes would today be without linguistic workers. Did God open the door to Mexico for us to shut it in the
face of over half who apply to come with us when there are so
many languages still without linguistic workers to give them the
Word of God in their own language? Are we willing to say we will
not accept volunteers to go to them if they do not have any better
qualifications than Ed Sywulka, Bill Sedat, Chips Smallwood,
Eunice Pike and Florence Hansen? Personally, I would rather accept five so-called failures, a thing incidentally that has not yet happened, and get a Bill Sedat or a Chips Smallwood or any of the
other "unqualified" workers mentioned than accept the responsibility
of denying God's Word to a single tribe on account of standards
that God has laughed at and utterly disregarded time and time
again. It is, however, up to the rest of you to decide. This matter,

therefore, should be put up for a vote in a careful way which will make the issues clear to everyone.

Cam signed off on this long letter to Max with warmest greetings to his wife Elizabeth and the "darling youngsters." He then added a P.S.

May I ask why the committee decided to take the risk in including Bible and seminary credentials as standards in the articles of organization of a linguistic society? Since Mexico is sensitive about such things, we have always been careful about the language we use. I am sending copies of this letter to the voting members and to Mr. Legters. But let it be understood to those who have come from Bible institutes that they are doing good work.[1]

Throughout his life, Cam wrote notes of encouragement, spoke a word of commendation and praised a member's contribution whenever he could. His purpose was to create and maintain through such encouragement a cohesive harmony among opposites. Given the highly intelligent, highly motivated, and highly individualistic nature of most group members, achieving such harmony was no small task. Yet Cam was generally able to achieve this collaborative spirit by the charm and charisma of his own personality. He and Legters were, after all, a living example of such a creative synthesis. And it fell to Legters to gently remind Cam that the harmony he wanted to establish may have been damaged by the tone of his letter to Max Lathrop:

About your letter on the constitution to Max. You used a very strong voice. I wonder how wise it is to be as hard on him as you were. I

---

1 The roster of 1939 (sixth) session of SIL and Camp Wycliffe that was held at the Baptist Assembly Grounds near Siloam Springs, Arkansas notes that of the almost thirty students, three were from John Brown University, one was from a seminary, seven were from the Bible Institute of Los Angeles (BIOLA, which is now a University). The remainder were from a variety of Bible Institutes including Moody and Columbia Bible College. It is also interesting to note the achievements of those who came from these Bible institutes. Some like William Wonderly went on to earn a Ph.D. Others like Hazel Spotts, Marjorie Davis, and Herman Aschmann, each translated a New Testament for an ethnic people. In the case of Herman Aschmann who was from Moody Bible Institute, he with his co-translators translated three New Testaments for three related Totonac people groups.

> do not know how I would have reacted had I been in his place. I
> do, of course, agree with you on this constitutional matter.

Fortunately, Max Lathrop seemed not to have felt Cam was unduly hard on him. His February 7 letter of response said simply that he had read Cam's letter over several times and admitted that he was in error for introducing the changes without prior consultation. In an offhanded way he said he hadn't taken the old constitution as seriously as he should have. Max then informed Cam of other changes the executive committee had made. The most far-reaching was the name used in referring to the SIL group in Mexico. Formally it had called itself, "La Brigada Mexicana." This was changed to the Mexican Branch of SIL (and later changed to the Mexico Branch of SIL).

People who knew Cameron Townsend well, knew he lived his life by certain principles. Perhaps the most fundamental of these was "service to others in the spirit of true Christian love." It was such a basic principle that Cam wanted each member to follow it and whenever he could, he provided positive examples of this principle. Often these examples took the form of a special meal in honor of a Mexican official. On July 4, 1939, Cam sent a letter inviting friends and churches in Southern California to attend a picnic in Agua Caliente just south of Tijuana, Mexico. In part, the letter read:

> The President of the Republic of Mexico, General Lázaro
> Cárdenas, has kindly consented to be the guest of honor together
> with his official staff at an open-air picnic. [The Summer Institute of
> Linguistics] has planned this picnic as an expression of gratitude for
> the help and encouragement he has extended to our group of lin-
> guists and Bible translators now working among the Indian peoples
> of his nation.

Borrowing a phrase from President Roosevelt, Cam advertised this event as a "Good Neighbor Picnic," but the deeper principle Cam wanted both the Mexicans and the SIL group to understand was that of love. When Cam exhorted the group, as he did throughout his life until he died, "to serve one another in love," he meant what the psychiatrist M. Scott Peck said of love: "Love is the will to extend one's self for the purpose of nurturing one's own or another's spiritual growth." And

from the many personal testimonies and speeches given that July 7th afternoon, this was clearly Cam's intention toward his friend, the president, and the country he represented.

During the days immediately following that historic event, Cam sent a
flood of letters and telegrams to friends and supporters brimming with
praise to the Lord for the picnic's success. (Cárdenas himself sent a seventy-five word telegram to Cam to thank him for the picnic.) Cam's first
telegram after the picnic was to Elvira who was once again ill and under
doctor's care in the American Baptist Hospital in Puebla, Mexico.

From all accounts the picnic was indeed a success. However, in their
haste, the planners of the picnic forgot one important item. Said Cam:

> I doubt if the Mexican officials really enjoyed our American food. If
> they did not, they were good sports for they ate heartily. Unfortu-
> nately, we should have been more thoughtful of our guests and pro-
> vided some Tabasco sauce, but it completely slipped my mind.

While Cam was trying to be thoughtful of his guests, not everyone was
tying to be thoughtful of Cam. From a few within the group and from a
number on the outside, the picnic became a flash point and served as a
launching pad for some to openly criticize Cam for "fraternizing with
the government when he could have been doing Christian work." This
charge from within his own ranks caused Cam great pain and on November 29 it occasioned the following response:

> I am writing this in answer to those who have criticized our policy of
> cooperation with the Mexico University, the Mexican government
> and with scientific bodies in the United States such as the Linguistic
> Society of America. Let me say at once that this policy has been
> signally blessed of God. It is true we often have to work with secu-
> lar people, even atheists, both in Mexico and the United States.
> But our cooperation with them has been constructive in matters that
> were vital to our program, such as linguistic research. And never
> has our association with such people been in any way destructive
> to our faith or morals. However, this policy has been subject to
> constant criticism. This was to be expected since our procedure
> was a departure from the norm and the people who criticized did

not know or understand the unusual way in which we were led of God to walk in an unbeaten path.

This criticism made most of us, and me in particular since I was responsible for the policies we were following, review the remarkable step-by-step guidance I had received in coming to Mexico. When I did this, the Lord gave peace and the assurance that if we continued, we would one day see a great spiritual awakening in Mexico.

Most of you have felt the same way about this. A few, however, have been unhappy with our policies. We love one another and would not consciously harm one another, and yet I can see trouble ahead unless we stop and think this matter through. It seems to me there are at least two policies that Christian workers should follow in Mexico. The first is the frank cooperation with and commendation of government projects that we can heartily endorse while carefully abstaining from anything that could be considered as [being in] opposition to [Christian principles].

The second is strict neutrality concerning government policies, neither commending nor criticizing them. Those of our number who cannot conscientiously endorse the first policy need only to consistently follow the second to avoid getting us into trouble. And that is what I am now pleading with you to do. Just be consistently neutral. Any kind of censorship of the government or the established church could result in deadly opposition to our work. *Therefore, if we cannot commend, let us be careful not to oppose.*

Remember we are in Mexico to serve, not to dictate policies to the government. Our task is to give the Word of God to the people. Furthermore, we are called not to pass judgment on the rulers of a nation, but to obey and pray for them. Let us be consistent. If anyone feels he cannot cooperate and wishes to hold himself aloof from the government, let him also hold himself aloof from criticism.

Please note also that if our policy of cooperation leads me a little further afield from the direct task of Scripture translation than the rest of you, please be lenient in judging me. I have prayed carefully over each step I have taken and am confident that He has led me to do it for your sakes and the gospel's. However, if any of you have observed detrimental effects from it, please let me know.

The charge that I am not doing "Christian" work bothered me at first, but since my Savior led me to do what I am doing just as definitely as he led the Apostle Paul to spend long hours making tents, I forge ahead unperturbed and receive amazing opportunities for sharing my faith.

The one thing that does disturb me greatly, however, is to have new recruits criticized and placed in a position where they feel they must leave Mexico in order to feel they are involved in "Christian" work. In the meantime, twenty million ethnic peoples in Latin America wait to see the spirit of the Gospel demonstrated in a way they can comprehend and to hear the Word of God in a language they can understand.

Our linguistic group must make both a [personal] demonstration of the gospel and the translation of the Word. I do not believe there is another way to do this other than by patiently following the path by faith and the humble path of cooperation in which God has so signally blessed us thus far.

With much love in the Lord and a burden of prayer, I remain yours in Romans 15:20, (signed) W. Cameron Townsend.

Eugene Nida, Claudio Iglesias (speaker of the Kuna language of Panama and visiting teacher at SIL), Eunice Pike, and Eunice Pike's older brother, Ken Pike. 1941.

Chapter Eleven
Casting Aside Pious Piffle

T he Western Union telegram addressed to W.C. Townsend dated December 24, 1939, contained a single sentence. "Father passed away tonight funeral Wednesday." The telegram was signed by Cam's sister (Evelyn Griset's mother). Cam's much beloved father had died. In two of his last letters to Cam, written in May and August of 1939, his father wrote:

> I can't rest at night. I just dream all the time when not awake. I seem to get lost and can't find my way home again. It's not pleasant. I want to keep writing but it seems like the tabernacle is fast giving out. Please remember me in prayer that God's strength may be perfected in my weakness. I told my doctor that my flesh and my heart fail me but God is the strength of my heart and my portion forever.

In his last letter to his father, written on November 3, Cam apologized for not writing as often as he would have liked. His reason, he said, was that he had set himself a daily schedule of writing or revising 2,500 words on his Cárdenas biography. Speaking of biography, Cam wrote:

I've been reading a wonderful biography of Abraham Lincoln and have been impressed more than ever with his greatness. He certainly lived to serve his fellowman. During the last months of his life he seemed to draw nearer to God. Here is a quote from him that I like very much. "If it were not for my firm belief in an overruling Providence, it would be difficult for me, in the midst of such complications of affairs, to keep my reason in its seat. I am confident the Almighty has His plans and will work them out, and whether we see it or not, they will be the wisest and best for us."

Six months later, on May 18, 1940, these very words returned to both haunt and console Cameron Townsend. The reason: his friend, confidant and cofounder of Camp Wycliffe and SIL, L.L. Legters, died suddenly at age sixty-seven.

Beside his role as field secretary of the Pioneer Mission Agency and all that entailed, Legters had the responsibility as director of Camp Wycliffe. It was he who received and processed the applications from prospective SIL students. But as early as November 2, 1939, Legters, the man who for years had been the tireless spokesman for the cause of Bible translation and given hundreds of rousing sermons across the length and breadth of the States, had sent Cam an uncharacteristic letter. When one reads it in retrospect, it appears prophetic:

I am not promising to be at Camp next summer. I just do not know what the Lord wants me to do. Therefore, I am making no engagements with anyone. Not even Camp. The Lord has given me no freedom to make any plans after April 1. I have received many speaking invitations, enough for two years, but I am saying no to every one, even to W.C. Townsend about next year.

L.L. Legters' role in the development of Camp Wycliffe and SIL, and his support of Cam, plus the many hundreds he encouraged and pointed into mission service is inestimable. Few people realize that Legters significantly influenced Cam's life at several crucial moments in time. One of the first was in January of 1921 in Guatemala when Cam had invited him to be a conference speaker.[1] Later, when Cam was undecided about

---

1 See *Wycliffe in the Making*, p. 35 ff.

how and when to implement his dream of a linguistic training school, it was Legters who suggested, in 1933, that the time was not yet ripe. "Better to wait," said Legters, "until we have a definite opening in Mexico so that we will have something to work toward." In his eulogy of Legters, Cam wrote:

> L.L. Legters was a rugged pioneer missionary, Bible teacher, friend and leader upon whom I could always depend. There was nothing uncertain or halfway about him. With absolute devotion he threw his great energy, his very life into vital things. The "vital things" for L.L. Legters was to point Christians away from self to the all-powerful ever-triumphant God. His further passion was to point Christians to the unfinished missionary task of the church and to stir believers to action on behalf of the overlooked and unevangelized areas of the world. Mr. Legters bluntly denounced as "pious piffle" all the devout teaching that excused defeat in the Christian's life rather than experiencing a triumphant walk in a victorious Christ.

Dr. Arthur Glasser, a professor at the Fuller School of World Mission, who knew Legters well, gives further insight into what Legters meant by "pious piffle":

> L.L. Legters practiced, lived and preached a classical form of the *Keswick victorious life* way of looking at the Christian life. This meant personal surrender to Jesus Christ, separation from the world and all that the "world" meant in the 1930s, disciplined reflection, plus obedience to the Holy Scripture. It also included the fullness of the Holy Spirit, which in those days meant tolerating no issue in one's life that was manifestly contrary to the will of God. The slogans most often heard in victorious life circles were "no unresolved controversies with God," "keep the ascended Christ central in your vision," and "trust the indwelling Christ to enable you to meet all the demands He is making of you."

In the same letter that told of Legters' death, Cam reported that the seventh SIL with forty men and women was the largest enrollment of the camp's history. In view of world events in 1940, Cam's faith in God and what God could do with forty dedicated Bible translators was analogous to David going up against the giant Goliath with his sling:

> At this moment, when young men are offering themselves by the millions to serve the god of war, forty men and women training for pioneer Bible translation work seems like an insignificant number. But as these young people make it vital to obey the Great Commission and go to unevangelized places, they will accomplish more than large armies.
>
> I write this letter in memory of Mr. Legters and of his do-or-die attitude toward vital things. Therefore, in the realization of the momentous times in which we live, let us cast aside all "pious piffle" and secondary issues, and let us press forward until every ethnic person has heard the story of His infinite love. Let us follow Him to victory! Acts 20:24.

One couple who had heard Legters speak and been influenced by him to prioritize their lives and "cast aside pious piffle" was Dick and Kay Pittman. In 1940, Dick was just twenty-five. In the course of time, he became Cam's understudy, earned a Ph.D. in linguistics and became director of the SIL linguistic courses at the University of North Dakota, a post he held for twenty-five years. In addition he would become the director of several SIL branches and the Pacific area director. From his early and close association with Cameron Townsend, Dick wrote a number of important books that specifically interpreted Cam's principles and leadership style. But while young adults like the Pittmans and others would play key roles in the development and growth of SIL, a number of Cam's early friends were getting older and dying.

In fact, death was very much a part of Cam and Elvira's experience in 1940. Cam's dear friend Luther Reese died, as did Elvira's mother. And incomprehensibly, L.L. Legters' wife Edna died of lung cancer. Her funeral service was held in the same chapel of the Central Presbyterian Church of Chambersburg, Pennsylvania, on September 23, 1940, where her husband's funeral service was held exactly four months before. However, on May 26, before Edna Legters died, Cam sent her the following letter from Mexico City:

This morning, all the translators who were in the capital, some eight of us, together with Mr. Marroquín, met in memory of Mr. Legters in the office across from the Bible Society. We read Psalm 139 and recalled the way Mr. Legters would have emphasized certain verses with his inimitable gestures and expressions. Of course, we sang "Faith mighty Faith, the Promise sees, and Looks to God Alone."

I pointed out that Mr. Legters and I had worked together in a common vision for twenty-one years. As each of the translators spoke about their memories of your husband, the one word that came up over and over was the word "rugged." We recalled how your husband had left his Carolina parish to work among the Indians in Oklahoma under most difficult circumstances.

We recalled also how he made arduous and dangerous linguistic survey trips through the interiors of South and Central America. And we recalled that this same hardy enthusiasm and profound love for the Lord and His Word enabled him to impart truth from the Book so that many who heard him learned, at times with a start, yet with deepest joy, that we are *in* Christ and that the Holy Spirit lives in us.

We all knew how deep was his passion for missions, but none of us knew how "rugged" it was. We have only learned recently that he was personally supporting several pioneer missionaries. And because of his passion to "find men and money" for missions, we are establishing an L.L. Legters memorial fund with the prayer that the money from this fund will perpetuate the work he so deeply loved.

By mid-1940, the effects of SIL's specialized linguistic training of young people to prepare them for a career in Bible translation was being felt on four continents. Cam was continually receiving letters of appreciation from former students who thanked him for SIL's unique training. One such letter came from Grace Armstrong working in China:

You know that I am here in Soochow, Kiangsu for language study. While I struggle with the difficult sounds and characters, I want to tell you how glad I am that I studied phonetics at Camp Wycliffe. Because of Kenneth Pike's good drilling, I have surprised my teacher with my ability to pronounce some of the most difficult words.

While former students like Grace Armstrong were deeply appreciative of the practical skills they had learned at SIL and Camp Wycliffe, not everyone understood why Townsend insisted there be two organizations. In a September 3, 1940, letter to Dr. Oscar Boyd of the American Bible Society, Cam answered this question for the Bible Society, who were still a little unsure of Cam's vision:

> Just as a commercial bank has to organize independently for its savings department, so too do we need two permanent and separate organizations. One organization, with its own director and board, handles the practical and spiritual side of our activities, including Camp Wycliffe. The other organization, also with its own director and board, handles our scientific activities (linguistic courses, etc.). This year I have asked Professor Nida and Kenneth Pike to jointly direct SIL at Camp Wycliffe [to replace L.L. Legters]. I am to direct the Institute in Mexico. This seems to be the opposite to what you would expect when you know our respective gifts and training, because certainly Nida and Pike are far better prepared to direct the Institute than I am. However, I find it advantageous in Mexico to be the director of a scientific organization.

Years later, as President Emeritus of SIL, Ken Pike gave a historic explanation and rationale for the two organizations:

> In a nutshell, SIL prepares people to learn unwritten languages and teaches them how to communicate across cultural barriers. Wycliffe Bible Translators (as a sister organization) recruits people to do Bible translation and achieves this goal primarily through SIL field work. WBT is concerned with its members' spiritual and doctrinal standards, while SIL is concerned with training WBT members. Uncle Cam's insight into the possibilities of serving God through the science of linguistics has had a tremendous impact upon all of us. From the beginning he insisted we do linguistic work with Bible translation. And this is what SIL and WBT are all about.

One of the things Cameron Townsend "was about" in 1940 and 1941 was the promotion of bilingual education for minority peoples. In a time when educators in the U.S. and Canada were forcibly placing minority children in government-run boarding schools and punishing them for speaking their mother tongue on the playing field at school, Townsend's approach was twenty-five years ahead of the curve. In a letter that had a certain poetic lyricism to it, written to Mexico's Professor Luis Alvarez Barret, Sub-Director General of Rural Education, Cam wrote:

> I believe bilingual education is of the utmost importance. After working for twenty-two years in Indian communities, I have witnessed many sad and sorrowful experiences of injustices perpetuated against a people whose innate abilities, if once developed, would be of inestimable value to their nation. I consider it a great tragedy for such people to remain century after century with the blindness of illiteracy over their eyes, the burden of exploitation upon their backs, and their feet hobbled with chains of superstition and drunkenness.
>
> Bilingual education will greatly expedite the removal of that blindfold, and with the blindfold removed, the Indian will himself be able to see how to untie his feet and remove his burdensome load. Some have the attitude that if the Indian is permitted to receive rudimentary instruction through the vehicle of his own mother tongue, he will have no desire to proceed further and learn Spanish (or the national language) as almost everyone wishes him to do.
>
> From my own experience and the experience of the language investigators of the Summer Institute of Linguistics, I have to say such a fear is groundless. For an Indian to learn to read first in his own language does not stifle the Indian's ambition to learn the national language or culture. On the contrary, it stimulates that ambition. Furthermore, it convinces him that he is capable of attaining knowledge contained in books. And this has the effect of helping him overcome his inferiority complex, a complex that told him he was an inferior person, and therefore could not learn to read. My experience has been that once ethnic persons have their minds awakened by a little learning, it gives them the confidence and de-

sire to learn more, and this includes learning their national language.

As logical and as persuasive as this argument was, it wasn't strong enough to convince the head of the Department of Indian Affairs in Mexico. After a conversation with Cam and Max Lathrop on this subject, Cam learned the Mexican educator bitterly opposed the use of Indian languages even in the initial steps of education. Further, the man viewed departures from Spanish orthography with disdain.

Clearly Cam was on the horns of a dilemma. From the influence of his father, Cam had been taught early in his life to use his own judgment and to have the courage to stand up for what was right, even if the odds of winning were against him. In this case it was a violation of a basic premise of his life and ministry, namely, the right of all people to learn to read and write in their own language.

On the other hand, Cam had repeatedly urged the SIL members to submit to the authorities of the host country. The solution? He would circumvent the educator's bias against the use of the vernacular language by producing diglot materials that used an orthography that, as much as possible, adhered to the Spanish alphabet. In a letter to the SIL membership dated March 3, 1941, Cam presented the following game plan:

> At a recent meeting with over a dozen workers representing three different mission agencies, plus three educated Indians, it was decided that a greater emphasis should be placed on teaching Scripture and memorization of the Word in the vernacular languages.
>
> In view of our conversation with the head of Indian Affairs who opposes the use of vernacular languages, I propose the following. One, that we publish all translations only in diglot, i.e., the vernacular language on one side of the page, and the corresponding text in Spanish on the opposite side. I believe it is humiliating to a non-speaker of a vernacular language to see a book published for fellow Mexicans that he cannot read. It makes him suspicious of the contents. It also makes him feel that the division between peoples of the same nation is being emphasized and perpetuated. A diglot publication however, helps the ethnic person learn Spanish without an affront to his dignity. Further, we should, wherever possible, adhere to the Spanish orthography.

By the end of February 1941, the SIL membership had grown to thirty-seven people who were working among eighteen language groups. The average age of the group member was twenty-seven. Of the thirty-seven, eleven were married couples, eleven were single women and the four remaining were single men. However, there were soon to be twelve married couples. On Valentine's Day, February 14, 1941, Bill Bentley hiked a hard seven hours over rugged mountain trails to give Marianna Slocum a large heart-shaped cookie that had been baked by the wife of the German coffee plantation owner on which he had been living. Bill and Marianna were officially engaged and the wedding date set for August 21, 1941.

When the group heard the news of Bill's and Marianna's engagement, it was met with happy approval. If any two people were meant for each other, it was surely Bill and Marianna. The poised, soft-spoken Marianna graduated from Wilson College in Chambersberg, near Philadelphia, *cum laude* with special honors in French, Greek, Latin and Hebrew. Her father, a Ph.D in civil engineering and professor at the University of Cincinnati, was a deeply committed Christian, as were Marianna's mother, her two brothers and sister.

Bill Bentley came from Topeka, Kansas and had all-American chiseled good looks. And like Marianna's, Bill's family members were also committed believers. Everyone who knew and observed Bill and Marianna during the days prior to August 21 was touched by their infectious love for each other and absolute commitment to giving the New Testament to the Tzeltal people whom Bill had been working for seven years. The remarkable story of the birth and growth of the Tzeltal church is recorded in two books, *The Good Seed*, and *Never Touch a Tiger* [1]

The stories in these two books, however, tell more than the remarkable growth of the Tzeltal Church. Intertwined is the story of Marianna's profound pain and indomitable courage in the face of Bill Bentley's death six days before their wedding. On the day they were to have been married, Marianna was at Camp Wycliffe en route to Mexico to work among the fiercely independent Tzeltals. An hour after her father had discovered Bill's body on Sunday morning, August 21, Marianna, in a state of grief and shock, and too numb to weep, nevertheless called Uncle Cam and

---

1 Marianna Slocum with Grace Watkins, *The Good Seed*, (Orange, California: Promise Publishers Co., 1988). Hugh Steven, *Never Touch a Tiger*, (Nashville: Thomas Nelson Publishers, 1980), p. 41 ff.

asked permission to return to the Tzeltals to continue the work Bill had begun. Without a moment's hesitation, Cam said "Yes." At the memorial service at Camp Wycliffe held on Monday August 25, Ken Pike read the passage from Hebrews 11:17-19 and then said:

> Although Bill has gone, yet we can offer him up willingly, saying that God has done all things well. Metaphorically, we shall receive him back, for God, through the continuing of the work through our prayers, will raise up fruit from this sorrow. "Except a corn of wheat fall into the ground and die, it abideth alone: but if it die, it bringeth forth much fruit."[1]

Without the help and moral support of L.L. Legters, the summer work load at the 1941 Camp Wycliffe was particularly heavy for Cam. With fifty-three students and staff, it was the largest Camp Wycliffe yet. In his report to the Pioneer Mission Agency, Cam pointed out that there wasn't a single seminary graduate among them. In fact, to Reuben Allen, Jr., age twenty-two, who had written asking about seminary training, Cam wrote, "Rather than go to a seminary, I strongly urge you to spend a year taking advanced Bible work and Greek at a graduate school like Columbia Bible College." Cam ended his letter by saying he never regretted going to the mission field at age twenty-one, even though it cost him the seminary training he had planned on taking.

One of the many difficulties Cam, Ken Pike and other staff members faced that summer was Eugene Nida's unexplained weakness and fatigue. So concerned was Cam over this that he and Nida checked into the Mayo Clinic (Cam was also suffering from fatigue) . The diagnoses for both were that there wasn't anything organically wrong. They had just been working too hard. The recommendation from the Mayo Clinic was that both men should take a rest from "intellectual work and responsibility." To a missionary in Point Barrow, Alaska, Cam wrote:

> The doctors at the clinic told Nida that his trouble was simply overexertion of the brain. This doesn't prevent him from enjoying life as long as he doesn't use his head. Of course, this is a hardship on anyone who loves books and mental exercise the way Nida does.

---

1 John 12:24 (KJV)

There is no indication that Cam himself took the doctors' advice. He did, however, relieve Nida of his teaching responsibilities at Camp and divided it between himself and Ken Pike. Ken assumed this responsibility even though he had to be absent for two weeks to take his oral examination for his Doctor of Philosophy degree in linguistics at Ann Arbor, Michigan.

In yet another letter to the council of the Pioneer Mission Agency, Cam reported, with justified satisfaction, that the whole New Testament in the Mazatec language had been completed in first draft. It had taken Florence Hansen and Eunice Pike five years to accomplish this. Cam acknowledged that he thought it would take two more years of careful revision before it would be ready for publication.[1] Nevertheless, he praised this as a memorable event: "This is the first time in the history of Mexico that so much of God's Word has been placed into the language of any indigenous people. This is indeed a milestone in the work which we have undertaken to give the Word of Life to all the indigenous groups of this land."

While Cam was pleased and proud of the two women for this accomplishment, it only heightened the reality of how much work remained and of the need for many more workers. Cam's report to the Pioneer Missionary Agency written a day later on September 10, 1941, very likely had the council members shaking their heads and wondering if he weren't just too much of a dreamer:

---

1 One of Cameron Townsend's virtues was his quickness to praise the SIL member and to see progress in the most optimistic light. Sometimes, however, his optimism needed to be interpreted. Dr. George Cowan, who joined SIL and WBT in 1942, married Florence Hansen and became part of the team that translated the Mazatec New Testament, gives a more realistic and accurate historical account of the actual date of publication. "Florrie had completed the first draft of the Mazetec New Testament with each verse on three by five cards (no computers in those days). After I joined the team, we went through it again with other speakers of the language. We typed up a composite for checking yet again with speakers of the language and began submitting individual books to the Bible Society. When the war came and we would send a manuscript across the border to the States, it would be held up for six months. The reason was the censors could not read it and they were suspicious of its content. Later an entire first draft of the Gospel of John was lost in some baggage that was being shipped. Meanwhile, over half of the New Testament was in use in separate booklets. However, because of these and other interruptions, the actual publication date of the Mazatec New Testament in a single volume didn't occur until 1961."

It has taken the Church nearly two thousand years to produce slightly over one thousand translations of the Bible in whole or in part (half are in part). If we are this slow in producing translations for the remaining thousand ethnic groups, many are doomed to a very long wait and the church will definitely have to view with shame a God-given task whose completion is long overdue.[1]

If two young women, utilizing the training that modern science provides, can translate the whole New Testament into a difficult tonal language in five years, it is easy to see that the whole task can be completed by a group of several hundred scientifically trained linguists in this generation. Already over a hundred young people have gone out from Camp Wycliffe under nineteen different mission boards, all trained to do Bible translation.

Within a few years we expect to see at least five hundred young people trained in the comparatively new science of [descriptive] linguistics and scattered all over the earth wherever the Bible has not been translated into an indigenous language. In view of the great stress which we must place on the scientific part of our work, and because I personally feel I lack this kind of scientific training, and because I feel my calling and gifts are in pioneer work on the mission field itself, I am asking the Institute to elect Dr. Kenneth L. Pike to be the director of the Summer Institute of Linguistics in my place.[2]

Cam's father had taught Cam to be a critical thinker and to use his own judgment. And his judgment on the eve of America's involvement in World War II was that just as Uncle Sam needed personnel to fight a terrible tyranny of war, so too, did Cameron Townsend need personnel to fight the tyranny of illiteracy and spiritual emptiness. And the only way he knew of recruiting such people was to ask them. Since the most

---

1 Cam's understanding of the actual number of ethnic peoples without the Scripture was based upon the best available information at the time. With the advent of more sophisticated survey data recording, the SIL Ethnologue database update of October 1996 lists the number of languages in the world to be 6,701.

2 Dr. Kenneth Lee Pike was elected President of the Summer Institute of Linguistics in September 1942. Pike held this position with great distinction for thirty-seven years, from 1942, the year of SIL's incorporation, to 1979, the year of his retirement.

effective tool in Cam's arsenal was his ability to write letters, he wrote a special letter on November 14, 1941, not to the general public, but to the forty-four members of SIL and The Wycliffe Bible Translators Group. It was a letter that was to have a profound effect on the future leadership and destiny of SIL and WBT.

Chapter Twelve

Lengthened Cords

In one way or another, people throughout the ages have asked, "Why must a world built on love include so much hate and cruelty?" On December 8, 1941, the day after U.S. President Roosevelt said "was a day that will live in infamy," Ken Pike wrote:

> Today the radio gives us the news of war with Japan. Isn't it strange to start heavy translation on such a day?

On December 13, Cameron Townsend wrote:

> At this time when the whole world is torn with strife, the message of love and goodwill which has been entrusted to us by the Prince of Peace appears to be ridiculously impotent. However, we continue to believe that Christ's' love is the greatest power in the world. I look forward to the day when not only the tribes in Mexico, but the rest of the thousands of unreached tribes of earth may come to know the power of God unto Salvation.

The "impotence" of the church, as Cam put it, to address itself to the spiritual needs of the groups of earth was constantly on Cam's mind.

Prior to December 7, 1941, American isolationism in places like the Midwest was still strong. Many felt the war in Europe was not the business of the U.S.A. In Cam's thinking, of course, the mandate of the Great Commission transcended any and all cultural trends. And he believed there was no greater cause than translating the Bible.

On November 3, 1941, Cam wrote a daring letter of faith to the forty-four members of SIL. The uniqueness of this letter is that Cam seems almost to enter into a dialogue between himself and God, the kind of dialogue one might expect between God and an Old Testament prophet. The letter is also noteworthy for Cam's display of audacious faith. It shows that even in this early stage, Cam's vision for SIL was greater than just Mexico.

> I began this letter while Elvira and I were visiting our dear friend ex-President Cárdenas in his home in Pátzcuaro, Michoacán. The president has been ill with malaria. I wanted to assure him of our continuing friendship and prayers for his recovery. On our return trip to Tetelcingo, we visited Max and Elizabeth Lathrop working among the Tarascan people on Lake Pátzcuaro. While we were there, the Lord put a fresh burden on our hearts for the thirty-two ethnic groups in this land who are still without a gospel witness.[1] The devil has tempted some of us to forget the smaller language groups. The temptation has been that since many of the tribal groups are small, we shouldn't expect talented men or women to dedicate ten or more years of their lives learning the language of a few hundred people and to translate the New Testament for them. (The officials have asked us to send workers to the Lacandon and the Seri.)
>
> However, when the temptation came to bypass these smaller groups, the Lord spoke to me and reminded me He had commanded us to go to "*every creature.*" I know it's true that some are

---

1 In 1941 there had not been a thorough linguistic survey made of the ethnic minority groups of Mexico. The best available information at the time was that there were about fifty or sixty language groups that needed a translation. Cam reasoned that since there was SIL personnel at work in twenty-five language groups, there were only about thirty-two groups remaining in the country. Later, linguistic surveys revealed that there are in excess of one hundred and eighty ethnic groups requiring their own translation of the Scriptures.

called to shepherd the ninety and nine, but others are called to go out into the wilderness in quest of the one lost sheep. I said, "All right, Lord, this being the case, we will look to you to raise up one or two workers for each of the remaining tribes in Mexico." But the question remains, "How soon?" The war conditions are closing mission opportunities in certain parts of the world.

The logical conclusion would be to expect an increase in the number of volunteers for fields that are open. Therefore, why not finish the Bible translation task in Mexico now? But then I said, "Lord, that would take at least fifty more workers, and how could they be supported?" And then the Lord said, "Have I failed yet to supply the needs of this rapidly growing work?" I had to confess that He had not, even though friends often wondered how support money could come in for so many new workers with no human organizational sponsoring agency behind them.

In faith we are asking God for *fifty* more Bible translators for twenty-five more tribes in Mexico. Will you join me in prayer for this and will each of you please make yourselves responsible before the Lord for one new recruit for this Bible translation project? This would mean forty-four new workers. However, I am sure the Lord would give us six extra people for good measure.

Any lengthening of the cords, of course, entails extra work and new problems. But God is able to take care of such things. One problem will be the allocation of the new workers when they come. How many of you would be willing to help open up a new station next fall and give one month of your time to this task? Wouldn't it be wonderful to have all the tribes in Mexico taken care of when so many other fields are closed? Then when the hindrances for other unreached fields, such as Siberia, have been removed, we would be ready for a new opportunity to serve. God is able to give the Word to all the ethnic groups in this generation if we look to Him for it.

The gauntlet was now down. So certain was Cam that God was going to answer this request for fifty new workers that he reminded members who would be sending out the letters to urge their friends to apply to the 1942 SIL session by June 1. In the meantime, Cam had other more immediate reminders for the group. In a November 14, 1941, letter he told the group of the sudden death by pleurisy of his longtime friend, and Mexican Ambassador to Peru Dr. Moisés Sáenz. Dr. Sáenz was the man whom Cam had met in Guatemala and who later wrote Cam a letter of invitation to do in Mexico what he had done in Guatemala. Cam's letter also told of U.S. Ambassador Josephus Daniels' wife's ill health and of Daniels' resignation and return to North Carolina. From the beginning days in Mexico, Ambassador Daniels had been a strong supporter of Cam and his vision for Bible translation in Mexico, which, he said, was "the greatest work in the world."

For six years Cam had two powerful friends and allies at court, President Cárdenas and Ambassador Daniels and by extension, their deputies. Now at the end of 1941, the political scene in Mexico had shifted dramatically. One of the first evidences of this was the nonrenewal of the subsidies a few SIL field members had received from the Mexican Department of Education. And then came this warning from Uncle Cam:

> May I urge you to be careful about your work. Unless you are certain the Lord would have you witness in Spanish it would be wise to give your gospel testimony using the Indian language. Richmond McKinney was thrown in jail (for an hour) last Sunday afternoon. He was accused of doing the work of a minister instead of a linguist.
>
> The University is backing him up, and I am sure it will come out all right in the end. In the meantime, let me remind you all that God has brought us here to do a difficult task of giving the Scriptures to people who have been deprived of them for nineteen long centuries. Our task is *singular*, therefore we look to the Lord in faith to lead out others, as indeed He is able, to testify in Spanish.
>
> This refers primarily to fields where you are working. There are also many exceptions. In Tetelecingo, where we have had six years of government backing and goodwill behind us, it is somewhat different. However, let us remember that even though we do have government backing to a degree, and the constitution of the land guarantees religious liberty, our strong point should always be Christian love and courtesy rather than insistence on our rights.
>
> Nine times out of ten, loving deeds of service and a humble forgiving spirit will accomplish much more than stern orders from some army general or officer in Mexico City. Here again there are bound to be exceptions, but let us make love and gentleness our chief weapons.

Cam was more accurate than he realized when he said that a larger membership would generate new and greater logistical problems. In 1941 the SIL group occupied a small downtown office in Mexico City, where for a time, when they were not living in Tetelcingo, Elvira assumed the role of office manager. With just forty-four members, the task of answering and forwarding mail, writing reports, and keeping track of where and what the translators were doing and needed in the way of supplies and medicines was already more than Elvira and Cam could handle.

Dick Pittman, with his wife Kay, working with Cam and Elvira in Tetelicingo, became Deputy Director. The Pittmans along with Ardis Needham, and later her sister Doris, who was a full-time and much over-worked office secretary made up the office staff. Others were occasionally asked to take time out from their linguistic and translation work to do what came to be known as "group service." This need for people other than translators to work in a nontechnical capacity on the field opened the way for a new kind of personnel who came to be known as "support workers."

One year Florrie Hansen spent her entire summer typing Cam's biography of Cárdenas. It was a task she did with love, but it took valuable time away from the translation desk. Clearly, in the interests of good stewardship, it would have been a better use of Florrie's time and skills to have had someone unskilled in linguistics, but with skills as a typist, relieve her.

This need for support workers came into sharp focus on November 8, 1941, when Cam learned indirectly from Brainerd Legters that the Pioneer Mission Agency was beginning to feel SIL had grown too large and their needs too complex for the Agency to handle. The Agency's recommendation to Cam was that SIL incorporate and form their own working organization. This news seems to have taken Cam by surprise. Part of Cam's November 14 response to the Pioneer Mission Agency council is uncharacteristically convoluted. Cam's letters were usually clear, unambiguous and to the point. This letter seems as if he were thinking out loud on this unexpected turn of events. There were a large number of strikeouts which hardly ever occurred in his letters. In the one paragraph that was clearer and to the point, Cam said:

> I learned recently that the PMA feels the task of handling funds which come through the office for the group of translators here [in

Mexico] has reached a stage by its size of being a burden on the Agency. Perhaps it's time that the translators themselves complete the maturity of their growth by forming an organization in the States to act as their representatives. However, this cannot be accomplished immediately, but we will lay it before the Lord for His leading.

Part of the reason for Cam's ambiguity at first seems to be his uncertainty about the Agency's full intention. However, a second letter from Rowan C. Pearce, Chairman of the PMA council, left no doubt in Cam's mind that the time had come for Wycliffe Bible Translators and the Summer Institute of Linguistics to be legally incorporated with their own board of directors:

As you know, the Pioneer Mission Agency is not a board. But we realize that some group must sponsor your work, and we have done what we could. You have estimated that there is a need for at least fifty new workers to complete the work in Mexico. We therefore believe this work should be under the supervision of a board who can give the time that is necessary to really think and pray through the many problems and considerations that must be dealt with.

In view of this, we of the PMA council believe the time has come to carefully consider the whole problem of our relationship with you. It is therefore most important that you should meet with us as soon as possible.

Cam had two dates from which to choose, April 9 or May 9. Reluctantly he chose the latter. Cam was usually most accommodating to outsiders, but he considered this trip to Philadelphia in May too expensive and believed it would steal his time from more important duties.

In January 1942, under pressure from the group who believed Cam needed a rest, he and Elvira took a short furlough in Southern California. Their address was to be the home of their longtime friends in Glendale, California, William (Bill) and Etta Nyman.

In some ways, it was a "busman's holiday," since another old friend, General Cárdenas, had invited Cam to hold special Bible classes among the Mexican soldiers stationed at Ensenada in Baja California. The Mexican government had appointed Cárdenas to be the Commander in Chief of the Mexican defenses along Mexico's Pacific Coast. To Gene Nida, Cam wrote:

> The General has invited me to spend several months with him holding meetings for his soldiers. As much as I would like to do this, I will have to decline since the group has sent us home to rest. I have suggested Captain Taylor join the General's staff for such meetings. Perhaps a bit later on in the year I will be able to give some time to the General's request without defeating the purpose of the Group in giving us a partial furlough.

While Cam admitted in several of his letters that his energy level wasn't as high as it once was (he was now forty-five), he had accepted the group's suggestion of a mini-furlough without protest. Elvira's heath had been a major concern for Cam and indeed for Elvira who for years had been a semi-invalid. However, anyone reading her upbeat correspondence for 1942 and 1943 would have to conclude that she was far from being an invalid. Inexplicably, her health had greatly improved. There is no obvious reason given for this dramatic improvement, except perhaps that in 1942 Elvira was much in demand in her own right. Actually, it would be more correct to say that her book, *Latin American Courtesy*, was in demand. Cam and others had been trying to interest Fleming H. Revell in publishing her book. Revell almost took it, but somehow it fell through the cracks. Finally, Cam was able to arrange a joint publishing venture between The National University Linguistic Institute in Mexico and SIL. The book was released in November 1941, and by the first three months of 1942, people and organizations were ordering multiple copies. It had become an instant best seller. Much of the work for this is credited to Elvira herself who worked hard sending out personal letters and sample copies to a host of people and organizations. She even sent a copy to editors of the *Ladies Home Journal* who said they could run a small advertisement for the book. But it was people like L. K. Anderson, Secretary of the Board of Foreign Missions of the Presbyterian Church, who clearly energized Elvira when he wrote, "I spent part of Christmas day reading L.A.C. and was delighted with your sympathetic and common sense approach to a problem which is of greater importance than many people realize." And then there was

Clarence Jones, co-director of radio station HCJB out of Quito, Ecuador who wrote:

> I only wish that I could have a had a book like yours twelve years ago when I first came to Ecuador. In my estimation, your book makes a tremendous contribution and is such a practical example of good neighborliness that we would like to offer this free to our North American listeners. Would it be possible to secure five hundred, or a thousand copies? I consider your work in *Latin American Courtesy* of such importance that I would like to do everything I possibly can to give it the widest distribution.

Here were words, special words of commendation and affirmation, that defined a significant moment in Elvira's life and ministry. Perhaps for the first time she was being singled out for an accomplishment that was uniquely her own. The result was renewed energy that allowed her to take a greater part in SIL's rapid growth.

Growth was very much on Cam's mind in 1942. Repeatedly he told people they were definitely planning for fifty new recruits to attend the ninth session of SIL from June 3 to August 8. This was to be held for the first time at the University of Oklahoma at Norman. Sponsored by the Department of Modern Languages, the courses were taught by SIL staff and listed as part of the regular university curriculum with the university giving credit for the course.

In her book, *Two Thousand Tongues to Go*, Ethel Wallis devoted an entire chapter to the remarkable story of how God led Della Brunstetter, a French teacher at the University of Oklahoma to invite SIL to the university. With permission I include a condensation of those details:[1]

> While teaching French at the University of Oklahoma Della had become fascinated by the Cherokee language spoken by a large number of Indians in Oklahoma. For some time, the University had talked about offering a course in Cherokee. However, before it could be adequately taught, someone needed to study the language and write it down in modern script. Miss Brunstetter was elected. At the Cherokee centennial celebration in Oklahoma, Della

---

1 Ethel E. Wallis and Mary Bennett, *Two Thousand Tongues to Go* (New York: Harper and Row, 1959,) p. 106-110.

had learned something of the history of the Cherokee people and the remarkable syllabary of the complicated tonal language invented by Chief Sequoya. Della attempted to study the difficult language and to write some of it by using French phonetic characters.

On her way to Washington to confer with government authorities, Della visited the original Cherokee region of North Carolina. (In 1838 the Cherokee people had been forced to move from North Carolina to Oklahoma over the painful "trail of tears.") There she met George Owl, a leader of the Cherokee people, who gave Della valuable information about his people. When she returned to the University of Oklahoma, Della, with the help of a native speaker of Cherokee, tried to settle into a solid study of the Cherokee language. However, she soon discovered the French phonetics could not handle all the different sounds in the Cherokee language.

It was then that Della heard about the University of Michigan's summer session where a new method for analyzing all languages was being taught. Della attended the 1940 summer session but found the technical jargon beyond her. Then a friend told her about a new school called the Summer Institute of Linguistics and two men, Kenneth Pike and Eugene Nida, who could give her practical suggestions for how to study Cherokee.

With a Cherokee-speaking woman, Della attended the 1941 session of SIL held then in the Ozarks where she learned linguistics "from scratch." In spite of the rustic living conditions, Della said she had a "wonderful summer both intellectually and spiritually." At the conclusion of the summer course, Della saw the potential for SIL's growth and need for larger quarters. She decided that SIL should be held at the University of Oklahoma.

That fall, when Della returned to Oklahoma, she contacted the Board of Regents, and made a special trip to the home of the President of the University of Oklahoma to plead the cause of SIL. A week after her visit, Della heard the news that the Summer Institute of Linguistics was going to be invited to the campus of the University of Oklahoma. That was indeed a great day for Della and for SIL. But there was still another great day to come for Della. George Owl had made a trip from North Carolina to Oklahoma. And in the summer of 1942, it was Mrs. Della Brunstetter Owl who joined the staff of SIL to teach linguistics on the campus of the University of Oklahoma at Norman.

When people first learned that SIL was to be held at the University of Oklahoma, they would often, with raised eyebrows, question Cam about where he thought the new students would come from, and had he thought about the complexity of doubling the size of the group in a single year? Cam said simply:

> It seems like a big order, but God is able and our confidence is in Him. In the meantime, we are endeavoring to organize and prepare our present workers to help take care of the new arrivals. Won't it be wonderful, should our Lord not return before, to see the Word of God placed in the hands of half a hundred tribes in Mexico in the next ten years? I believe God is able to do this in spite of the war. Further, I believe the ethnic groups in Mexico should be taken care of before we advance to other unreached tribes that will be opened up as a result of the war, or in spite of it. These are difficult days for mission endeavor, but God will overrule. I still believe the world is to be evangelized in this generation.

Cam had reason for his optimism. He was greatly encouraged by the way God had brought SIL from two students in 1934 studying in an abandoned farm house to a State University with more than a hundred students. In the meantime, there were many practical considerations to be taken care of in 1942. Throughout the spring of that year, Cam and Elvira spent time going back and forth to Ensenada where Cárdenas had given Cam free rein to speak if he wished and to distribute Scriptures among the Mexican soldiers. In April, Cam spoke at several missionary rallies in Los Angeles. Prior to his May 9 meeting with the PMA, Cam was invited to take part in a large missionary rally on May 5 at Moody Church in Chicago. On May 10, a day after his meeting with the PMA, Cam wrote his friend William Nyman in Glendale, California:

> The Lord blessed wonderfully in our meeting yesterday. The PMA council consented to help us until we can consummate our organization. But they did so with an urgent request that we do so with all

speed possible inasmuch as they are swamped with work. In fact, they cannot take on any more SIL workers. We therefore must make other provisions to care for our new workers.

Cam then made a request that ranked in importance with asking L.L. Legters to help him when he said:

> Bill, we have been offered a fully-equipped office in Chicago, but we don't feel God leading us to go there. What would your advice be? If we could secure a competent office secretary and locate in Southern California, could you give your time in sufficient quantity to be the Home Secretary of the organization? Could you with your present state of health [Mr. Nyman had a serious heart condition and was forced into early retirement from his Chicago lumber business] take on this responsibility of organizing the office, the deputation work, etc.? If possible, the office should be functioning by July 1.
>
> It looks as though we will have between seventy-five and a hundred students at Camp and it seems quite certain that we will have our fifty students for Mexico. I'm speaking now from actual figures and not as before from faith alone. Isn't our God wonderful? What a marvelous Saviour and Leader we have! How did He ever give us the faith to ask for fifty workers in November? After Pearl Harbor it wouldn't have been so hard, but He put the burden and faith in our hearts before. Praise His name! He'll see the whole project through.

On May 12, 1942, William G. Nyman, a man with serious heart problems, ordered by his doctor to resign from at least a half dozen boards of Christian organizations, answered Cam's letter:

> Your letter of the 10th calls for praise. I am glad everything is progressing smoothly in Philadelphia. To separate from the Pioneer Mission Agency is no easy matter. Now to answer your questions.
>
> First, last and always I am prayerfully anxious that the *Bible Translation Movement* continue its God-given task of giving the Bible to every person in his own language. To this end I am willing and ready to do all I can to further this enterprise until the job is done. If you and your associates are agreed that a council should

organize here in Los Angeles and desire that I should serve as a member of this council, I shall be glad to do so.

Cam was desirous of making Mr. Nyman a member of the board and also of becoming the first Secretary-Treasurer. In a tourist court in Norman, Oklahoma on June 14, 1942, five men full of faith met to draft two documents for the incorporation of SIL and WBT. The Articles of Incorporation for The Summer Institute of Linguistics were filed two months later in the office of the County Clerk of Los Angeles, California, on August 12, 1942. WBT was incorporated a day later on August 13.

On September 15, 1942, the first meeting of the board of directors met in Mexico City's popular Shirley Courts, room 59, to elect the officers of the corporation. They were, William Cameron Townsend, General Director, Dr. Kenneth L. Pike, President, Mr. Gene Nida, Vice President and William G. Nyman, Secretary-Treasurer.

When Mr. Nyman met with Cameron Townsend, Ken Pike and Eugene Nida at the historic organizational June 14 meeting in Norman, Mr. Nyman, drawing on his wide experience from other mission boards he had served on, gave the first of his wise administrative and financial counsel that was to guide the group for the next eighteen years. Knowing Nida and Pike were strong independent thinkers with their own ideas that were at times at variance with Townsend's, and knowing further the fragile nature of any beginning organization, Nyman asked all three men to bow in prayer with him and covenant before God to remain together for the next five years, no matter what.

In a letter to the Pioneer Mission Agency, Cam spelled out Wycliffe's vision statement:

> The purpose of Wycliffe Bible Translators will be to forward in every way possible the project of putting the Word of God into all tribal tongues of earth in which it does not yet exist. Wycliffe will seek to assist all pioneer evangelical missionaries to receive specialized linguistic training, written helps and expert counsel for their task of reducing languages to writing, translating the Scriptures into them and teaching people to read the Word when it has been made available.

On September 1, Cam gave PMA a further progress report:

In consultation with interested friends, we have asked Mr. William G. Nyman to become secretary-treasurer of the new organization which will have its headquarters in California. Mr. and Mrs. Nyman came to Norman, Oklahoma to discuss the matter with the executive committee of the Mexico group and other workers. After much discussion, it was decided to call the new organization WYCLIFFE BIBLE TRANSLATORS, INC. The incorporation papers, both for this organization and the SUMMER INSTITUTE OF LINGUISTICS, have been duly authorized by the State of California. Mr. Nyman is coming to Mexico (this week) to meet with us and to draw up the bylaws. Under Mr. Nyman's direction, the new office at 1305 N. Louise St., Glendale, California,[1] is already functioning beautifully. This is due in part to Mr. Nyman's long experience in business and missionary affairs. There is also a full-time office secretary in the person of Mrs. Ethel Lambotte.

Cam was more than pleased with the smooth transition of the two organizations into legal entities with a functioning Board of Directors. Cam had seen to it that the four men (Pike, Nida, Nyman and himself) who had done the incorporating were on the board. With them were three others from the constituency: Mr. E.S. Goodner, Dawson Trotman (head of Navigators) and Dr. John A. Hubbard. Cam also installed a policy he had long championed, namely, that SIL personnel actually working in Mexico would be the ones to elect the Board of Directors for the homeland. And then in October, Cam gave a fuller report to the PMA and his prayer partners:

As you know, Camp Wycliffe was held this year at the University of Oklahoma at Norman. There were one hundred and thirty people from thirty-two states and twelve foreign countries. We could not have accommodated so many at Siloam Springs. As you also

---

1 This first home office for WBT was a three-room converted apartment over the Nymans' garage where Cam and Elvira had lived during a visit to California in 1933. In 1949 this office moved to a store front building in downtown Glendale. This office functioned with a limited staff until 1960 when it was moved to a converted church building on Broadway and Walnut Streets in Santa Ana, California. In March, 1974, the very much overcrowded Santa Ana office moved to new facilities in Huntington Beach, California. In July, 1999, the headquarters moved again to Orlando, Florida.

know, we have been praying for fifty new workers for Mexico. Forty-two of the fifty have materialized! We are still praying for the remaining eight.

One of the people who wrote several letters of inquiry about joining SIL that summer was a highly competent educator named Elaine Mielke. For some time, Cam had been concerned about the educational needs of the growing number of translators' children. He wanted someone to assume this responsibility:

> Mrs. Townsend and I were delighted to receive your good letter of October 23 and to know that Mexico is on your heart. Yes, we are still anxious to provide schooling for the children of our translators. We could also use you most advantageously when you were not working directly with the children. We are planning to give more attention to reading campaigns among the Indian groups. Let us know when we can look for you in Mexico.
>
> P.S. Word has just come that the United States government has requested us to give our linguistic course to one hundred officers of the Army and Navy beginning May 1, 1943, at Norman. Please pray for preparations for this important step.

Chapter Thirteen

If God Is For Us, Who Can Be Against Us?

In 1942 and 43, most Americans and Canadians, in one way or another, were involved in the war effort. Hollywood personalities entertained the troops and sold war bonds. Children of all ages gathered string and tin foil, rolled them into balls, and deposited these, along with empty toothpaste tubes, at their schools or local receiving stations.

While Cameron Townsend wasn't collecting critical metals for the war effort, he was aware that he would like to contribute something worthwhile and voiced that concern in a letter to Ken Pike and Gene Nida. Specifically he said, "If the war continues, I feel we as a group will need to take a more active part somehow in Mexico's contribution to the war effort." The answer came sooner than he expected.

On November 17, 1942, Eugene Nida wrote Cam to tell him that he had been asked by the University of Oklahoma if SIL would give its intensive courses in linguistics and language learning to approximately one hundred Army and Navy officers. For the services of a staff of six, the government would pay one thousand dollars per month. The courses would be scheduled to begin May 1, 1943. Nida, who took Cam at his word, wrote:

> It has always been our policy to cooperate and help wherever we can. I believe we can do a signal service and at the same time advance the cause of missions throughout the world through appropriate contacts and development of our techniques.

Cam could not have agreed more with Nida's decision to offer SIL's expertise to the government's war effort. On November 27, 1942, he officially announced this decision to the group and then said:

> If you are called upon by the authorities [Mexican or American] to cooperate with them somehow in the war effort, please remember Titus 3:1: "Put them in mind to be subject to principalities and powers, to obey magistrates, to be ready to do every good work, to speak evil of no man, to be no brawlers, but gentle, showing all *meekness* unto all men." Our master was "meek and lowly" and when he was reviled, reviled not again. It is in becoming servants we are like our Lord.

At the end of that November letter, it is unclear whether he is asking a question of himself or others in leadership:

> We still lack workers for five or six tribes that should be reached this year. I sometimes wonder if a mistake hasn't been made by those of us you have placed in positions of leadership. If we did err, and for that reason the fifty workers we needed haven't materialized, do pray, please, that God will overrule our error even yet. To delay the evangelization of six tribes another year would be a terrible thing. Several would-be translators are writing about coming next fall and two others hope to arrive early next year. But we asked for fifty this year and had expected more than we asked for (Ephesians 3:20).

Cam's original prayer was for God to double the membership, which would have been forty-four people. He then decided to ask God for an extra portion and prayed for fifty. In his official report to the group in 1943, Cam wrote:

> Truly it is a miracle of God that we now have forty-seven new work-
> ers and two sponsored workers [non-SIL members but supported
> by a church]. All this happened in a *brief nine months.*"

As grateful to God as he was for these forty-seven new workers, Cam
could not forget that he had asked God for fifty. But then in a letter to
Mr. Nyman dated Summer 1943, Cam said he now realized that God
had given him fifty-one new workers, one more person than he had
asked for:

> Do you realize that when we count in you folks there in the [home]
> office, we now have fifty-one new workers to add to our forces in
> one year, and we asked God for fifty? Our hearts rejoice over the
> wonderful way the Lord has taken care of our group during this past
> year.

In 1943, the war took a decisive turn for the Allies with the capture of
Tunis in North Africa and the invasion of Sicily and what General Ei-
senhower called "the first stage of the liberation of the European continent." The Allies were on the offensive. They had come of age. So too,
were SIL and WBT coming of age in 1943. With a total membership of
almost a hundred workers in thirty-six different languages, people from
other organizations were beginning to take notice of this new unusual
group of people.

Dr. Eric North of the American Bible Society wrote to tell Cam that the
Society would like to offer financial assistance in the amount of five hundred dollars to those translators who were doing "good work" but might
be hampered in their work because they lacked financial support.

Dr. Frank Laubach, the renowned literacy expert, came calling. He was
particularly interested in the way Cam and others had prepared their literacy reading materials. Said Cam:

> Dr. Laubach's visit stirred up considerable interest among educa-
> tors in Mexico City. He also visited two areas where we have work-
> ers. One team is teaching reading using his method. Others of our
> group are preparing materials according to our own psy-
> cho-phonetic system which is quite different from Dr. Laubach's

method since our method is based on the phonemic structure of the languages involved.

Ken Pike's scholarship was also beginning to come of age with the publication of his books and monographs. In 1942, he published a preliminary work, *Pronunciation: An Intensive Course in English for Latin American Students*, Vol.1. This was replaced in 1943 with his book *Phonetics and Phonemics: A Critical Analysis of Phonetic Theory and a Technique for the Practical Description of Sounds*. Pike wrote this for Dr. Fries' English Language Institute. While Cam was pleased with Ken's technical publications, he also knew that most Wycliffe constituents needed a non-technical popular publication that would give them firsthand accounts of God becoming known through the academic and practical work of SIL translators. Thus, with the design and printing done by Max Lathrop and editing done by Marianna Slocum and Ethel Wallis[1] and partially financed by Marianna, the first issue of *Translation* magazine[2] was sent out to thirty-six hundred people. From that small beginning, *Translation's* constituency has grown to over two hundred thousand in the 1990s.

The woman who has been called the "Mother of the American Sunday School Movement," Henrietta Mears, also came to pay Cam a visit in 1943. At one point Cam thought he might ask her permission to use the fine retreat facilities she had begun at Forest Home, California for a second SIL school on the West Coast The tenth SIL session was very much on Cam's mind in 1943. The University of Oklahoma was willing for SIL to return, but this was wartime, and the U.S. Navy occupied most of the University's facilities. The in-house *Wycliffe Chronicle* said:

> Due to the training of so many armed forces personnel at the University of Oklahoma, it was impossible to hold Camp Wycliffe at Norman as planned. But it would be difficult to find a truer atmosphere for Camp Wycliffe's tenth session than Bacone College

1 Besides working on the Mezquital Otomi and the Cercasian New Testaments, Ethel Wallis became one of Wycliffe's first popular writers with such significant books as *Two Thousand Tongues to Go* and *The Dayuma Story*. Ethel was also a great encourager and mentor for many beginning writers in Wycliffe, including this writer.

2 *Translation* retained this name until January, 1975, when its name was changed to *In Other Words*.

(near Muskogee, Oklahoma). On this campus we found Choctaws, Cherokees, Creeks and other Native American Indian groups.

As early as the end of January, 1943, the SIL staff had received fifty applications for the 1943 summer session. Amazingly, twenty-one of the applicants were from Canada. One reason for this early registration and high interest from Canada was Oswald J. Smith, the energetic pastor of The People's Church in Toronto. Smith's interest in world mission was legendary. George Cowan, who was to become the President of Wycliffe Bible Translators and who was partially supported by People's Church, said, "Smith's energies were directed at getting as many Canadian young people to the mission field as possible. His philosophy was to partially support a large number of people rather than a few who were fully supported."

With the coming of age of WBT and SIL and their growing membership came larger and more complex problems that fell primarily on Cam's shoulders. There were new concerns over linking single women with the right partner. While this was a Christian organization with high Christian values, there were still problems with compatibility. Occasionally there were difficulties between married couples. One couple in particular occupied a substantial amount of Cam's emotional energy. Cam, too, was always concerned about the physical safety of single women who worked in isolated areas.

On one occasion, Marianna and her companion, Martha Moennich, who was asked by Cam to write a book on SIL and Mexico's ethnic groups, were suddenly ambushed by a group of drunken road workers on the outskirts of Las Casas, Chiapas, in southern Mexico. One of the men grabbed the reins of the mule Marianna was riding and tried to pull her from the saddle, but Marianna held tight to the saddle horn. In the middle of this skirmish, the foreman of the work crew happened along and ordered the men to leave the women alone. Later Martha Moennich said: "We fought for our freedom and got it. This, we realize, was by God's grace."

Then there was the frequent problem of ill health among the workers. Malaria for people working in the low, hot tropical areas of Mexico was of major concern, as was tuberculosis. Another concerned a translator who had broken his leg and had to be sent back to the States because it had been set incorrectly and wasn't healing.

And then there was the problem with some who were unhappy with the principles of operation that had been voted on and set in place by the members of the Mexico branch in September 1942. Mr. Nyman, who had seen the difficulty of the "pool" system of missionary support, enthusiastically approved of the plan of the Mexico group to assess themselves ten percent of all monies they received to be used for overhead and office expenses. Five percent would support the field office and five percent would be used to run the home office. This meant that each worker would receive ninety percent of all money designated for him or her. No one, not Mr. Townsend or anyone in the directorate, would receive a salary. WBT and SIL was then, and is today, totally dependent upon God and the free-will gifts from friends and churches who are in partnership with each individual.

However, a few early members tried to avoid the ten percent assessment by having their gifts sent directly to them, thus bypassing the home office. (This sometimes occurs today, but members are on their honor to report such gifts in order that they can be ten-percented.) When Cam learned from Mr. Nyman that one member had become angry when confronted by her indiscretion, he jettisoned his indirect method of making his wishes known and said "If this is the case, she should be asked to leave the group at once." In his letter to her, Cam was firm but more conciliatory:

> It shocked me to learn that you sent letters to your supporters requesting them not to send funds through the Glendale office. This grieves me as it does Mr. Nyman who gives so generously of his time and money for the advancement of the work. Of course, you may not have stopped to consider how much service the group gives just in bookkeeping and the running of errands, and also in obtaining immigration permits and other government documents. Would you like us to stop handling your government papers now that you refuse to support the office?
>
> Further, don't you appreciate the financial help we have been able to send your partner just because the group as a whole is willing to spend ten percent on general expenses? Don't you want to have a part in keeping Camp Wycliffe operating and the extension of our work to other unreached areas of the world? In other words, would you like the Glendale office to close down and all our litera-

ture stopped? If not, and of course you don't, please send in at once a report on how much you have received that is assessable, with joyous instructions for us to take the ten percent of your share for the entire cause. Also please write your friends explaining that you hadn't thought the matter through and to send your funds through the regular channels to the Glendale office.

Of course, if you have been suffering want, all unknown to us, you are exonerated, and we would like to help you until such time as the Lord supplies your needs adequately. The last request, however, is absolutely essential, and I shall appreciate having a copy of the paragraph you write your friends on the subject. We are with you in the task and want you to be reassured as to your standing with us and the group.

But by far the most difficult, and in some way the most troublesome problem Cam had to deal with in 1943, came to be known as the "Pentecostal Matter." At issue was Cam's strong personal stance of being nonsectarian which was at variance with some members of the board. In fact so conservative were some of the board members that they voiced their opposition to WBT, SIL and Cam himself to fellowship with Pentecostals or anyone from the Presbyterian Board (U.S.A). In a letter to Mr. Nyman dated February 23, 1943, Cam gave this response:

I refer to the matter of our relationships with people of Pentecostal leanings, beliefs or connections. It seems to me that I am out of harmony with the other members of the board on this question. It is not an attitude I can easily brush aside or leave in the background while the rest of you follow the wishes of the majority.

If our organization were dedicated to the propagation of some special system of theology, practice or discipline as are the denominational missions (and to a certain extent most faith missions), my attitude would be quite unreasonable. But we are not like other [mission] organizations. God brought us into being to give the Bible to people who have never before had it in their language. Our task is not to extend existing denominations or to found new ones, as faith missions do on most fields.

To accomplish our task, we need to harness the consecration and energies of all who genuinely love the Lord and are vitally concerned about fulfilling the Great Commission. If someone wants to help us who is affiliated with what you and I consider to be people who hold doctrines different from our own, whether of the nature of those held by John Wesley, A.B. Simpson, or any other saint of God, that should not be given too much consideration. Particularly is this true if we are to build an organization like the American Bible Society, and to give the Word to all the tribes of earth.

The main argument that has been presented to me is that the doctrinal sector to which almost all of us belong will not support us if we are as broad in our fellowship as I desire. The Secretary of the Independent Board of Foreign Missions told me they would probably not be represented on our Advisory Council if we invite anyone from the Presbyterian Board (U.S.A). And now you tell me that the Church of the Open Door [Cam's home and main supporting church] would not have a certain one of our missionaries on its Rally program. I have an answer and also a partial preventive to this danger. The answer is this: *"If God be for us, who can be against us?"*

Usually Cameron Townsend's personal correspondence can be characterized as warm, instructive, well thought out, often hard edged and free of abstract generalities. While his personal convictions show through, what is often absent are his own emotional feelings about the way things are. The one exception to this is his correspondence with Mr. Nyman. Both Cam and Elvira seemed to feel at ease in using the Nymans as a sounding board for their ideas and in giving vent to their feelings. With Etta Nyman, Elvira was not above indulging in a bit of "back fence" chatter over the way certain people conducted their personal lives, or her feelings that a certain person was not working as hard as she thought they should. As Cam's February letter on the "Pentecostal Matter" to Mr. Nyman continued, it is notable for its autobiographical peek into his heart, emotional feelings, and indeed into his soul:

Last summer I was made most unhappy by the attitude of my colleagues toward my spiritual leadership of the Camp, and my desire to be tolerant toward "pentecostalists" of good testimony. I felt bad about it, not only because my convictions in the matter are so deep seated, but also because I could see I was making others unhappy. And the last thing I want to do or be is in a place where I make others unhappy, especially my beloved and overworked colleagues.

If we are going to be so careful about nonbasic doctrines as the basis of fellowship, should we not be just as careful concerning matters of purity, love, mercy and humble service? I know things about the various organizations that want to exclude these people that sorely grieve our blessed Lord.

There are things in the Wycliffe family, wonderful as it is, that should humble us all. We need constant warming spiritually and our national believers need it as well. We can't take ourselves as standards, nor the organizations from which we come. Let us stick to the Bible as our gauge—no broader and no narrower—as exclusive but with a love that is as inclusive. *What we know, or think we know, about the Book and the way we live it should not be the mold we pass on to the world. Rather it should be the Book itself.*

This is my attitude, but in practice, I'm more careful than that sounds. I dislike Pentecostalism just as I detest formalism, ritualism and professionalism. While I was in charge at Camp, I always endeavored to hold both extremes in check. I did not want other folks praying out loud while I was praying, any more than I wanted the pipe organ to be playing while I was speaking or praying. The "Pentecostals" who have been at Camp, whether as students or speakers, have been perfectly proper. No one did anything that might have bothered or upset the rest of the group. Personally I am more afraid of the Camp becoming too formal in its worship than of leaning in the other direction.

Under God we are building something new. And there are many points where we have found it necessary to diverge from the old methods. We are building a worldwide organization dedicated to the task of translating the Scriptures into all languages in this generation. Within fifteen years we will have a thousand members in all parts of the unevangelized world. We will be serving evangelical missionary organizations with all kinds of doctrinal peculiarities. The more we can serve them, the more accurate and efficient their work will be. Let's not limit our sphere of service by officially condemning their pet theories. If our spirit of tolerance should in time prove to be

a handicap rather than a help, we can take action based upon experience, but let's not make a change yet.

To further make his point that he was nonsectarian, and that the WBT
and SIL membership and member constituency should understand the
ideals (as Cam had formulated them) of nonsectarianism, Cam wrote
the following policy statement:

> To both our denominational and nondenominational friends who
> feel inclined to criticize us because we place our emphasis on the
> Book rather than on their various interpretations of it, we give this
> word of explanation.
>
> We do not represent any of the established ecclesiastical organi-
> zations, nor are we endeavoring to build up one of our own. A rep-
> resentative of the great National University of Mexico, in a public
> address, described our attitude as follows: "These young people
> have brought a message that is far above Catholicism and far
> above Protestantism. It is the gospel of love and service."
>
> We strive to serve and we put to the front what we believe to be
> the most basic and important service we can render. It is not unilat-
> eral: it is universal. It is to give the Book that is universal in its ap-
> peal and power to all peoples who have not yet received it in their
> own language.
>
> We invite *all* who love it and have experienced its transforming
> power to link hands with us in the task of giving it, in this genera-
> tion, to the thousands of people groups who have been denied it.
> Invariably and irresistibly, the Bible will bear fruit though sometimes
> that fruit may fall into baskets not of our own weaving.

It was important for Cam personally to formulate his views, but not everyone in the group fully understood or agreed with Cam's policy. Mr.
Nyman was somewhat puzzled and asked Cam to withdraw it from being published in *Translation* magazine until the whole group had an opportunity to discuss it. Ken Pike and Gene Nida also questioned Cam
more fully on what he meant. While Cam knew perfectly well what he
meant, others did not, and the interpretation of Cam's policy would be
debated and argued for many years. In the seventies, it would rise again

to become a major discussion on the floor of SIL's International Conference.

In the meantime, Cam had other concerns. One of these was writing letters of explanation to draft boards for some of the men to receive their 4-D deferment. In most cases, this was routine. There was, however, a problem with some men being denied passports. While he had no empirical proof other than the nongranting of these passports, Cam believed there was a calculated pressure on the State Department by Rome to somehow block evangelical gospel workers from entering Mexico. Acting on this belief, Cam wrote a long two-page letter to Franklin D. Roosevelt. The letter is more of a manifesto than a personal letter. In it, Cam asks the president, on behalf of the principles of tolerance and love and in the defense of common democratic principles, that he act upon his Good Neighbor policy and overrule any government policy that might in any way hinder SIL people from receiving their passports and being allowed to leave the country.

There is nothing in the archives to indicate that President Roosevelt answered Cam's letter. But Ambrose (Amby) McMahon, for whom Cam wrote, did eventually get his passport and permission to leave the country, as did others that followed.

One of the other curious wartime anomalies the SIL group had to contend with was the problem of transporting linguistic language data, plus other notes and documents, including cameras and film across the U.S. border. Since the U.S. customs officers could not read the strange looking language data, it was considered suspect. The customs officers had to assume it might be some kind of encrypted code destined for enemy intelligence. It was widely believed that there were active German spies operating in the mountains of Mexico who were sending counter intelligence out of the country. One customs office confiscated a translator's personal Bible because he thought the red underlining of certain verses might constitute a secret message. On another occasion, U.S. customs officials routinely detained manuscripts of books of the Mázatec New Testament that were being sent out of Mexico to be published by the American Bible Society.

By May of 1943, it had become clear to Cameron Townsend that the demands of the group had grown far beyond his physical capabilities. No longer could he handle all the intricate administrative details demanded by a hundred energetic independent thinkers. It also became clear that he had to fine tune and bring into focus WBT's and SIL's purpose. In a letter to Mr. Nyman dated May 13, 1943, Cam spelled out for the first time Wycliffe's Five Basic Working Policies. Cam also admitted that the demands on his time exceeded his energy level. In order to more fully share the weight of responsibilities, he suggested (since this was war time) that Mr. Nyman, Gene Nida and Ken Pike become like generals in an army. In his May 13 letter, he explained how this would work.

Chapter Fourteen

What Are We?

Cameron Townsend began his May 13, 1943 letter to Mr. Nyman
with "Dear Will:" Mr. Nyman was usually addressed as Will before he
became part of WBT, but most now addressed him as "Bill." Curiously,
Cam never once addressed L.L. Legters as "Len," or" Leonard." It was
always "Mr. Legters." Clearly, in William G. Nyman Cam had a true
soul mate, one who understood and supported him in his vision, even
when he occasionally failed or stumbled:

> It was my intention to have a decent report ready for the last board
> meeting, but the best I could do was to send eleven pages of dic-
> tated material that didn't arrive in time for the meeting. I must con-
> fess my energy level hasn't been equal to do the absolutely
> essential tasks, like reading and correcting the eleven pages of ma-
> terial.
>
> With the rapid growth of the work, I feel there needs to be a
> greater distribution of responsibility. It is important to understand
> there are certain basic principles about our work, many of them
> unique, that we should not depart from except with the consent of
> the organization. But within those guidelines, I would like to see dif-
> ferent ones of us have almost full responsibility. You, for instance,

should have complete charge of business matters, Nida for public relations in the States as it relates to schools and boards, and Pike as it relates to our scientific connections. I will continue to assume responsibility for the field advancement of our work. We each can be like generals in our particular field, the board like Congress and the workers and translators on the field to have voting power that gives them ultimate control.

The board, too, should eventually distribute its responsibility. The China Inland Mission, for example, couldn't be responsible for four-teen hundred missionaries if it had only one board. You men on the board will have your hands more than full with five hundred workers before many years. You will need sub-councils in different parts of the country composed of men whose hearts God has already touched to the point where they have already rolled up their sleeves and gone to work for us. When God Himself has chosen the men, we can trust them with jobs. We don't need to be afraid of their lack of reputation or even that they aren't accepted in the inner circle of certain doctrinal groups.

In Mexico we have seen God work through the most unlikely of men. Never try to cramp the Lord by setting up our judgment against His. God has raised up men like Clarence Erickson in Chi-cago and Oswald Smith in Canada to help us. If I had been the one to choose, I would have picked Louis Talbot and Harry Ironside, men whom I have known for years and whose interest we have all worked for, but while they are interested, I see little evidence of it compared with the burden God has put on the hearts of the other two men. Let's not be afraid of the men God sends us. Let me now give you some of the distinctive points about our organization:

1. We specialize on giving the Scriptures to tribal peoples now without them.

2. We pioneer, going preferably to closed fields.

3. We cooperate with missions, governments, scientific organiza-tions and philanthropic organizations. Always cooperate and serve, never compete.

4. We follow the linguistic approach.

5. We dare to follow even when God leads in strange paths. We lean not to our own understanding. We follow and trust, counting Him faithful who promised.

6. We are not sectarian or ecclesiastical, not even dogmatic. We give people the Word of God, but don't try to force them into any type of denominational or non-denominational mold.

7. We look to God to raise up the men [and women] and the financial means to do our work. We also look to God to open doors of opportunity. We do not look to the reputation or wealth of men to open doors, but God alone. We do, however, try to be strictly scientific both in linguistics, methods, and attitudes. I feel we should use all the aids science gives us as the occasion arises, including radio, airplanes, etc. when going to jungle tribes.

8. We expect to finish in this generation.

These eight basic policies were later refined to what has become known as the Five Basic Policies that reflect Wycliffe and SIL's basic mandate for ministry:

1. SIL must constantly pioneer.

2. SIL must consistently follow the linguistic approach. We seek to be scientific in our linguistic work and participate in scientific gatherings and contribute to scientific publications.

4. We *serve* everybody we can possibly serve, and let them serve us, and we serve them in *love*. We *cooperate*, not compete. We give the government in the countries where we work credit for the work we do, and in all of this we find that we silence our opposition.

5. We must take God at HIS word. He told us to evangelize the world, to go to every creature. He says to GO, and that all power is given to Him. So we go and rely on His inexhaustible power to take us through the stone walls. Go nowhere God doesn't lead you; go anywhere He does.

Implicit in Cam's five basic principles is the essence of the two great commandments of Scripture, "Love God... and your neighbor as yourself... on those two commandments hang all the law and the Prophets."[1]

---

1   Matthew 22:37,39.

Also implicit is the reality that these principles came from the very essence of Cam's being and in a significant way defined him as a person. They were Cam's gift to the group and the wider mission community, a gift he expected each one in leadership and each member to apply to his or her own life and ministry.

Sometimes in the midst of his writings, his heavy administrative load, caring for Elvira and renovating his house in Tetelcingo (he built an extra room to house their mimeograph machine), Cam would lay down his tools and take a day off to do personal witnessing. At the end of June, 1943, Cam and another friend took a day trip to a nearby large town and made what Cam said were "some contacts for the Lord." At the end of the day Cam noted in his diary: "How I wish there was more time, and I had more energy for this type of work."

One area where Cam was expending considerable energy in 1943 was in trying to educate the SIL staff and others about the unique roles and distinction between SIL and WBT. He had just published the eight principles that in the minds of most SIL staffers could apply to both organizations. However, Gene Nida and Marianna Slocum, who was the editor and writer for the *Wycliffe Chronicle*, suggested that since the *Chronicle* was published only in the summer and dealt with news and happenings relating to SIL's summer session at Camp Wycliffe, the name should be changed to become an organ of the Summer Institute of Linguistics.

By return mail on July 14, Cam addressed his letter to Gene and members of the staff in an effort to try to untangle the confusion that evidently existed in their minds between SIL and WBT:

> I understand you want to change the name of the *Chronicle* and make it an organ of SIL. SIL is a scientific organization, therefore how can it logically be the main sponsor of the *Chronicle*? It seems to me that Wycliffe Bible Translators should sponsor it. I object to the change at this time. As long as they are together and Wycliffe Bible Translators sends workers to pioneer fields such as Mexico, it is only natural that poorly informed people could confuse our ministry of linguistic training with that of actual Bible translation.

To help the public more clearly understand the nature and purpose of SIL and WBT, Cam wrote a three-page position paper from his village home in Tetelcingo, under the heading, *Wycliffe Bible Translators, What are we?*:

> No one refers to the American Bible Society as a mission. The organization, Wycliffe Bible Translators, Inc., is not a mission either. Just as the American Bible Society does not build ecclesiastical organizations on the field but turns over the fruits of its labors to mission boards and national churches that are willing and competent to take care for the ongoing growth and development of a people, so too do we render scientific and spiritual service and then move on to fields where our services are needed.
>
> Our doctrinal statement is the same as that of the China Inland Mission [later called Overseas Missionary Fellowship] and is broad enough to facilitate our cooperation with all evangelical missions. What are we? We are a fellowship of scientific pioneers who are determined to see the Great Commission carried out and are willing to leave lesser details to ecclesiastical organizations. We are two organizations with a single vision. Or we can say we are one organization with three aspects: (1) the academic courses each summer, (2) The scientific linguistic research in many lands, and (3) the giving of the Word of God wherever we go. In a word, we are *Wycliffe Bible Translators* at the service of all.

In his list of Wycliffe's five basic working policies, Cam listed pioneering as the number one priority. At first, most of the SIL and WBT members thought this meant pioneering into so-called third world countries in out-of-the-way jungle areas. And indeed, for the first several decades, that was true of the organizations. But when Cam called the membership to pioneer, he included much more than simply living in a primitive jungle area learning to speak an unwritten language. Cam, and others like Ken Pike, Dick Pittman and Gene Nida, were themselves on the cutting edge of linguistic theory. In order for Cam's prediction that SIL would one day make the "scientific linguistic community sit up and take notice," SIL members would have to publish their data. In a special memo to the membership in which he advocated the motto "Prepare to Publish," Dick Pittman wrote:

> When I say we need to "prepare to publish," I am not thinking primarily of our Scripture publications, but rather our scientific publications. If our work isn't good enough to be published in a scientific magazine, perhaps we should ask ourselves whether it is fit to be published as a Bible translation. I don't think it is too high a standard to set to say that each of us, by the time we finish and publish our New Testaments, should have in hand and in good shape the makings of a creditable, if not exhaustive, grammar, dictionary, and books of texts and primers.

From his own experience with the translation of the Cakchiquel New Testament in Guatemala, Cam knew that most translators move some distance into their translation project before the enormous complexity and size of the task they have assumed strikes them. He agreed with Dick, but did not want the translators to flounder and collapse under the complex implications of their task. Therefore, in July 1943, Cam sent out a letter asking that all translators come together at a special conference site for what was in reality SIL's first translation workshop:[1]

> I am asking all our people to come out of their locations and meet the last week of August through September. Bible translation must be done with the greatest accuracy possible. We have among us some outstanding linguistic talent and we want all of you to benefit from the help these experts can give you.
>
> We will also have a time of spiritual refreshment and an opportunity to meet the board and discuss about how to go about reaching the "closed fields."

While most of the new SIL workers were just settling into their work in Mexico, Cam was looking ahead to the end of the war when governments would relax their restrictions and access to new fields would be

---

1 Today there is in place a series of regular translation, linguistic and literacy workshops where beginning translators can talk over their problems and receive expert help and guidance. However, it wasn't until the early sixties, under the leadership of Dr. Benjamin Elson, then director of the Mexico Branch, that a coordinated system of checking and consultant help was in place. The board appointed John Beekman to become SIL's first international translation coordinator. For further information, see Hugh Steven, *The Man with the Noisy Heart, The John Beekman Story* (Chicago: Moody Press, 1979).

easier. With Ken Pike and Dick Pittman, Cam was making plans for an "initial expedition of twenty-five workers to begin work in South America." In September of 1943, Ken Pike, at the request of the American Bible Society who paid for his flight and gave him a stipend of three hundred dollars, made a four-month trip to Peru, Bolivia, and Ecuador.

In addition to his long-range planning to send workers to South America, Cam wanted to open up at least two more SIL schools in the U.S and one in Canada. In 1942, five Canadian students were accepted to attend SIL but were denied exit passports. Of the twenty-one Canadian students who had applied to attend the 1943 summer session of SIL, only ten were given permission by Canada to leave the country.

Given Oswald Smith's energetic interest in Wycliffe and the difficulty with crossing borders during wartime, Cam thought it critical to start a linguistic school in Canada. One person most interested in beginning that school was Sinclair Whittaker, President of Briercrest Bible Institute, Briercrest, Saskatchewan. He wrote Cam and offered the use of the school facilities at a reduced rate if SIL Canada would come to Briercrest. However, to open another school in Canada would require a director plus a competent staff of teachers. Cam said he would present the matter to the board of directors.

There was also among the young SIL membership several people who were fine platform speakers. One of these was George Cowan. George, a Canadian from Manitoba, had worked with Cloyd Stewart among the Amuzgo people and, like others, including Cloyd, had become engaged to be married. When Cam learned that George and Florrie Hansen had announced their engagement in August and were planning to be married at the Church of the Open Door in Los Angeles in November, Cam's public relations antenna shot up. He suggested to George that their wedding would provide a wonderful opportunity to present the work of Wycliffe.

In those days, the Church of the Open Door drew hundreds of people from all over Southern California to their Sunday afternoon rally, including many servicemen and women. People would come for the afternoon rally and then stay on for the evening service. With a captive wedding audience of several hundred people, Cam felt it would be wasting a grand opportunity not to present a missionary challenge.

For all his sensitivity and concern for people, Cam sometimes displayed certain blind spots. If there was an opportunity to be with a government official and the business at hand took him past a scheduled dinner hour with a member, Cam deferred to the government official. The "work" always came first. In what seems almost to be an insensitivity for the solemnity of George and Florrie's wedding, Cam wrote the following to Mr. Nyman on October 19:

> Florence Hansen seems to be in accord with the idea of having the wedding serve as a means of rallying friends of Wycliffe Bible Translators. [Actually, Florrie had wanted a quiet, unobtrusive wedding.] When I see her, I'll ask her again. I think that George will be willing to bring a missionary message at the start of the afternoon session. George is a good speaker. I would then suggest that Miss Henrietta Mears, Dawson Trotman and you follow with a brief message. George could then leave the platform as soon as he finished speaking and dress for the wedding while you all were speaking. The wedding could come at the close of the meeting.
>
> With announcements going out to all the Wycliffe mailing list coupled with announcements over the air by Mr. Talbot and First Mate Bob, we should have a big attendance and arouse a lot of interest. Folks at home aren't used to taking advantage of weddings for the glory of the Lord. But why not? We find many wonderful opportunities on the field for this. American weddings are generally very selfish affairs, the ones I have seen. They say this is not the case among the Mennonites.

Six days later Cam wrote Mr. Nyman, in response to the criticism for overzealousness and commercialization of George and Florrie's wedding:

> A few people seemed to have gotten the impression that we are planning to commercialize the wedding. George spoke to me about it, and while I didn't get a chance to speak to Florence as I should have, my impression is that they are perfectly willing to go ahead with the plan to use the wedding as a means of focusing the attention on the friends of Wycliffe and our program of calling young people to make a decision for mission service.
>
> George and Florrie are anxious, and rightly so, to avoid anything that savors of sensationalism or commercializing. George felt that if

an offering were not taken up at the big meeting, this problem would be taken care of. Let us ask instead of an offering that a large number of young people consecrate themselves at the meeting for pioneer service. May I suggest that the Glendale office and the office in Mexico pay for the wedding decorations.

On November 22, 1943, the day after George and Florrie's wedding, Mr. Nyman wrote Cam the following:

Everything went well at the rally yesterday afternoon. We had a fine attendance, perhaps fifteen hundred people. George spoke well. He seemed not the least nervous, though his talk preceded his wedding. Dr. Talbot supported the meeting with a few remarks.

I was very tired from the effort, but very much satisfied with the way everything went.

Cam, too, was very much satisfied with the wedding, partly because it had been an avenue to acquaint more people with Wycliffe's work, and partly because Cam now had an answer to the problem of staffing the Canadian SIL. On November 25, Cam wrote two letters, the first to Sinclair Whittaker and the other to Mr. Nyman:

The advisability of our starting a Canadian Wycliffe and providing properly trained staff and teachers for our growing institute in Oklahoma as well as Canada has caused our faith to stagger. Personally, I feel there was something providential about your call that will enable the directors of our courses to undertake this added responsibility.

You will be interested to know that simultaneously with your letter came a telegram from Dr. Pike telling us that the Minister of Education of one of the South American countries that has been closed to ordinary missionaries has extended an invitation for our organization to begin work there. *There is nothing impossible for God.*

I personally think the call of God is upon us to open a school in Canada. Please show the correspondence to George and Florrie. I believe they are the ones to direct the Canadian school at least for the first year. I believe we could give them a good staff of helpers without robbing the mother institute too much. My vote is to accept

> the invitation from Mr. Whittaker and hold our first Canadian SIL be-
> ginning mid-July 1944 at Briercrest, Saskatchewan.

On December 16, 1943, the board of directors wired Cam that they had met and were in favor of his proposal for a Canadian Wycliffe and authorized him to negotiate the details.

The telegram that told Cam that SIL had been invited to work in Peru was in itself extraordinary. But more extraordinary was the chain of events that resulted in Ken Pike securing the "formal" invitation to begin work in Peru. In every way the events were similar to Cameron Townsend's own unique chain of events that led to the open door of service in Mexico. "In both instances," said Ken Pike, "it was the hand of Jehovah Lord God Almighty, Maker of Heaven and Earth."[1]

In 1942, Ken Pike had been appointed to a half-time position as Research Associate with the English Language Institute at the University of Michigan. Ken's mentor, friend and supervisor was Professor Charles Fries. When Ken told Fries he had been invited to go to South America, Fries suggested he first stop in Ann Arbor on his way from Mexico City in order that he could give Ken certain letters of introduction. America was still deeply involved with the war in 1943 and before anyone could leave the country they needed a passport approved by the U.S. Selective Service. Some years later in 1963, Ken related the events of that trip in his own unique style of writing and speaking:

> When I got the letter from the American Bible Society asking if I
> would give them some advice on the alphabet of the Quechuas in
> Ecuador, Bolivia and Peru, I asked Uncle Cam if I should accept.
> When he learned they would pay my way and give me expense
> money, he said yes, by all means take it.
>
> This meant I had to get out of the United States, but it was diffi-
> cult to get out except in the uniform of a service man, especially
> since I was of draft age and not exempt. I was classified at the time
> a 3-A. So I wrote Fries and he told me to come and see him. When
> I did, he wrote letters of introduction to the cultural relations office in
> Ecuador, Bolivia and Peru and also to a cultural relations officer in
> Washington, D.C., to someone by the name of Thompson.

1 For fuller details of these events see, Eunice Pike, *Ken Pike, Scholar and Christian* (Dallas: Summer Institute of Linguistics, 1981).

I went to Washington to try and get a passport. They said passports for Latin America had to be okayed by cultural relations. I tried to see a man called Thompson to whom Fries had addressed my letter and who controlled all passports out of the U.S. into Latin America. Unfortunately I discovered he wouldn't be available for two days.

I felt impatient, so asked if his assistant would see me. He would. I walked in and presented my letter from Fries which said, "This is Pike. He is going to South America for the American Bible Society to work on orthographies of Quechua. He has also helped to write our textbooks on teaching English for Latin Americans. He is our preeminent specialist and he is going to give some lectures there for the University of Michigan."

"Oh, you're Pike." said the man.

"Yes," I said.

"You helped Fries write textbooks?"

"Yes."

At that moment the man swivelled around in his chair and pulled a book off the shelf behind him. It was the English Language Institute book on pronunciation. The man opened it up to the preface and found where it said that Dr. Kenneth L. Pike was responsible for the book and then closed the book and put it back on the shelf.

He looked at me and said, "Your passport has to come across my desk, and when it does, I'll okay it." Now I tell you, *this was the hand of Jehovah, Lord God Almighty, Maker of Heaven and Earth.* However, it took the FBI three weeks to give me my routine clearance.

When Ken arrived in Peru, he realized he only had forty-eight hours in Lima. Feeling alone, young, incompetent and very scared, Ken knelt by his bed, opened his New Testament to First Timothy, chapter two where it exhorts believers to pray for kings and everyone in authority. Said Ken:

The exhortation is that we might lead a godly life in all honesty and sincerity, for this is good and acceptable to God our Saviour. What I noticed for the first time was that praying for kings and those in authority was tied into the progress of the gospel around the world. [1] This was a completely new thought to me. I said, "Lord, here I am without competence in this matter. I am not a public relations man, I am a scholar, not a diplomat. God, You've put me here. Please Jehovah, Lord of Heaven and Earth, where is the God of Elijah? Slap the waters and let's see what happens." I went to the Department of Education, climbed up the big central stairs and gave my card to a secretary.

The Minister of Education invited me in and since my Spanish was lousy, we spoke in English. It was fortunate that he had studied at Columbia University. Also fortunate was the fact that he understood American scholarship and was interested in my book *Phonetics* that had just been published by the University of Michigan.

The minister asked if I would give a series of fifteen lectures in cooperation with the cultural relations [department] which had just been set up in Lima with the Department of Education. When he asked me what I was doing in Mexico, I said we were doing a threefold job of scientific work which was our professional capacity. That we tried to help people with a variety of practical community development programs including teaching indigenous people to read and write their own language. I said when we teach people to read and write this appeals only to one dimension of man's need. Our founder Cameron Townsend believes that one must deal with the spiritual as well as the physical side of man. Translating the Bible is our spiritual contribution.

The minister turned to the man next to him and said, "Well, why don't you do the same thing here? (I found out later that man represented the papal nuncio.) When the minister said that, I felt like Nehemiah and breathed a prayer to God of heaven and said, "This is what I have come for. Lord, help!" When the minister asked me why we didn't do it in his country, I said, "We haven't been asked." After he checked with the man next to him, he asked me how much it cost and how much we were paid. I said that President Cárdenas in Mexico had given our translators twelve dollars per month for several years, but mostly they gave us facilities.

---

1 First Timothy 2:1ff.

Then in typical Latin American style, the minister said, "If there is anything we can do to help you, let us know." So again I breathed a prayer to the God of heaven and earth and said, "Well, we'd like visas because sometimes your consular officers are slow to grant visas." He replied, "Come back in a day or two and we'll see what we can do."

I went back to my hotel. I just had a couple of days before I had to leave and prayed again to God, Maker of Heaven and Earth who lives, who knows us by name and acts with us as individuals. Once again I climbed up the big white central stairs all the time wondering if I would have to leave the country forever without the work done that Uncle Cam needed done, which really was God's work. As I walked along the big corridor toward the office of the Director of Education, a young man walked down the corridor toward me with a few papers in his hand and said, "Oh hello, Pike." I said "Hello." "You taught at the University of Michigan?" "Yes." He said, "Look what I've got in my hand. I just drafted the letter for you and I am taking it to the Director of Education. Come along."

So with a letter in hand inviting SIL to Peru, the young man took me into the office of the Director of Education and said to the secretary, "This is Pike. He taught at the University of Michigan." "Oh, you know Pike?" "Yes," said the young man, "and this is a letter for the Minister to sign." The secretary took the letter, trotted into the Minister's office and in a few minutes returned with the signature and handed me the letter.

I say again we need to learn to recognize the hand of Jehovah, Lord God Almighty, Maker of Heaven and Earth, whom we know by name as an individual God, and who knows us each by name as individuals.

Chapter Fifteen

The Mystery of Community

Who walks with God must take His way,
Across far distances and gray,
To goals that others do not see,
Where others do not care to be.
Who walks with God must have no fear,
When danger and defeat appear,
Nor stop when every hope seems gone,
For our God moves forever on.

Cameron Townsend sent this poem as an encouragement to the membership in his January 1944 newsletter. Eleven months later, on Christmas Eve, he would himself be called upon to face one of the biggest tests of his life and to find comfort in the truth of his own words. Meanwhile, with his customary optimism, he wrote:

> There have been important advances for our organization, marvelous answers to prayer, and in our personal lives there has been, I trust, marked progress as well. Surely each one of us loves more, trusts more, rejoices more, serves more, is more unselfish, is more diligent than a year ago. What are the expectations for the coming year? In our lives we must see growth, a closer approximation "unto a perfect man [woman] unto the measure of the stature of the fullness of Christ."

What Cameron Townsend was building in those early days was more than just an organization. He was building *community*. Henri Nouwen, scholar and author who worked with the L'Arche Christian communities for handicapped adults in France and Canada wrote:

> Community has little to do with natural compatibility. Community is grounded in God, who calls us together, and not in the attractiveness of people to each other. There are many groups that have been formed to protect their own interests, to defend their own sta-

tus, or promote their own causes, but none of these is a Christian community. The mystery of community is precisely that it embraces *all* people, whatever their individual differences may be, and allows them to live [and work] together as brothers and sisters of Christ and sons and daughters of his heavenly father.[1]

One of the important legacies Cameron Townsend left and demonstrated, by his own example, to the "community" he founded, was that of working in harmony with diverse people. As idealistic as this notion was, Cam's own spiritual insight told him such harmony was something to be worked at, to be learned and deliberately added to one's personal faith. Without using the term, he was urging the membership to take seriously the *disciplines* of the Christian life. And the ever practical Townsend suggested concrete ways to incorporate these disciplines into one's character. His prayer was for workers to demonstrate a Christ-like life, particularly in the areas of service and love. He, therefore, continued with his 1944 circular letter to the SIL and WBT membership outlining his goals for that year:

My desire would be that our companions would be able to see at the end of this New Year that we are much more like our Lord than ever before. May we also see many of the people who live around us added to the Lord–in each indigenous community an "increase of the body unto the edifying of itself in love." Now may I suggest some other goals for us to strive toward:

1. Systematic Bible study for new believers.
2. Better facilities in Mexico for printing translations and scientific materials.
3. The [publishing] of a linguistic magazine and linguistic literature.
4. More Mexican linguists whose talents are dedicated to God and their fellow men.
5. New Mexico City headquarters, preferably a long lease, rather than a purchase.

---

1 Henri Nouwen, *The Modern Spirituality Series* (Springfield, Illinois: Templegate Publishers, 1988), p. 73.

6. Adequate staff and facilities for teaching our children together with some of the most promising Indian children.

7. Gospels published in at least twelve languages–one a month.

8. Reading campaigns with visual aids in at least four different language groups.

9. New translators allocated in each of the remaining language groups in Mexico.

10. Guidance and practical training for twenty-five workers who will go to Peru.

11. More group interest in demonstrating the spirit of Christ in service through the group projects in Tetelcingo and other places.

12. A business manager in the Mexico City office.

13. Three helicopters, one for states of Chiapas and Oaxaca and one for the central and northern parts of the Republic.

14. Five hundred new students for Camp Wycliffe and its Canadian branch to be held this summer in Briercrest, Saskatchewan.

15. And finally, that our organization may grow steadily in vision, harmony, efficiency and faith–ever serving and never hindering.

These were clearly ambitious goals. And according to Dick Pittman, who was appointed director *pro tem* of the Mexico branch in January of 1944 while Cam was involved with other projects, that reflected Cam's willingness to put God to the test. "Uncle Cam liked to fly test balloons," said Dick, "knowing that some would fail, but others would succeed."

Many of these goals were modified and some took several years before they were reached. One, like his long-held dream of using aircraft to reach remote areas in Guatemala and Mexico became the responsibility of Mission Aviation Fellowship (MAF) who began their Mexico service in 1947. (MAF used fixed-wing aircraft rather than the high maintenance helicopters that Cam had suggested.) The organization Cam named *Jungle Aviation and Radio Service* (JAARS) would, after much resistance from the SIL board, be formed in 1948. But that's another story.

One goal that could be implemented quickly was the reading campaigns. The person he chose, and the most qualified to execute this, was 31-year-old Elaine Mielke. Before joining Wycliffe, Elaine had been a literacy specialist and supervisor of education for mentally handicapped children in three hundred schools for Chicago's Board of Education. Since her arrival in Mexico a year before in 1943, Elaine had taught translators' children in a village adjacent to Tetelcingo. In addition to teaching school, she had worked with the Townsends in Tetelcingo. A native of Chicago with Scandinavian roots, as was Elvira, Elaine and Elvira became fast friends.

In letters to her friend Etta Nyman, Elvira often wrote about the amount of work she had to do in the office. She spoke about how hard it was to cut stencils, run the mimeograph machine, readdress the increasingly large volume of mail for the SIL workers living in remote areas plus many other secretarial and office duties. In fact, Elvira's letters to Etta Nyman were sometimes a lament over the office work that often overwhelmed her.

In January, Elvira wrote Etta that her niece Evelyn Pike and Elaine Mielke had "taken a great load off my shoulders" and had given her a "grand help" in the office. Elvira said she was sorry that Elaine would be moving on to a literacy project. However, just before Elaine was to begin her first literacy assignment in 1944, she was called back to Chicago for a short visit to help her grandmother who had fallen and broken her hip.

In the meantime, Cam had other important projects to occupy his attention. One of the most pressing was the opening in July of the first Canadian SIL on the campus of the Briercrest Bible Institute, in Saskatchewan. While Cam had assigned the basic responsibility to Gene Nida, he was in constant communication with him, deliberating over the dozens of details that had to be arranged. One of the most crucial was securing teaching and administrative staff for Briercrest, as well as for the eleventh session of SIL that was to be held at Bacone College in Muskogee, Oklahoma. In addition to this, Gene was in correspondence with the regents at the University of Oklahoma at Norman to look into the possibility of moving SIL back to that campus. For unexplained reasons, the president of Bacone College was becoming increasingly uncooperative even to denying the SIL students access to the library.

Besides having to run interference with a difficult college president, Cam had to deal with the occasional problems of personnel who were at odds with some aspect of SIL's polices and stated goals. The one policy that continued to trouble some of the new workers was the ten percent assessment. For others it was taking direction from the general director. In answer to a couple who had tendered their resignation over these matters, Cam wrote:

> The matter of direction is something that is inherent to all combined efforts. Only if you work absolutely by yourself can you avoid taking or giving direction. If you build a house and hire a man to help, you tell him what to do. Or if you help another man build a house, you accept his direction. If you travel, you obey the rules of the railroad. If you go to school, you obey the rules of the institution.
>
> In Christian teamwork, the ideal would be for each person to know perfectly the mind of God and to follow the leading of the Spirit without having to consult with others. This would result in perfect and immediate coordination of effort. The reality is that none of us is infallible in knowing the mind of God. God is a God of order. In dealing with men, He has chosen again and again to deal with the many through the one or the few. This was the order of the Old Testament. And in the New Testament God gave special gifts of "governments" to some believers. They exercised this authority, locally and at a distance. Troubles in the early Church came when men set themselves up to rule when they did not have this gift, or when men who had it did not depend upon the guidance of the Holy Spirit in exercising the authority derived from it.

In addition to his burden and the concerns of staffing an office, of juggling personnel for two SIL schools and trying to interpret the uniqueness of SIL and WBT to ultraconservative members, Cam revealed to Will and Etta Nyman on February 5 that Elvira was not well.

> Today is D.L. Moody's birthday, and it makes me think more than ever about the need for a nationwide spiritual awakening in this and other lands. I have written Dr. Edman, president of Wheaton College, that when the war ends, we should be ready for an unprece-

dented advance into the corners of the earth where the Gospel has never gone–a truly pioneer movement.

Elvira has been having quite a bit of pain in her heart lately, as well as edema. I took her to an outstanding heart specialist and after careful examination, including a cardiograph, she was ordered to have complete rest for six days and to eat only fruits, strained vegetables, milk and gelatin.

On February 15, Elvira wrote from Tetelcingo to assure Etta and Will that after five days in bed, which she rather enjoyed, she was feeling much better. In fact, she was well enough for her and Cam to celebrate their twenty-fifth anniversary of becoming engaged with a special dinner at a hotel in nearby Cuautla. As cheery and positive as her remarks were, Elvira was far from well. Yet her strong-willed commitment to duty and the organization seemed to override her weakening body. In March she confided to Etta:

It isn't that I am in love with the work–it's just a case of doing work that no one else cares to do and which seems necessary. But with so much other "office work" to attend to here at my home office in Tetelcingo, it gives me little or no time for my own correspondence. We now have workers in forty-five tribes and dialects. If only I had proper help, much more could be accomplished. In addition to that, Mr. Townsend is making arrangements to visit Peru.

Ever since Ken Pike had returned from Peru with a clear invitation from the Peruvian government for SIL to begin work among the indigenous peoples of Amazonia, Cam had been petitioning the U.S. State Department for a passport to visit that country. Cam particularly wanted to meet Dr. Enrique Laroza, Minister of Public Education, from whom the initial invitation had come. Meanwhile, ever eager to promote goodwill and solidarity of the Americas, Cam sponsored what he called "Amerinova." He explained it all to Will Nyman in a March 7 letter:

I am sending you a copy of the Mexico City daily *El Nacional* for March 2 in which is announced the contest that we are sponsoring together with the newspaper itself for a hymn to the United Western Hemisphere for which we have coined the name "Amerinova." We

> have put up a thousand pesos for prize money. It is my hope that
> on my trip to South America I will be able to get some of the news-
> papers and poets interested. It will put our institute before those
> countries in a good light while it helps foment goodwill toward our
> country.

In faith, and without a passport in hand, Can booked a flight to Peru for
April 5. On March 21, still without a passport, Cam wrote Will Nyman:

> My passport hasn't had time to come through yet from Washington,
> but I am getting ready to leave early in April. Dick [Pittman] will be in
> charge. Elvira will look after the many details here in Tetelcingo. Elaine
> Mielke will also be here. She and Elvira make a wonderful team.

In a March 30 letter to Etta, Elvira confirmed that Elaine Mielke was indeed a great teammate:

> I want to say that Elaine Mielke is a pal. She sees many things to
> do as I do, and does them without being told. She is a good house-
> keeper, neat and efficient in whatever she undertakes to do. This
> has meant that we can do a lot of teamwork together. And when I
> am under the weather, I know I can call on her to help. It means a
> lot to me to know that she can cut a stencil, oversee the young men
> who work in the mimeograph room, take care of guests, to say
> nothing of working with the local congregation.

In her April newsletter, Elaine told her friends that in order to be closer
to the school children she was teaching, she had moved into a
three-room adobe hut next to the schoolhouse. At the close of the letter,
she casually mentioned that the Lord had been watching over her in a
special way.

> This is the season when scorpions are plentiful. One night we killed
> four in the living room. Within the last three weeks we have killed
> eight more in the house. So you see how thankful I am for His lov-
> ing care.

For the few friends who knew, there was more to that last sentence than
met the eye. In her natural exuberance and open friendliness to share
the love of Christ with a particular class of young men in their twenties

(she being in her thirties), Elaine had urged them to love their fellowman as Christ had loved them. One young man wrote Elaine a note that said, "Since you told us to love everyone, I write to tell you that I love you."

Shortly after receiving that note, Elaine was awakened in the middle of the night when she heard her door open, then footsteps, then suddenly she felt a hand touch her. Instinctively she screamed, and the intruder fled.

Assuming it was the same young man who had written the note, Elaine reported the incident the next morning to don Martín, leader of the local church, and recommended that the young man be disciplined. To her surprise, don Martín said, "It's all your fault." In utter amazement, Elaine asked how such an action could possibly be her fault. "It is because you talk with your eyes."

Several days later, Dr. Elena Trejo, the young woman from Guatemala whom Cam and Elvira had sponsored and helped to get her medical degree, came to visit. When Elaine told her what had happened and what don Martín had said, Elena said that she too had the same experience with the young men of the village misinterpreting her friendliness. When Elaine asked how she had corrected the problem, Elena said, "I began wearing sunglasses." And that's how Elaine conducted her future Sunday School classes, wearing sunglasses.

On April 4, the day before Cam was scheduled to leave for Peru, he wrote to Will Nyman to tell him his passport hadn't yet come, but that he was optimistic it would come after Holy Week [Easter]. On April 12, Cam sent a telegram to Will that read, "Washington slow about passport. Trip Peru delayed." Elvira was not altogether unhappy about this delay. She had hoped they could celebrate their twenty-fifth wedding anniversary together. Had Cam gone to Peru as planned, he would have missed it. In a letter to Etta, Elvira wrote:

> Cameron is sort of in a daze these days, walking around in another world thinking about his trip to Peru. Personally, I don't think about it. There will be plenty of time later when I am alone and longing to see him before he can get back. However, things are so uncertain these days. Cameron had wanted me to take a trip to Guatemala, but I feel that if Cameron goes and can't get back for our twenty-fifth wedding anniversary, I would far rather bear the disap-

pointment at home alone than with others. I am just selfish enough to hope that we can at least be together on that day. But I am willing for the Lord's will to be done in the matter.

On April 14, Cam wrote Will Nyman to tell him once again that his passport hadn't come and perhaps it wasn't the Lord's time for him to go. With a rare admission, Cam said he would try to relax a bit at home since he really wasn't in the best of shape to take a trip south. He concluded his letter with the disquieting news that an assassin had tried, but failed, to shoot his dear friend General Cárdenas. "The attempt on the life of the [former] president last Monday in the patio of the *Palacio* has given him extra cares. We are rejoicing that the bullet missed."

A few weeks later Cam admitted to Will Nyman that he agreed with the State Department's decision not to issue him a passport. He believed this was the Lord's timing because he could now turn his attention to securing a piece of property in the jungles of Chiapas. Cam wanted a place to serve as a boot camp to train new translators who were assigned to work in Peru. It would later be called Jungle Camp:

> We hope to get a training center ready by next September in a jungle section of southern Mexico with mosquito-proof shelters for twenty-five workers, a mess hall, doctor's quarters, a hangar for a helicopter and radio equipment for keeping in touch with small parties that will be going back and forth in the jungle with Indian groups. We hope to have a clearing large enough to do some farming for food and experience. Our object is to train and test, at the smallest possible expense and risk, a brigade of pioneers for the desperately difficult regions in South America where we will be working.

In his letters to Will Nyman, Cam routinely reported on the progress of at least a half dozen projects—projects that were far-reaching and complex. At the end of his typewritten letters, often in his own hand, he would ask prayer for Elvira's heart problem, which he said was "losing ground."

On July 9, Elvira was to get her wish to celebrate their twenty-fifth wedding anniversary together as well as Cam's forty-eighth birthday. There was, however, a kind of pre-celebration in the form of a vacation that the board of directors and Elvira's doctor insisted she take. On June 20 Cam wrote to longtime friend Dr. Harry Ironside, pastor of Moody Memorial Church in Chicago, to tell him their plans:

> The doctor wants me to get Elvira out of the high elevation of Mexico City and completely away from work. We have heard of a little hotel on a lonely beach north of Veracruz where they only charge a dollar a day for board and room. We are going to take a vacation there.

Then Cam wrote a sentence that, given Elvira's state of mind and health, is inexplicable. Without missing a beat, he invited Harry Ironside to join them on their vacation! Wisely, Dr. Ironside declined. Later, when Dr. Ironside learned from a letter that Cam wrote to Will Nyman of their misadventures, he was doubly glad he had declined. On June 27, Cam wrote the following:

> We left Mexico City on Wednesday anticipating a wonderful rest. However, that first day, we only got as far as Puebla [a city about two hours away]. Our car broke down. On Thursday, things went a bit better. We were looking for a little beach hotel we had been told about called *El Paraiso* [Paradise]. A few miles before the beach hotel, we left the paved highway onto a dirt road and just before nightfall, got stuck in the mud. I had no idea how we were going to get out when a truck came along. He really didn't want to help us, but since I was blocking the road, he had no alternative. He pulled us out, but it was a tough job.
>
> When we finally arrived at *El Paraiso*, we discovered it had slipped badly from when my friend who recommended it had visited it. Not that it had been anything more than frontier ranch house. There was no protection from mosquitoes, the toilets were filthy, the sea breeze didn't reach our bedroom, the roof was undergoing repair, a bunch of laborers made the dining room noisy and the beach had been washed away by what they called a *golpe del mar* [sea surge] that had left a bad drop to the water.
>
> We did, however, have an exceptional waiter. He wore a big sombrero while serving, but no shoes. His overalls were rolled up to one knee on one leg and just above the ankle on the other. The hair

on his chest fairly bristled and his old faded shirt made little effort to cover it. He once tried to keep the cat away from our table and kicked at it. He missed and hit his toes on our table legs hard enough to knock over a bottle of chile.

The letter continued, and from Cam's point of view, things got better once they were able to secure mosquito netting for their beds. Both Cam and Elvira enjoyed the surf, went boating on a nearby river and, with the protection of the mosquito nets, slept soundly. Elvira's badly swollen ankles began to improve. Cam ended his letter by thanking Will and the board for making the vacation possible, and assuring them they were making this vacation "a real honeymoon."

Elvira, however had a slightly different opinion of their vacation:

Our vacation was restful even though I believe they had the world's worst cook. We had fish, badly prepared, three times a day! No good tortillas, only sour bread. Every morning for breakfast we had fish soup! And, of course, there wasn't the slightest hint of anything modern or of conveniences of any sort. But in spite of these things, we did have a restful time. The ocean beach was perfect. It was simply fun to be alone with each other for a change, with no problems or cares. It did us both a lot of good. I think both Cameron and I could take a lot more of just rest and carefreeness.

On July 9, Cam and Elvira celebrated their twenty-fifth wedding anniversary by going to a quaint little hotel in Cuernavaca, "Where there was," said Elvira, "a large patio with trees, flowers, birds and a trickling fountain." Both Cam and Elvira said it reminded them of similar patios in the city of Antigua in Guatemala where they first began their married life and ministry together.

The newsletter to friends that told about their anniversary also mentioned there were one hundred and fifty students enrolled for the 1944 SIL school and that they very much wanted to go to the new SIL school in Briercrest, Saskatchewan. However, what the letter didn't say was that once Elvira returned to the higher elevation of Mexico City and Tetelcingo, her health problems returned. To Will and Etta, Cam wrote:

Elvira felt fine at sea level but just as soon as we returned to the highlands, she began to suffer from her old symptoms–weakness, irregular pulse, nervousness, sleeplessness and distress of other kinds. We are wondering if the Lord would have us spend a few months at sea level. It seems it would make a tremendous difference to Elvira. I am also torn about leaving Tetelcingo, since the main pastor is at a low spiritual ebb. We are wondering if we should also return to California after SIL. We would like to have yours and the others' direction on this matter. If we did return to California, Elvira could regain her strength, and I could perhaps get x-ray treatments for my face. Two years ago the doctor told me it would take several months of treatment to clear up those little rough spots, and though they have increased in number since you last saw me, the doctor might be able to speed up the treatment and get my face cleared up by December. I don't think there is any danger of them turning into skin cancer, but I would like to check on them.

On September 16, after a busy summer Elvira wrote to Etta from Siloam Springs, Arkansas, telling her that when they arrived at the home of Dr. Bast, he said he had never seen any two people look as bad as they both did in the two years since he last saw them. But after a couple of weeks eating good food and resting, Dr. Bast said he could see a decided improvement in their appearance. The October progress report sent from Mexico to the SIL Board gave notice that after October 13, Cam and Elvira would be staying at the home of Mr. A.M. Johnson, 7333 Franklin, Avenue, Hollywood, California. The board earlier had unanimously recommended, in view of Elvira's deteriorating health, that they return to California for an extended rest.

On December 24, 1944, Dick Pittman, Deputy Director of SIL in Mexico, received the following telegram from Cameron Townsend:

ELVIRA TOWNSEND HAD A STROKE LAST NIGHT. STILL IN DEEP COMA.

Chapter Sixteen

A Heavenly Citation

One of the "must see" attractions listed in the Automobile Club of Southern California's *Desert Area Handbook* is the extravagant Spanish Moorish-styled museum known as "Scotty's Castle." In reality, the "castle" was once the winter residence of Albert (A.M.) Johnson, a Chicago insurance millionaire[1] and friend of Townsend.

In one of those amazing ways that Cameron Townsend had of "accidentally" meeting interesting and often significant people, like Dr. Moisés Sáenz while walking along a lake front in Guatemala and President Cárdenas in a dusty village plaza in Mexico, Cam met A.M. Johnson while Johnson was sick in bed in Mexico City. It's not clear how Cam knew this man was ill in a hotel room in Mexico City. On January 20 and 26, 1944, Cam wrote to Will Nyman and explained the unusual circumstances under which he and Johnson became friends:

---

1 "The name Scotty's Castle comes from Walter Scott, a cowboy, prospector, publicity hound, prevaricator, storyteller and friend of Johnson's. Scotty, whose enthusiastic flamboyance was financed by Johnson, managed to convince many that the Castle was his personal domain." From *California Desert Areas*, Automobile Club of Southern California (Los Angeles, California, 1996), pp. 192-194.

> I found Mr. A.M Johnson sick in bed in a hotel in Mexico City. He
> had become ill with tonsillitis and was in bed for a week. When he
> was feeling better, I invited him to Kay Pittman's birthday party. He
> said he read our *Translation* magazine from cover to cover. He also
> expressed keen interest in our work and even talked of helping with
> our need of new headquarters in Mexico City.

Before he left Mexico in March, A.M. Johnson took Cam and Elvira on a
six-day all-expense-paid vacation to Veracruz. Then as a parting gift, he
gave Cam twelve hundred and fifty pesos to purchase the small plot of
land that they had been renting for their trailer and small house in
Tetelcingo. When Johnson learned Cam and Elvira were returning to
California, he offered them the use of his Hollywood home. The location was ideal for both Cam and Elvira. It was close to family and
friends and the Wycliffe office in Glendale where the Nymans lived. It
was also close to the doctor who was treating Cam for the cancer-like
spots on his face. And while there were stairs to climb, Elvira said she
could cope with this for a while.

In spite of Elvira's fragile health, there was much that was positive
about the summer of 1944. Elvira found strength to give several lectures
from her book on Latin American courtesy. George Cowan, director of the
Canadian SIL, reported the school was going well. There were more than
a dozen newly-assigned workers in Mexico, including a nurse for the future Jungle Camp. There was also the SIL's sponsorship of work among
the Navajos in the U.S. with Fay Edgerton and Turner and Helen Blount
joining the SIL team. Cam planned to meet them at Window Rock, Ari-
zona and allocate them in their new location. And from Ken Pike came
word that God had answered prayer for SIL to become officially associated with the University of Oklahoma at Norman. The 1945 session of SIL
would once again be held at Norman.

In August and September, Elaine Mielke sent Cam regular reports on
the various reading campaigns she was directing. Her reports were enthusiastic saying that all was going well. Then in October came a report from
Cam to the Board of Directors:

> Severe weather storms have swept across the southern part of the
> country. In the states of Chiapas, Oaxaca, and Veracruz railroad,

bus transportation and mail service had been disrupted. We are attempting to find out about our people in these stricken areas.

On Sunday, October 1, Elaine Mielke who was in the central highlands in the state of Oaxaca in the village of Papálo, wrote the following report to Cam and Mr. Nyman:

> I don't know when you will get this report. The flood caused by the cyclone has shut us off from all communication. The people say it will be six months before the trains can run again. This is because all bridges have been completely washed away. People were killed in every town around us, but the Lord kept us safe here in Papálo.
>
> I am here with Marge Davis and Doris Needham conducting a reading campaign. We began the classes a week ago and already we have reached over fifty people. Classes for men are held at night in the only store in town. The women meet every afternoon in the schoolhouse. In the morning we all go out to their homes and teach the women while they make tortillas. I am not sure when I will be able to leave since the river is still high. Some say we will be able to cross at the end of the month. In the meantime, there is still a lot of work I can do here.

To her friend Ardis Needham who was working in the Mexico City office, Elaine reported on October 10 that the "Lord had opened doors" in the village of Papálo with seventy-four people learning to read. Elaine said she hoped to leave the village on October 28. She concluded her letter by saying she thought she might have to swim across the river in order to get back to Mexico City!

As it turned out, Elaine did not have to swim, but she, Marge and Doris, had to cross the river on a bosun's chair attached to a sagging cable strung across the river.

On November 10, Cam reported to the membership that he and Elvira had spent eight wonderful days of rest and relaxation as guests of A.M. Johnson at Scotty's Castle in Death Valley. Then on December 26, 1944, Mrs. J. Harvey Borton, Secretary of the Pioneer Mission Agency in Philadelphia received the following telegram:

ELVIRA ASLEEP IN JESUS. FUNERAL THURSDAY AFTERNOON. WITH MIS-
SIONARY CHALLENGE. W. CAMERON TOWNSEND

Elvira Townsend died Christmas Eve in Cam's arms as he held her close
to an open window in an attempt to give her more fresh air. She was
fifty-two. The official word from Wycliffe said:

> On Christmas Eve, Elvira received her heavenly citation. Though
> she suffered from a severe form of heart trouble for twelve years,
> the blood clot or cerebral hemorrhage that took her life came as a
> shock to us who remain. Her death came at the close of a busy day
> spent in the service of others.

Elvira's funeral service that was held at 2:30 on December 28, 1944 at the
Church of the Recessional, Forest Lawn Memorial Park, Glendale, California, emphasized victory through Christ. Mr. Townsend had re-
quested that in place of flowers, the farewell tribute should be New
Testaments for the people of the countries where Elvira served. But
among the floral pieces at her casket that gave comfort to all, was a
large *V* made with red flowers, with the words: "O grave, where is thy
victory? Thanks be unto God which giveth us the VICTORY through our
Lord Jesus Christ."

With the news of Elvira's death came letters and telegrams of condo-
lence. Mrs. Borton wrote:

> Your telegram a real shock. All send sincere sympathy. Second Co-
> rinthians one, three and four. Underneath are the everlasting arms.
> His grace is sufficient.

From two dear Cakchiquel friends, Lucia de Rayán, and Juan Rayán
(written in Cakchiquel), came this letter:

> In His name, our Lord Jesus Christ, we send our greetings to you
> and may He help you with all His goodness. We know that God al-
> ways does what He wills. Because of that, we believe God has
> done His will with our sister Elvira in that He took her to heaven.
> Thanks to Him that our God made ready a beautiful home there
> with Him where He gives peace and where always there is light.

God reward you both because of all the kindness that you have shown to us. We are asking the Father that He will take care of you in your life and that He will bless you with the work you are doing among the brethren that are there. May God comfort your heart with His Word from these following passages: Psalm 116:15, I Thessalonians 4:13-17, I Corinthians 15: 51-55.

In a letter to Dr. Ironside on December 30, Cam wrote:

God was present in power at the funeral yesterday. He and many wonderful relatives and friends stood by in such precious ways that the hard experience was greatly lessened. I'm sure I'll have to make a lot of adjustments. I am also sure that I'll never again have a home of my own. I want Ken and Evie to take over our home in Tetelcingo if they can do their work there.

Mr. Johnson was wonderful to us. For the last three months of Elvira's life, he did everything in the world for her comfort and happiness. And since the Lord called Elvira home, Mr. Johnson has been like a father to me, standing with me in loving compassion in my bereavement. He took care of all the funeral expenses and made it twice as beautiful as I could have done. I had to hold him back on the expenses. I wanted the funeral to be modest in keeping with the life of a pioneer missionary. He was considerate of my wishes and yet gave Elvira a wonderful burial in a beautiful spot in Forest Lawn Cemetery.

A great many people attended the funeral. I prayed that all might receive a fresh inspiration of the hope we have in God. I am returning to Mexico soon, and if God permits, will attend the memorial service that you have so kindly arranged at Moody Church on March 25. I am not sure when I should plan to go to South America, perhaps in March or April. With deep appreciation, as ever.

By January 1945, it was clear that Allied forces would soon have complete mastery of the European theater of war. But not without some of the bloodiest and most horrific battles yet to be fought. On April 25, British, Canadian, American and Soviet forces met with toasts and embraces on the Elbe River. Seven days later, on May 2, Berlin fell and on

May 8, 1945, five years and eight months after it started, the war in Europe was officially over. There was, of course, yet to be the Enola Gay and Hiroshima.

In the six hundred letters written by Cameron Townsend during 1941 to 1945, there is surprisingly little reference to the war. After Cam's nephew, Lt. Lorin Griset was captured in France in December 1944, Cam frequently reminded colleagues to pray for him.[1] When news came on August 14, 1945 that the war in the Pacific had ended, Cam asked the group to spend a half day of prayer in thanksgiving to God and for new workers to join in the Bible translation task. But this is getting a little ahead of ourselves in the story.

During the first weeks of January 1945 after Elvira's death, Cam's letters were bittersweet as he reached out in expressions of love to the many friends and colleagues who had sent their condolences. He wrote that he was finding strength and a "new sweetness in communion with the Lord, with colleagues and friends, and indeed with humanity in general."

Cam's January thank-you letter to his friends paid tribute to Elvira's consummate skill as letter writer, organizer of the household finances, homemaker and gracious host. In several letters Cam said that even though Elvira had often referred to the way they had lived as "a gypsy's life," he was saddened at the thought of perhaps never again having a real home of his own. He warned his friends that he might not be able to communicate with them as regularly as he had done in the past. "The reason for this," wrote Cam, "is because I must not neglect the responsibilities God has given me in His service." So keenly did Cam feel this responsibility and so desirous to be free from anything that might encumber him, Cam issued an unprecedented directive to the SIL group finance office in Mexico City:

> I am closing out my bank account and putting the money into the Elvira Townsend Memorial Fund. Most of this money will be earmarked for a local memorial in Tetelcingo to build a sewing room to be used for the women of the village. I am closing out my bank account as I do not want the burden of trying to keep track of my funds. If I should ever have a balance in my account at the Mexico

---

1 For a fuller account of Lorin Griset's harrowing account as a prisoner of war during the last days of the war, see *It Takes Two to Untangle Tongues* by Ethel Emily Wallis.

> City office of more than a hundred dollars, I have asked that the ex-
> tra automatically be given to some project in the work. In this way I
> will never have to be bothered with keeping books.

By mid-February Cam, who had driven to Mexico City in the company
of A.M. (Uncle Al) Johnson, was fully occupied with the affairs of the
group in Mexico. Chief among his concerns was larger housing facilities
for SIL workers living and passing through the city. To Mr. Nyman he
wrote:

> Our two homes here in Mexico City are overcrowded. The
> Pittmans, with their three kiddies, live in one room. Kenneth and
> Evelyn and baby Judy live in another room (about seven feet wide).
> There are four other families besides five others and myself. There
> is also a language helper from one of the villages and the live-in do-
> mestic help. It seems most urgent that we obtain larger living quar-
> ters as well as larger office space.

In addition to the evident need for more adequate living quarters, Cam
had several other concerns. The most immediate was arranging staff
and a special display illustrating SIL's teaching and educational methods to be held at the Palace of Fine Arts in Mexico City the last week of
February. To draw attention to the importance of reading, the President
of Mexico, Manuel Avila Camacho commissioned the Ministry of Education to sponsor this special symposium and asked that those who
knew how to read teach someone who didn't know how. Since Elaine
Mielke (who herself had just returned to Mexico in February from caring for her grandmother) was the one most recently involved in teaching indigenous peoples to read in their own language, Cam asked her to
be in charge of the display.

There were two other important projects on Cam's mind in the spring
of 1945. One was his upcoming trip to Peru. He was scheduled to leave on
April 25 and return to Mexico in July to lend his energies to the development of the next most important project, the Jungle Training Camp in
Chiapas.

Cameron Townsend's official report of his trip to Peru (May 29 to July
7, 1945) comprised nineteen pages of single-spaced typewritten copy. In

his report, he described his many miles of air and river travel, of important government people he had met, plus missionaries and educators. Cam's report is too long and detailed to be included in this volume. There are, however, two letters (one of many he wrote) that capture something of the essence of his experience. The first is dated May 23, 1945 written on board the riverboat "Ancón" on the Ucayali River, Peru:

> The big boat that had promised to pick me up didn't come. So when this little boat came in sight, I decided to take it. The captain says the other ship is waiting for freight to accumulate. This boat should reach Iquitos in four or five days. What is time in the jungle?
>
> The river is pretty and the weather not too hot this time of year. In fact, the nights have been cold, with the thermometer going below fifty degrees. What is BAD, is the utter lack of cleanliness about the preparation and serving of food. Dishwashing is a revelation of indifference to germs. I commit myself to the care of God and eat without concern—also without much relish. There are about eighty people on this small ship. I haven't found a place to hang my hammock, but by night I'll find a way to crisscross it among the rest of the people. The staterooms are all taken.
>
> The captain and passengers are all nice to me so I'm enjoying myself and wouldn't trade places with anyone. My visit to Roaboya, Loreto, Peru was timed perfectly and I am sure will result in the furtherance of Bible translation work by other organizations than our own. It is appalling how this aspect of the work has been neglected. There is a tremendous job to be done and in spite of what some leaders think, *it can be done*. Modern means of travel and linguistics are essential though.

Cam's second letter was written from Iquitos on June 2 while he waited for a government plane to pick him up:

> My heart is greatly burdened for the indigenous peoples. The things I have seen and read and hear make me yearn to do something for them. We'll need strong, capable, big-hearted workers and plenty of money. God is able! The Consul General of Colombia has become greatly interested and suggests we begin work in his country.

The commander of the Peruvian air force in this region had told me he was going to send me on two trips but neither one materialized. However, I have had a long and worthwhile conference with a number of people who have given me a great deal of helpful information. I have also had time to gather data from a number of books and magazines that have been loaned to me.

You may wonder why I wait for the plane instead of going by riverboat. Had I continued on by riverboat, any of the trips would have been over two thousand miles due to the curves and slowness of river travel. The distance by air is only four hundred miles. Since my time is limited, I knew I wouldn't get very far by boat. One trip that took me two and half hours by air, took some Adventist missionaries twenty-seven days on a barge. The river was so rough in places that any craft except a barge would have capsized or been grounded due to the shallowness of the river in some places. I can wait a week for a plane and still save a lot of time and gather information while I wait.

Cam's trip to Peru can best be described in a single word, "exhilarating." From Lima he wrote: "I'm having a wonderful time. At times my heart nearly explodes with joy as I watch Him work." For years Cam had dreamed of a way for SIL to have its own airplanes to serve the translators' needs in getting to and from difficult and inaccessible indigenous village areas. And if nothing else, his trip to Peru convinced Cam once again that this dream must become a reality. As if to confirm he was on the right track, Cam received a letter from Elizabeth (Betty) Greene, former Women's Air Force Service Pilot (WASP) and Secretary for the Christian Airmen's Fellowship (CAMF), later changed to Mission Aviation Fellowship (MAF.) The letter was written May 23, 1945 and reached Cam while he was still in Peru.

The letter explained that the CAMF was a growing organization of Christian airmen from the military (she was their only woman pilot) whose vision was to use their flying talent and expertise in the Lord's service:

> Six months ago God clearly led us to open our offices here in Los Angeles. We are endeavoring to contact missions for the purpose of studying their fields in relation to the practicability of aircraft oper-

ation. We also want to be of assistance to any who are contemplating such air service. We are looking into the possibility of training certain missionaries how to fly, and are preparing for more extensive and helpful service after the war.

We keenly respect you for your life of service and for what you represent in the Wycliffe Bible Translators. We believe CAMF needs to be in touch with the work of Wycliffe. We also realize that you have the work of world mission on your heart. For this reason we invite you to serve as an official member of our Advisory Council.

Cam immediately wired his acceptance to be on the CAMF Advisory Council, and followed with a letter written July 11, 1945:

Your letter reached me in Peru and I wired my acceptance to serve on your Advisory Board. I have returned from my Peruvian trip more convinced than ever that if ever the people who live in the jungles of Amazonia are to be reached with the gospel, it will be absolutely necessary to use airplane transportation.

By way of interest, you will be happy to know that we (SIL) have signed a formal agreement with the government of Peru to work among fifty tribal groups. For this work, we are going to need an expert pilot.

The formal agreement Cam mentioned came from Peru's Ministry of Public Education dated June 26, 1945 and was confirmed by Supreme Resolution No. 2420:

After due consideration, the accompanying agreement between the Ministry of Public Education and Mr. William Cameron Townsend, as the General Director of the Summer Institute of Linguistics, Inc. of the University of Oklahoma, U.S.A., for the purpose of carrying out a program of cooperation for the study of Indian languages in this Republic, especially those of the Amazonian Jungle. It is important to preserve, for the national science and history of our country, its linguistic wealth before it disappears. To entrust the Department of Artistic Education and Cultural Extension with the carrying out of this Resolution. Initialed by HIS EXCELLENCY THE PRESIDENT OF THE REPUBLIC. (Signed) Enrique Laroza Minister of Public Education.

For all intents and purposes, the SIL group in Mexico was very much a large family. (There were a now hundred twenty full time workers and four guest helpers.) And like most families, they frequently engaged in good-natured banter. By June 1945, much of the bantering and conversation centered around who might become the second Mrs. Townsend. From time to time, some of the women of the group were not above playing a discreet game of Cupid. There is no positive proof if Cam's niece, Evelyn Pike, was playing such a role. There is, however, Cam's revealing answer to what must have been Evelyn's attempt at playing matchmaker. From Lima, Peru, Cam wrote the following to his niece:

> It was lovely of you, Evie, to write as you did. I knew from your remarks that you would be pleased to have me observe Elaine's many virtues. And to tell you the truth, I have already observed them enough to feel that if I want to keep my single estate, I should stay away from Tetelcingo. I didn't keep away enough and then came that weekend in Mexico City when I said more to her than I should have said, until I was sure of the Lord's will about having a home again.
>
> If He doesn't want me to be free for this traveling ministry and gives me liberty to marry again, I can't imagine a better partner, particularly for me with my big Wycliffe family, my many responsibilities, my vision and programs, my hard-boiled adherence to certain convictions and ideas that would irk, try and vex many a wonderful woman.
>
> She knows I don't have liberty from the Lord to make a definite proposal yet. I am convinced that all of 1946 is going to be so full of travels, etc. for me that there will be no time to establish a new home. These next years will be a period of great advance for our work and I must be free to give every bit of my energy and time to it. Perhaps 1947, that will be my year of Jubilee. I will be fifty you know.
>
> Also, Elaine needs to give all of 1946 to reading campaigns. By the time she sees how hard-boiled I can be, she may say "no thank you," and I wouldn't blame her. As long as I am single, the work comes first. That's why I was wrong in speaking to her before I knew the Lord's will. I must say that I love receiving her letters and I love writing to her. The one thing I can say for sure, if it is anyone, it

will be her. I am, however, determined that my head shall steer my heart for the group's sake as well as my own. And my head says Elaine, and my heart rejoices over the choice *if* it is the Lord's will. Please don't let anyone else in on this matter.

Chapter Seventeen
A New Era

The poignant photograph of John F. Kennedy, Jr. saluting his father's coffin is one of the twentieth century's most defining moments. So, too, eighteen years before, did the photographs of a black woman's face wet with tears and another with her handkerchief pressed to her lips and wearing a look of great distress define for a nation the depth of grief and unease at the death of Franklin D. Roosevelt. And on April 12, 1945, it fell to an untested Harry S. Truman to be the helmsman of one of the world's three mightiest nations. The decisions that would end the war in the Pacific and shape a new era were largely his to make.

In 1945, Cameron Townsend and world missions were also on the brink of a new era. The war had left hundreds of thousands of people spiritually and emotionally drained, shattered and barren as the rubble of war. Wrote one historian, "There is an overpowering need for faith, for a mystique, for a moral revival in the midst of moral collapse".[1]

Seeing this obvious need, many parachurch organizations responded to try to fill this vacuum. Most of these groups believed the vacuum should be filled with the foundation of all moral truth, as found in Holy Scriptures. One new group that responded was Mission Aviation Fellowship

1 William Manchester, *American Caesar, Douglas MacArthur 1880-1964*, (New York: Dell, 1983), p. 547

(MAF). They wanted to be of service to Wycliffe Bible Translators and to other groups in Mexico. And under the auspices of the Evangelical Student Foreign Missions Fellowship of the Inter-Varsity Christian Fellowship, the first-ever Convention For Missionary Advance under the leadership of J. Christy Wilson was gearing up for a massive rally that was to be held in Toronto, Canada, beginning December 27, 1946. This was the forerunner of the great Urbana student mission conferences held every three years at the University of Illinois at Champagne-Urbana. It would become one of the preeminent channels for serious students to learn about cross-cultural mission opportunities.

The problem for Cam in 1945 was that as important as this conference was to become to Wycliffe and other groups, it was still a year away, and Cam needed volunteers to go with him to Peru in the Spring of 1946. To Dick Pittman on June 11, 1945, Cam wrote:

> You doubtless know by now of the wonderful openings the Lord has given us to begin work in Peru. The agreement I signed with the government calls for all aspects of the work we are doing in Mexico and then some. We are going to need new recruits as well as modern equipment to carry out the program, but our God is able.
>
> However, I was sorry to learn through Pike that there are practically no volunteers at Norman for our South American project. This throws the bigger burden on the Canadians at Briercrest. I know Briercrest is small, but God can use small things.

Never one to wring his hands over a difficult or impossible situation, Cam, on that same day, wrote his old friend Charles Fuller. After explaining about the new opportunity for service in Peru and the need for volunteers, Cam asked Dr. Fuller for a favor:

> I am wondering if you could come to our rescue by preaching a strong missionary sermon over your worldwide broadcast. God could use you to stir many young lives to volunteer, and we could arrange to hold a special linguistic institute to train them. Training is a must. In all the years of missions in the past for Peru's high and lowlands Indian peoples, only one gospel has been translated into one of the fifty indigenous languages. How can you reach people

without the Word of God, and without being able to speak their own language?

As one examines the life of Cameron Townsend it is soon evident that he has little time or patience for grumbling or lamenting. He seemed never to look back with regret for what had happened or hadn't happened. Thus, it was curiously out of character for him to admit to his niece Evelyn Pike that he probably shouldn't have said as much as he did to Elaine Mielke on that weekend in Mexico City.

Whatever it was that he said on that weekend, no one is telling. However, in Elaine's June 28 letter to Cam, in answer to his suggestion that she should consider dating younger men, Elaine's effusive greeting, "Good morning darling," clearly indicated that their relationship had moved beyond that of the general director and a group member:

> I appreciate your advice, dear, when you tell me to have dates with younger men, but please believe me, honey, when I say it is *you* I love and I know I would never be happy with anyone else. While I was home, I did have dates with younger men, but no one can compare with Cameron Townsend. I wanted to tell you face to face, but I just couldn't wait to tell you. You mentioned that your life was now one of travel. This is not an obstacle to me. I am sure that if it is the Lord's will that our lives be united in His service, He will work out every difficulty, no matter how big or small.

Elaine was correct about Cam's traveling schedule. There was, of course, his trip to Peru in April, May and June with a stopover in Venezuela. There Cam had a lengthy visit with President Rómulo Betancourt about the possibility of SIL establishing a work of Bible translation among Venezuela's indigenous peoples. On his return from Peru at the end of June, Cam flew to Panama, then to Tegucigalpa, Honduras, and Guatemala before returning to Mexico City. He just had time to catch his breath before leaving for SIL at Norman, Oklahoma. In a letter to a friend at Norman dated July 21, Cam reported that since April 29 he had spent ninety hours in the air. He said he was happy to report he was looking forward to traveling by train from Norman to the Canadian SIL at Briercrest, Saskatchewan. He was also planning to take the train from Canada to Chicago to visit family and to fulfill several mission speaking engagements.

In letters to Will and Etta Nyman, Cam outlined his travel plans and mentioned the people he would visit while he was in Chicago. There was no mention of visiting Elaine's parents. In his August 6 letter, however, there was this off-handed phrase. "Went to the Mielkes' for lunch." What the Nymans didn't know was that Cam, in a time-honored tradition, had gone to Elaine's father in private that weekend and asked his permission for his daughter's hand in marriage.

In their book *Uncle Cam*, Jim and Marti Hefley reported that Cam's visit to Chicago coincided with Elaine being in Chicago to attend her grandmother's funeral. The Hefleys also reported that Cam stopped in at Norman on his return trip from Briercrest and confided to his old friend Dawson Trotman that he had proposed to Elaine. Trotman was delighted with the news until Cam said he thought he should wait a year or more before getting married. "This will give me time to get things going in Peru," said Cam. Trotman is reported to have said, "That doesn't make sense. It seems to me that anyone marrying a tremendous woman like Elaine would want to spend as many years of his life with her as he could." [1]

There is no further record of that conversation, but it is evident from Cam's actions over the next few weeks that his intention was to take his friend's advice and make a formal engagement announcement and set a wedding date. Before doing this, however, the Hefleys reported that Cam, following an old Mexican custom, sought the approval of two old and trusted friends, General Cárdenas, and Mr. Marroquín, the Mexico representative of the American Bible Society. Both gave their enthusiastic approval. Thus the announcement of their engagement was made on October 6, 1945 at the SIL Mexico Branch Conference in the form of an Old English proclamation that John Wycliffe would have been comfortable reading:

> Mistress Elaine Mielke and Sir William Cameron Townsend hereby to all peoples make known ye words of troth. About the time of the Ides of March, when spring doth bring its joys and gladness and hath put to flight winter's hoary chill, and just before the labor of the

---

1   James and Marti Hefley, *Uncle Cam*. (Waco, Texas: Word Books 1974), p. 136.

great King demands that said twain set forth with emboldened heralds for jungle peoples below the earth's middle line, it hath been ordered that church portals in ye olden fair romantic land of Mexico be opened and bells pealen forth in gladsome note as maid and knight take their vows to plight thereafter to be one.

When one looks at the flourish surrounding the announcement of this special event, one may wonder why Cam, knowing he was going to be engaged, did not have an engagement ring to present to Elaine on that early October day. We learn from Will Nyman in a letter to Elaine dated October 23, that Cam asked him to select and buy the engagement ring and send it to Mexico with Uncle Al Johnson. While those who look down the corridors of time and wonder at what seems a glaring oversight, Elaine had no such concerns. Immediately after the Mexico Branch conference, she headed for the southern states of Chiapas and Oaxaca to conduct yet another series of reading campaigns. Cam went to Jungle Camp to help make it ready for the new workers who would leave for Peru in the spring.

Then on October 24, Elaine wrote a most remarkable letter to Cam. It's remarkable for the way she expresses her private emotions about the character of the man she will soon marry. The letter also seems to be written to reassure Cam that the disparity in their ages and experience makes not the slightest difference in her love for him:

> For years I have wondered if the Lord would ever bring into my life a companion whom I could love with all my heart. One whom I could admire because of his convictions and character, one whose interests were the same as mine, one who was thoughtful, understanding, loving, patient, one who loves children, is generous, hospitable, self-sacrificing with a dynamic personality, a leader, a pioneer in the Lord's work, one who practices what he preaches, a spiritual man of prayer. All these qualities I have found in you. And in answer to your question "Will you be mine as long as God spares our lives?" I can gladly say "YES." I am looking forward to many happy days with you.
>
> Now about the problem you thought I should consider carefully before answering, let me say this. I am sure the difference in our ages does not present any problem for the present, nor will it in the

future. If for any reason you might be bedridden during the last five years of our marriage, I would count it a privilege to take care of you. As far as a home is concerned, just being near you will be enough. I can't thank the Lord enough for bringing you into my life. It will be a happy day in March when the preacher asks me, "Do you take W. Cameron Townsend to be your wedded husband?" And I can tell the whole wide world, "I DO."

During the following weeks there were dozens of letters from Elaine, each filled with a warmth and ardor of love and understanding that could only have kindled a new rush of happiness in Cam's life. Almost from the beginning of their courtship, there were no cross purposes or lost energy on Elaine's part. She wrote as one who understood and believed implicitly in Cam's vision. Cam, who had wondered if he might ever again have the love of a woman and an established home, now had the devoted love of one whose energetic devotion to both him and his vision would make his companionship complete.

By mid-November 1945, Elaine had received her engagement ring, and pronounced it "exquisite." She, along with others, including Uncle Al Johnson, joined Cam at Jungle Camp where, after long days of work Cam and Elaine enjoyed moonlight strolls on the newly created airstrip. Cam, in a letter to Will Nyman, noted that there was wonderful cooperation from everyone involved in establishing the jungle training camp, from plastering mud on the cane walls of the thatched-roof huts, to helping with practical carpentering. And, of course, Cam was quick to praise Elaine for her help, saying that she was "an untold blessing to everyone here. She has organized the academic program, and is helping me with my correspondence before her reading campaign materials arrive."

In the same letter, Cam spoke highly of the flying skill and practical help of MAF's Betty Greene in selecting and surveying landing sites at Jungle Camp plus other sites in Chiapas and Oaxaca. From Cam's last letter of 1945 written from Jungle Camp on December 4, it becomes evident once again that Cam's mind is refocused on Peru:

I haven't seen a newspaper for months, nor do I have a radio. Doubtless things of importance have happened that we should know about, and eventually we will hear. However, when I think about this Christmas season, I think about the indigenous jungle peoples of Peru who have not yet heard about an exceedingly important event that happened centuries ago.

At Christmas we think of the angels who announced the Christmas massage as white fluffy creatures. The messengers we need now for the jungle tribes must have hardened muscles and be rugged like the environment they will face. These Bible translators will be angels of mercy, and Christians at home can wing them on their way by prayer.

Elaine's Christmas letter to the Nymans told about the near completion of the large hut that would serve as a single women's dorm. She wrote about sprinkling pine needles in the dining room and how sweet that smelled and how soft a carpet it made on the dirt floor. There was to be a Christmas fiesta where a calf would be killed and twenty of the local indigenous workers employed at Jungle Camp with their families would be invited to be part of the celebration. Elaine ended her letter by telling the Nymans that she and Cam had set the wedding date for March 23, 1946. (In actuality, the wedding date was postponed until April 4, 1946, because Cam's best man, General Cárdenas, had to attend the funeral of an aunt).

But before that day arrived, there was important work to be done. The first contingent of new workers that God had raised up to go to Peru had to be trained at the new Jungle Camp. Cam had hoped the Waco biplane that was being worked on by MAF pilot Nate Saint would be readied to ferry the twenty-three new workers (including six single women) into the remote Jungle Camp area, but when the day came for the campers to fly into camp, the Waco plane wasn't ready. As he had done in the past, Uncle Al Johnson came to the rescue and chartered a local bush pilot to fly in the campers.

For the next three months, the twenty-three campers conditioned themselves by hiking jungle mountain trails. On certain days the trails might be dry and hot, the next slick with mud from a tropical downpour. The campers learned the rudiments of first aid, how to identify various jungle plants and trees, some of which could provide water and food in an emergency. They learned how to handle a heavy dugout canoe and swim or scull feet first through boiling rapids, how to give injections and read a map and make a simple jungle hut out of vine and cane. But more important than all the practical skills they learned regarding survival in the jungle, was what they would learn about themselves.

The tensions and stress of working and living together in close proximity under primitive conditions often revealed hitherto unrecognized character traits in an individual. In some cases the training revealed strengths of leadership and self-sacrificial qualities the person was unaware they possessed. In others, certain weaknesses showed up that, when admitted by the person, became an occasion for building new strengths into their character. In all, Jungle Camp was a voyage of self-discovery.

By the end of March, Elaine, who had been spending her time with Marianna Slocum and Florence Gerdel among the Tzeltal people conducting a reading campaign, was anxious to forget all about teaching people to read and concentrate on preparations for her wedding. Once when Elaine had expressed her apprehension about not having enough time to get ready, Cam, in his "everything will work out fine" attitude, assured her she had nothing to worry about, that all things would be ready.

When April 4 finally came, Elaine discovered that Cam was right. Preparations had been taken care of by General Lázaro Cárdenas and his wife Amalia who served as Elaine's matron of honor. In their book, *Uncle Cam*, the Hefleys said of that moment, "The day dawned bright and sunny. The Nymans had come from California, Uncle Al Johnson was there as were several of Elaine's relatives including her mother and father. Mexico's leading anthropologist, Dr. Manuel Gamio, was there, together with six generals and other prominent Mexicans. The orchestra played. Mr. Marroquín's daughter Amanda sang 'The Love of God' in Spanish. The local mayor presided. As Elaine walked toward him (dressed in her elder sister's wedding dress), Cam thought, "She is wonderful!" The short ceremony was soon over and they were pronounced *Señor* and *Señora* William Cameron Townsend. The reception was a blur of picture-posing hugs and hand-shaking."[1]

Elaine recalls that Cam had spent the night before the wedding talking to General Cárdenas until after one a.m. In his attention to the general, Cam had forgotten one important detail. Namely, to make a hotel reservation for their first night. It wasn't until he and Elaine were about to leave the beautiful hilltop home of General and Mrs. Cárdenas overlooking Lake Patzcuaro, that Cam realized his *faux pas*. Once again it was Uncle Al

---

1 Ibid, p. 138.

Johnson to the rescue. He gave the newlyweds his room at the nearby don Vasco Hotel!

A week later on April 11, 1946, Cam and Elaine sent out their first letter as husband and wife. They told about a special banquet in Mexico City held in the newly purchased group house that was nicknamed "the Kettle." The special guests at that banquet were once again General and Mrs. Cárdenas along with the full number of young people who were going with Cam and Elaine to Peru. They ended their letter by saying they were leaving that night by plane for Peru by way of Venezuela.

As Yogi Berra said, "This was *déjá vu* all over again!" When Cam married Elvira in August 1919, they spent their first night at the home of a missionary friend. The following morning, as they left for their "honeymoon," Cam invited Elvira's brother, who had been his best man, to accompany them. (Their honeymoon was spent going on an evangelistic outreach to Cakchiquel churches.)

Now twenty-seven years later little had changed in Cam's order of priorities. The morning after their first night, Cam and Elaine had a quiet and leisurely breakfast before returning to the headquarters in Mexico City and then packed for their trip to Peru. The difference this time was that instead of a brother-in-law in tow, Cam and Elaine had nineteen young people for their companions, all eager to begin a new life of adventure in Peru. In April 1996, in celebration of SIL's fifty years of service in Peru, Elaine wrote:

> It is a great blessing for me to have been invited as a guest of the Peru Branch on April 18, 1996 to celebrate that special occasion. On April 4, 1946, fifty years ago, Cam and I were married at the beautiful summer home of General and Mrs. Cárdenas. Then on our honeymoon we took our first nineteen workers to Peru. [Others came on their own by boat.] It was then I realized I had not only married Cameron, but Wycliffe as well. I have no complaints on either account. In fact, the result has been nothing but a life of rich, wonderful blessings.

It is said that "God is to be found in the details of our lives." This being true, then one of the blessings Elaine remembered during those first days in Peru was the high excitement of being an eye witness to a new experiment in mission and seeing God at work in the details of establishing SIL's presence in Peru. Often they were simple things like having former Wycliffe workers John and Isabel Twentyman in Lima who willingly helped them rent a large home to serve as a group house. Or having the Christian Missionary Alliance Bible Institute lend the group extra beds and mattress. Said Cam:

> The house we rented is beautiful. We were told that houses of this kind are very scarce. But we found this one before it was advertised [thanks to the Twentymans]. The Lord answered our months of prayer for adequate accommodation in a wonderful way. When three of our fellows went to the customs office to retrieve our seventy-four pieces of luggage that had come via steamer from Mexico, the fellows showed the customs official our official agreement with the Ministry of Education and the customs official only opened three of the seventy-four pieces and passed everything on through duty free. John Twentyman told me it took him six weeks for his luggage to clear customs. We also got immediate results in setting up an official post office box to receive our mail. One person told me he had been waiting six months for a mailbox.

There were other concessions that Cam attributed to the Lord's special blessing, like the government's decision to waive the head tax levied on all foreigners. And then from the Foreign Liquidation Commission in Panama, there was the purchase of a U.S. Navy Amphibious Grumman Duck aircraft valued at over eighty thousand dollars that Cam with Betty Greene, after much negotiation were able to purchase for three thousand five hundred dollars, including spare parts and other extras. (That story is worthy of a complete chapter when the full story of SIL in Peru is written.)

But what is most interesting and nothing short of providential is the way Cameron Townsend brought his vitality and insight to bear in a new way in accomplishing his mission. Bob Schneider with his wife Lois, a registered nurse, had been with Cam in Mexico and were among the early members to arrive in Peru. During the first weeks and months in Peru. Bob was able to observe Cam at close range. After many years of reflection, Bob wrote:

When we arrived in Peru, Uncle Cam began immediately to build relationships and make friends by entertaining a whole host of government officials. He wanted to both make their friendship and to acquaint them with his vision of service to the country.   In many ways, Cam had a new kind of freedom in Peru that he didn't have in Mexico. In Peru he was able to explore avenues of service and cooperation with a variety of government agencies. Agencies like the Ministry of Aeronautics, the Ministry of the Treasury, Public Health and the Ministry of Public Education under which SIL developed the bilingual school system at our jungle center.

From a letter by Cam and Elaine to Will Nyman on November 4, 1946 written to thank the Nymans for their wedding gift of a radio, we gain a further insight into the impact SIL was having in a few short months :

The radio is a constant joy to us and to others when we are not here. I am enclosing a clipping from a local newspaper which gives the Minister of Education's decree making the alphabet that Ken Pike worked on so much as the official alphabet for publications in the Quechua and Aymara languages. It is interesting to think of how the Lord used Ken Pike to open the doors for us here in Peru, and now the Lord has allowed him to save the alphabet (which was on the point of being discarded) through our being here. I am delighted we could make this contribution on behalf of Scripture publication for several million indigenous peoples.

Today we are celebrating Elaine's birthday by taking a daughter of the Minister of Education and two others to lunch at the Bolivar Hotel. Every day I praise the Lord more and more for His love gift to me and the work. How very glad I am that Elaine and I were married before coming to Peru. She has been invaluable to me and the whole program.

And then on December 28, 1946, Cam and Elaine sent out the following letter:

Dear friends of Mother and Daddy,
    My name is Grace Lillie Townsend. I'm just a tiny baby (only six pounds, four ounces) but I am making quite a stir. Father was off in

the jungle on the other side of the Andes allocating translators, and
Mother was getting caught up on her primer work when I decided to
stage a surprise party by coming early yesterday.

About the middle of the letter that announced the arrival of their first
daughter[1] there was a paragraph that, from historical hindsight, had
frightening consequences:

Peru has been very good to Mother and Dad, and I intend to do my
bit to strengthen the Good Neighbor links that bind our American
continent together. This will require quite a bit of travel. I plan to
start my "journeying often" within four or five weeks. My first journey
will be to the jungle training camp in southern Mexico. Dad wants to
be with the recruits there who are preparing to come to Peru next
year. [2]

Cam concluded the year 1946 with the General Director's Report entitled, "A Vision of Advance for WBT." In essence, the report summed up
what God had done during the previous eight months. He told about a
new sixty-acre jungle center that had been established. Cam was more
than pleased with the purchase of the Grumman Duck aircraft, which at
the time of his report was due to "hop the Andean wall on its maiden
flight with Betty Greene of MAF as the pilot." (Cam had worked out an
arrangement whereby the Peruvian Ministries of Health and Education
paid half the cost of the plane and it could therefore be repaired in government facilities.)

   Translators were at work in four languages. A course in linguistics had
been given by SIL at the National University. Two bilingual primers had
been prepared and there had been a most successful Quechua/Aymara
literacy campaign for the Peruvian government (Elaine had been involved
high in the Andes near Lake Titicaca). And then, of course, Cam and

---

1 Cam and Elaine were to have a family of four children: Grace, Joy, Elainadel
and Bill. As of this writing, Elaine has nineteen grandchildren!

2 This trip to Jungle Camp resulted in a near fatal airplane crash that seriously
injusred both Cam and Elaine. In the annals of Wycliffe history, that accident is
claimed as the moment when JAARS (Jungle Aviation and Radio Service) was
born. For the report on the details of that accident, see Epilogue.

Elaine and others had entertained many visitors including cabinet ministers and three ambassadors. Cam ended his report with the following:

> In 1942 we prayed for fifty new workers and God sent fifty-one. Last summer we prayed for twenty-five recruits to take the Word of God to the indigenous jungle peoples of Peru and thought at the time it seemed impossible. We now have twenty-three and more in training at Jungle Camp in Mexico. We believe God would have us quicken the pace in the tremendous task of giving God's Word to all the many thousands of peoples who still have not received it in their own language.
>
> We plan to pray and work toward this objective in the strength of Him who time and again has done for us "exceeding abundantly above" during the twelve years that have elapsed since our small beginning. But in reality, we are only just beginning.

From top, Cameron Townsend, Elaine Townsend, daughters, Joy, Grace, Elainadel, and son, Bill, in 1963.

Epilogue
Carpe Diem

Early in his ministry, Cameron Townsend had learned to "seize the day." Whether it was a word of quiet witness for the Lord or explaining his vision for Bible translation, Cam was ever on the alert to "speak a word in season." Never is this seen more graphically than in the events surrounding a near fatal airplane crash that occurred on February 28, 1947 at Jungle Camp, Yaxoquintelá, Chiapas, Mexico.

During the first months after his arrival in Peru, Cam's dream of having adequate air transportation and radio communication for the translators living in remote areas had become an all-consuming passion. He knew translators and their families could not live and work in isolated jungle villages if they had to endure long, hazardous river travel. Air support in Amazonia was a must.

Immediately after the crash that nearly cost him his own life and the life of his wife and infant daughter, Cam was more concerned that people should take photos of the accident than he was of his own comfort.

> If we are to adequately serve the indigenous peoples of Amazonia, people in the homeland must be made aware of the need for good equipment, operated by well-qualified personnel.

In a March 4, 1947, extra edition of the new in-house publication of the Mexico Branch of SIL called *Steam from the Kettle,* came the following two reports. The first was written by Cameron Townsend three and a half hours after the accident. The second is eyewitness accounts from those on the ground:

> We praise God that it happened to us and not to any of the workers. We also praise God that Dr. Culley is here. You can imagine how busy he is giving injections and preparing to set bones. We hope the pilot's life may be spared. But at this point it looks doubtful. In one way we are thankful for the accident because it shows conclusively that for such an important project as the one in which we are engaged, it is absolutely necessary to have the best aircraft and pilots possible.

> Latest word from the Jungle Camp at Yaxoquintelá following the commercial airplane crash in which both Mr. and Mrs. Townsend were injured, indicates their condition is improving. Likewise the pilot, whose injuries at first were such that he wasn't expected to live, is showing signs of recovery. The plane was a Piper Super Cruiser operated commercially out of Tuxtla, Gutierrez. After the Townsends, with their infant daughter Gracie, boarded the plane, the pilot taxied to the end of the runway in preparation for takeoff. About midway down the strip, the pilot lifted off at about a forty-degree angle. Mr. Townsend was watching the speedometer and reported the plane left the ground at thirty-seven miles per hour and at no time did it get over forty miles per hour. There was not sufficient speed to keep on climbing so the pilot leveled off.
>
> For us standing on the ground it looked a little shaky, but we had no idea what was about to happen. After the plane cleared the hump at the end of the strip, it went straight ahead for a few seconds, then for some reason turned left toward higher ground. Immediately after the plane turned left, the tail struck the top of a tree and the front end crashed obliquely into the earth.
>
> By the hand of God alone, all escaped death because the plane struck one side of the ravine and leaped clear to the opposite bank before coming to a stop. Had it landed in the ravine, it would have probably meant death for all. Those of us on the ground rushed to

the scene of the crash and found Uncle Cam and Elaine lying on the ground near the front of the plane, from which gasoline was streaming all over the ground. A passing Indian man was already there holding little Gracie, unharmed, thank God! The pilot was unconscious and still in the plane with his head jammed hard against the instrument panel. After we turned off the switch (a miracle the current had not ignited the gasoline), we pulled the pilot from the plane. We could see clearly he was in terrible shape. We made everyone as comfortable as possible. Dr. Culley brought his medical kit and immediately went to work on Elaine. Later the doctor gave the following report.

Mr. Townsend. Fractured lower end of left tibia, leg up in traction. Hope to put in plaster cast in a few days. Also a very deep cut in left hip, making it difficult for him to lie flat.

Mrs. Townsend. Painful bruises. Open cut and bad dislocation of ankle, reduced under ether. Several cuts on left leg, necessitating stitches.

The Pilot. Fracture of jaw of left cheek bone, very severe, with ugly hole below left eye; packed with iodform gauze. Unconscious much of the time, requiring two men to hold him. Many cuts on his face and knee requiring sutures. Dr. Culley says, "Plenty of reasons to thank God, and the patients are very helpful." The doctor thinks it's possible that all may be moved in two weeks.

When the Townsends returned to Mexico City, they began a long recuperation at the group house on Héroes 53, fondly known as The Kettle. During the time they were recuperating in one of the back room apartments of The Kettle a newly hired Zapotec Indian youth was assigned to clean and sweep their room each day. The young man's name was Ricardo (Richard) Salvador. Richard had left his rural mountain village with a dream of studying in a secondary school in Mexico City.

When Richard arrived in Mexico City in February 1947, his only contact was his aunt who worked as a domestic at The Kettle. At first Richard's aunt was not too pleased with the arrival of her nephew. There was no room for him and she didn't think there was work for him. When Dick Pittman became aware of Richard's problem, he found him a place to live with another young man and gave him a job as an all-around domestic helper. Richard had been given the special task of cleaning the

Townsend's room. Years later he wrote his own feelings about that experience:

> One day the housekeeper gave me special orders to clean a particular room every day. She said I must be careful and do a good job. I did not know who was in the room. When I first went to the doorway and looked in, I was surprised to find a man and a woman lying on twin beds in casts and wrapped in bandages. I had never seen anything like this before. I was petrified. They looked like mummies. When the woman smiled and told me to come in, I was still more frightened. Then I learned they had been in an airplane crash.
>
> The man smiled, too, and asked me all sorts of questions. He wanted to know my name, how old I was, who were my people, and what village I had come from. He asked me why I had come to the city, and what I wanted to study. And then he asked me a strange question. He wanted to know if I knew Jesus Christ as my personal Saviour. I never before had been asked such a question. I did not know how to answer him.
>
> Then the man pointed to a black book lying on the coffee table, and said, "Would you do us a favor and read from the place where the bookmark is?" I read some words I had never heard before. "The Lord is my shepherd; I shall not want. He maketh me to lie down in green pastures: he leadeth me beside the still waters. He restoreth my soul: he leadeth me in the paths of righteousness for his name's sake..."[Psalm 23:1-3 KJV.]
>
> Every day I visited "the room of the mummies" and each day the man asked me to read from the black book, after which I cleaned the floor, the furniture and bath. One day I received a severe tongue lashing from the housekeeper for taking longer to clean the room than she thought I should. The next morning when the man asked me to read from the black book, I said I could not, and told him why. But the man said, "Don't worry, I am your boss's boss. You only need to let her know that we need you to read to us each day. Sit down and read to us."
>
> When the housekeeper learned that the boss of all the bosses in the building had asked me to stay and read to them, I never again received a tongue lashing. And knowing that such an important

man considered me to be his friend gave me a new sense of self-confidence. It made me feel important.

As time passed, the "mummies" began to take walks in the hall-ways, past the offices, and eventually to the lower level dining room. Always they were supported by some strange sticks that I later understood were called crutches. One day they began to walk normally, without support. Although I noticed the woman had the most difficulty walking.

At first I thought the man, once he got better, would have too much important business to talk to me. But such was not the case. Whenever he saw me, he smiled kindly and called me by my first name. Then he would ask about my spiritual well-being and encouraged me to read the Bible on my own. Soon after, the man arranged that all of us who worked in the building we called the Kettle, because it was always boiling over with people, were to have our own Bible study. It was in this way that I and others who worked at The Kettle came to know Jesus Christ as our Lord and Saviour.

Eight years passed before I saw the man everyone called Uncle Cam again. And before I could say "don Guillermo" [Cam's name in Spanish], this important man immediately called me by my first name and said, "Ricardo, I am very happy to see you and to know that you are faithful in the ways of the Lord. Elaine and I always remember you with love. May God bless you in all you do, and don't forget us because we are your friends."

I became a grown man, a head of a household, a university professor and a church founder, and while I never saw Uncle Cam again, I often heard of the ministry he was having through Latin America, and indeed throughout the world. Then in May 1982, I heard the news that Uncle Cam had died, that he had answered his final call on April 23. When I heard the news, my mind flew back to the "room of the mummies," and I thought of the love and kindness he and his wife had shown to a poor frightened Zapotec boy from the country many years before. I thought of the inner peace and joy and purpose that had come to me by knowing Jesus Christ as my Saviour. I thought of the Black Book and the words I read so haltingly for the first time. "The Lord is my shepherd. . . I will fear no evil. . . my cup runneth over. . ." I thought about the man who was

once all wrapped up in bandages who took the time to teach me
how to read out of his personal Bible and because he took time for
a young boy, today, as a man, my cup is full and "runneth over."

If there was one wish or legacy that William Cameron Townsend could
give to those in the family of faith and beyond, it might well be found in
the words of a poem he penned on the road in Guatemala on November
30, 1918:

Trust Him

Trust Him when dark doubts assail you,
Trust Him when your strength is small.
Trust Him when to simply trust Him
seems the hardest thing of all.
Trust Him, He is ever faithful.
Trust Him, for His will is best.
Trust Him, for the heart of Jesus,
Is the only place of rest.
Trust Him then through cloud and sunshine,
All your cares upon Him cast,
Till all the storms of life are over
And the trusting days are past.

Afterword

In 1917, when William Cameron Townsend applied to the Los Angeles Bible House to spend a year in Guatemala selling Scripture portions, he was interviewed by Mr. R.D. Smith. Smith looked at the skinny twenty-one-year-old Townsend and said to Cam's friend Robbie Robinson, "I don't think Townsend will last six weeks".

The skinny young man who wasn't supposed to last six weeks died on April 23, 1982, after sixty-five years in active mission service. During that period, he became, with William Carey and Hudson Taylor, one of the three outstanding mission statesmen of modern times. As of this writing, personnel with the three organizations he began are at work in 1,053 language translation projects around the world and have helped to complete New Testament translations in 432 languages.

A year after that near fatal airplane crash in Chiapas, Mexico, Cameron Townsend organized the Jungle Aviation and Radio Service (JAARS) with one airplane and one woman pilot. From that humble beginning, JAARS has grown to a fleet of forty aircraft worldwide. As the years passed, other services were added, including computer technology, telecommunications, purchasing, shipping, trucking, construction, and most recently vernacular media.

What began in Cameron Townsend's mind as a dream, has for over fifty years become a responsive provider of high quality technical support services for Wycliffe Bible Translators and the Summer Institute of Linguistics.

In 1970, Wycliffe personnel began working among the 500th people group. To mark the occasion, Cameron Townsend quoted from the man who, in 1916, first challenged him to consider cross-cultural mission. The man was the missionary statesman, John R. Mott, who wrote in his book, *The Evangelization of the World in This Generation*:

> It is a gigantic task to furnish in their own tongues to all races of mankind the revelation of God through the Scriptures, but it is indispensable to the enterprise of evangelization. There are also many languages still to be reduced to writing. What an undertaking, then, to translate the Gospel into hundreds of languages and dialects which do not today give expression to the glorious message. The taking of a knowledge of Christ to the whole world without delay is a most pressing duty.

The plane crash in southern Mexico, March, 1947, which Cameron Townsend, Elaine, and baby Grace survived.

Index

N